KISSING
FIDEL

T0119712

WINNER OF THE IOWA PRIZE FOR LITERARY NONFICTION

KISSING FIDEL

A MEMOIR OF
CUBAN AMERICAN TERRORISM
IN THE UNITED STATES

MAGDA MONTIEL DAVIS

UNIVERSITY OF IOWA PRESS | IOWA CITY

University of Iowa Press, Iowa City 52242
Copyright © 2020 Magda Montiel Davis
www.uipress.uiowa.edu

ISBN 978-1-60938-726-6 (pbk)
ISBN 978-1-60938-727-3 (ebk)

Printed in the United States of America

Cover design by Kimberly Glyder
Text design by April Leidig

Epigraph from *Scoundrel Time* by Lillian Hellman, copyright © 1976, 2000.
Reprinted by permission of Little, Brown and Company, an
imprint of Hachette Book Group, Inc.

No part of this book may be reproduced or used in any form or by any
means without permission in writing from the publisher. All reasonable steps
have been taken to contact copyright holders of material used in this book
with any whom it has not been possible to reach.

Printed on acid-free paper

Cataloging-in-Publication data is on file
with the Library of Congress.

To my children,
Katie, Paula, Maggie, Sadie, and Ben,
for allowing me the freedom
to grow up after they did.

———

To the Nonfiction Writing Program
at the University of Iowa,
for taking a chance on me.

———

And to Ira,
a hot, quirky love like ours comes once
every hundred years.
Then it goes.

¡MIL GRACIAS!

The Women

María Magdalena Hernández: Mami, for believing I could prevail over anything. My sister, Maggie DiFalco ("Do I need to sit down for this?"). Catherine Deming: I never feel as loved as when Cathy talks me down. Lazara Pittman ("Yeah, Magda? I'm just calling to tell you I'm not mad anymore," after years of not speaking.) And Havana's Ivelisse Blanco: Ive, *mataperreando* the hills of our Nuevo Vedado barrio with me since we were three.

The Men of Those Past, Distant Times

Ira Kurzban, and the fury that propelled me to finish and perfect. My father, José Ramón Montiel Someillán—*Bebo* to his lifelong friends, *Papín* to my sister and me. From him I learned to look at life in terms of strikeouts, home runs, maybe a walk to first.

The Descendants and
Descendants of the Descendants

Kathryn Montiel Davis: Katie, our own Vagina Doctor and her endearing *Mommie* notes. Paula Davis Hoffman, and her endearing screenshots of Cartoon Network's taco-selling, scheming grandmother, that she *claims* sending at my loving grandchildren's direction. Magda Arguelles: Maggie knows when to make me Abuela's soup and put me to bed. Sadie Kurzban: once a preteen Streetdancing next to me, now the founding 305Fitness exec expecting me to follow her dance moves. Ben Kurzban, whose loving eyes see in me the pop-icon likeness of Snape or Grimace.

Max and Matthew, Sasha and Jeremy, Ollie, Louie and Violet: I now understand the love Abuela had for their mamas, Katie, Paula, and Maggie, and for their Aunt Sadie, and Uncle Ben.

Backbone, Chutzpah, and Cojones

They risked their lives staying or coming to work with me: Irma Mendez, Sadie and Benny's office nanny, weathering attacks at my side. Miriam de la Torre, those garbled, harried messages: Sean *Penn*, or Imelda *Marcos* called. Mara Chemerinsky and her toddler son running buck naked down our office corridors. My *tío* Marino, what a way to step up for his *sobrina*, along with my sister. Raysa Aguiar, our polarized politics did not get in the way of her humanity.

Those who supported me noisily or with a quiet note in the mail. Quick-witted Eddie Levy (*el esposo de Xiomara*, as Fidel once said) and Xiomara Almaguer: they walked arm-in-arm with me at Miami International Airport during our most virulent *acto de repudio* (not included in this book; in the sequel, perhaps?). Andrés Gómez and the memory of "Aruca," Wilfredo, and Cachita; they live in me still. Marisol Zequeira, who prepared emergency cases from home, not succumbing to *cubanito*-colleague pressure. Debbie Smith, rallying support for a one-page ad in the *Miami Herald* about my freedom to speak. David Lawrence, then publisher of the *Herald*, once victimized as well, who readily accepted the ad for far less than its cost. Carmen Oliva's and the Haitian Refugee Center's / Steve Forrester's uplifting faxes; years later, still remembered. Carl Shusterman ("Let the dogs bark, Magda, but the caravan moves on"), Jack Pinnix ("Why the hell didn't you tell me you had a thing for beards?"), Marc Van der Hout, Ted Ruthizer—too many immigration lawyers to name.

The Exes

Every woman deserves an ex like Paul Davis; he dragged me to my first law exam and stood outside until he was sure I wouldn't run out. Kari Fonte: though ex–law partner, Kari will always be my law and everything-else partner. My ex-coworkers Marianna Cardona: the times she met with clients so that I could write said everything; and newlywed Susanna Hamadallah, the nights she stayed up to type 1,548 pages of manuscript said more than everything. Sandye Cole, Nancy Weese, and Francy Neal: since our inner-city school days, dynamic forces in my life.

And What Else but the Writing?
Always the Writing.

John D'Agata, director of University of Iowa's Nonfiction Writing Program (NWP) had me from day one, when he had us introduce ourselves by telling our most embarrassing story. (I think I won.) His dog Boeing, I'm convinced, reads our work to him as he drives cross-country or takes (not *Planes*, never planes) *Ships, Trains, and Automobiles* to sit (or not) in Plutarch's chair. My dream-team University of Iowa thesis committee:

Kerry Howley, director—I see Kerry's hand in my pages, hear her words of guidance and encouragement; Inara Verzemnieks, so patient for art and generous with her time; and from our Havana Sugar Kings days of childhood, DePaul's Felix Masud-Piloto, PhD, who stood behind me in line as I planted The Kiss heard around the world. Other NWP extraordinaires, Bonnie Sunstein, Jeff Porter, Patricia Foster; and visiting instructors, Dylan Nice and Bernard Cooper. Each of my classmates brought something of their eclectic selves into my writing that I carry with me still. *Sabe-lo-todo* Spenser Mestel ("Spenser, help! Pretend it's your mother . . . grandmother!") Who else but Spenser would have poured over an unedited version of the manuscript and lifted my waning spirit during that godawful year of queries?

The Iowa Summer Writing Festival (ISWF) jumpstarted me back to my love of writing. Amy Margolis's recommendation, I believe, was pivotal in securing my acceptance to the University of Iowa's Writing Program. ("Magda . . . the unlikely mother of 5 daughters, and a novice writer so urgent and spirited in her advances, I wondered when she approached me in the halls of EPB what chased after her and hoped very much if it arrived it wouldn't linger.") ISWF instructors, so terrific; bearing mention are Mary Kay Shanley, my "first"; Marilyn Abildskov, that tender prose! Suzanne Scanlon, those blue eyes! BK Loren, who named a character *Magda*; and Marc Nieson. A passage about meeting Fidel as originally written in Marc's metaphor class made it to the final version.

Born of the ISWF, my longstanding writing group: Arlyn Norris, Charlotte Hamilton, Michelle Cantwell, and James Joyce (for real, James Joyce; our own funny Jim). For their sage advice, *Profesores* Jesús Jambrina and Alfredo Estenoz. When we converge on Iowa, we increase the Cuban population by 100 percent.

The University of Iowa Press: James McCoy, Jacob Roosa, Allison Means, Suzanne Glemot, Susan Hill Newton, Meredith Stabel, Karen Copp, and Carolyn Brown—Carolyn!—my copy editor. How did I get so lucky? Hanif Abdurraqib, judge of the 2020 Iowa Prize for Literary Nonfiction, I am enthralled that a writer of his caliber chose me.

Por último, Fidel: though he'd protest that I didn't list him first, he got the last word.

It is not true that when the bell tolls it tolls for thee: if it were true we could not have elected, so few years later, Richard Nixon, a man who had been so closely allied with McCarthy. Mr. Nixon brought with him a group of high-powered operators who made Cohn and Schine look like cute little rascals from grammar school. . . . And one year after a presidential scandal of a magnitude still unknown, we have almost forgotten them, too. We are a people who do not want to keep much of the past in our heads. It is considered unhealthy in America to remember mistakes, neurotic to think about them, psychotic to dwell upon them.

———

Lillian Hellman, *Scoundrel Time*

KISSING
FIDEL

———

The stairs are black marbled, the carpet a thin red. I begin the climb, the Cuban national seal—her mountains, sea, star—on the wall behind me. At the top of the stairs, a face. Not an alive face, a sculpted face. José Martí, I think, our national poet and liberator. The wide forehead, bristly mustache, half-shut eyes. But no, not José Martí. COMPAÑERO FÉLIX GARCÍA RODRÍGUEZ, IN MEMORY, it reads. Young diplomat stationed here at the Cuban Mission to the United Nations. Slain here on the streets of New York by the exile terrorist group, Omega 7. Using silencer MAC-10 automatic machine guns, commandos of Omega 7 shot Felix in the face and neck. The execution date was the sixth anniversary of Omega's founding, September 11. Not September 11 as the people of the United States know it—September 11, 1980.

Minutes ago, as I made my way into the mission, I looked up at the building across Lexington Avenue, its half-opened windows. At protesters stretching a bit too far over NYPD barricades. Reporters quickly encircled me. *What did I think about President Obama's reestablishment of diplomatic relations with Cuba? Will I meet* el presidente *Raúl Castro at tonight's reception?* and, *Vindicated, do I feel vindicated?* A friend grabbed my elbow, pulled me the opposite way. "*Pendejo* reporters," she said. "If they catch up to you, tell them it's all behind you," and we half-laughed.

As the Cuban flag was raised over Washington this last July, a man a few feet from me rushed the embassy gate. Splattering red paint onto his white shirt, he yelled ¡*Sangre cubana!* Cuban blood. The handwriting, you could say, is on the wall. A month before, a reality-TV star descended a long escalator into the gilded basement lobby of his eponymous tower. Using the well-taught tactics of Roy Cohn, McCarthy mentor, Rosenberg prosecutor, and other things, Donald Trump kicked off his race for the

Oval Office. The first-ever presidential endorsement of Brigada de Asalto 2506—renamed the Bay of Pigs Veterans Association by the Trump campaign—was bestowed upon him. Against a backdrop of the brigade's gold banner of an armed soldier on the ready, Mr. Trump thanked the brigade for its first-ever award, but the Brigada de Asalto's only first-ever award was to General Pinochet of the Chilean junta. As Mr. Trump delivered his thank-you before news cameras, I wondered whether seated in the audience were those Brigada de Asalto members with histories of bombing US and state government buildings, weapons possession, and narcotics trafficking, plots to assassinate Fidel Castro, and the like. I wondered whether seated in the audience was the Brigada de Asalto member, cited in Human Rights Watch's *Dangerous Dialogue: Attacks on Freedom of Expression in Miami's Cuban Exile Community*, who made threats against a Cuba-activist colleague, and the Brigada de Asalto member who, one early morning on the thirty-fourth anniversary of the US-botched invasion, accosted me at the entrance to my neighborhood gym.

———

In the vast *sala de recepción*, its walls high, a creamy yellow, *¡Muchachita!* and *¿Que es de tu vida?* and kisses and touches and hugs. When the time is right, I slip away to a secluded corner. A roar overtakes the room. Someone says Raúl just entered. Guests abandon their Cuba libres and swell around him. But unlike Fidel, who towered over everyone and everything, I can't see Raúl from where I stand, I can't see him anywhere at all.

Joséfina Vidal, who led Cuba's negotiating team with Washington, spots me standing alone. She grabs my wrist, pulls me across the room. *"Perdón,"* says Joséfina, a succession of *perdóns* as she plows her way through the crowd circling Raúl. She positions me smack before him. I stand, not craning my neck as with big brother Fidel, but eye-to-eye with Raúl.

SchlickSchlickSchilck go the camera shutters. *"Oy vey,"* says Cuba's New York lawyer, "here we go again."

Most diplomatically, Joséfina steps to the sidelines. Then, hand to mouth, *"¡Raúl!"* she yells, *"¡Es Magda! ¡La del beso a Fidel!"*

"¡Ah, bueno!" says Raúl. *Well then.* "If she kissed Fidel, she's going to have to kiss me too."

PART ONE

ATREVIMIENTO

1

YOU THINK THAT'S RIGHT?

———

The news director of a Little Havana radio station, WQBA "La Cubanísima," speaks out against terrorism and violence in Miami. Not the terrorism and violence for which Miami is known, the inner-city brutality, the *Scarface* hype. It's the terrorism and violence one doesn't hear much about outside of exile circles—the bombing, mutilation, and execution-style assassinations of those who don't adhere to *el exilio*'s stance on Cuba.

After a series of such editorials, the news director, *un exiliado cubano* himself, exits the radio station at the end of the work day. A young Latina who works in the same building seeks his help. It's about a little boy she found on the street. He's lost. *No hay problema*, says the news director. *El manager del estudio contacta a la policía.* He walks to the abandoned lot next to the building, where he always parks his station wagon. He opens the driver's door, WQBA 1140 AM decal on its white-lacquered surface. He gets in his car. He turns the ignition. It is at 7:17 PM that the explosive device detonates.

The young woman will tell the *Miami Herald* and all major news stations that she saw dark flames and smoke. That she tried opening the car door

OPPOSITE: Fidel and me at a receiving line as Fidel greets hundreds of Cuban émigrés at the conclusion of the unprecedented, three-day conference, La Nación y la Emigración. The photograph, probably taken by a member of the Miami media, is from a video filmed by Cuba's press corps at a reception at Havana's Palace of the Revolution on the evening of April 24, 1994. The image of the traditional "hello" kiss, planted by Fidel on the cheeks of hundreds of other female guests, was repeatedly aired on television in my South Florida community and appeared in hundreds of local, national, and international publications.

but that it was too hot. That through the car window, she saw the man, his eyes. That his eyes were full of pain. That he shook and shook his hands but said nothing.

A young Latino will tell the *Miami Herald* that while walking on Calle Ocho, the heart of Little Havana, he saw the hood of the station wagon hurled one hundred feet in the air. That he rushed over. That blood was everywhere. That the man did not stop looking at him and at the young woman. That when the man spoke, he said, *No puedo moverme.* That he said, *¡Sácame!* and that together, he and the young woman tried to get him out but the door was jammed. They grabbed him by the belt, then tried to pull him up by the leg. But the leg, both legs, were severed below the knee.

When finally they got him out and the man saw his legs, he tried to get up. He pounded the pavement with his fists. There was mention of his bleeding to death. Efforts were made to stop the bleeding, but the bleeding would not stop. Firemen put the man into a shock suit. The shock suit would force blood into his vital organs, thereby preventing the news director from lapsing into shock.

The media was soon at the scene. A Miami city commissioner who heard the news immediately rushed to the site of the explosion. The *Miami Herald* will credit the city commissioner with saving the news director's life.

At the hospital, the news director's fifteen-year-old son will talk to the *Miami Herald* and City of Miami police. The wife and younger children will stare straight ahead. *My dad kept getting threats*, the boy will say. *Cállate, the callers would say.* Shut up about the bombings. *O te asesinamos.*

My father felt it was his right to speak. He took precautions but wasn't afraid. Later, the boy will say that he spoke of his father as if in the past because he thought his father was dead. A City of Miami detective assigned to the case will receive authorization to reveal the following: *The victim has been the target of many threats for the past several months after his editorials on his radio show*, Habla El Pueblo, *against terrorists here in this town*. His radio show, *The People Speak*. Here, in this town. The threats came, were coming still from several paramilitary terrorist organizations run by a few select members of *el exilio* trained by the Central Intelligence Agency. Some trained while still in the homeland. Others trained in Central America. All were—are—indefatigable fighters for *la causa cubana*, indefatigably fighting to return to the homeland to the same kind of freedom they enjoyed pre-Fidel. *Antes De*: AD—that's the joke. Or BC, Before Castro. That's the other joke.

Like his bombers, the victim was a fierce anticommunist fighting for *la causa cubana.* Like the rest of us, he'd left the homeland shortly after the January 1, 1959, rise of the revolution. He too was fighting to bring freedom to Cuba, the same kind of freedom it is said we enjoyed BC. But unlike his bombers, the victim thought that the way to return to the homeland was not through terrorism and violence. And he spoke out.

The victim alerted the authorities immediately upon receipt of the first death threat. City of Miami police then put a watch over his home. The children were instructed not to answer the telephone, open mail or packages.

It won't take much of an investigation to determine that the bomb was planted under the hood of the victim's car during daylight hours in the heart of Little Havana. Nor that the victim had driven the station wagon home during lunch to eat *un sándwich cubano* or maybe *una medianoche* with his wife. No one at the press conference will ask the detective why Miami police did not put a watch over the radio station where the victim broadcast his editorials that led to the death threats, to the bombing, and though not to his death, to the loss of both his legs and to eleven surgeries in five months.

Prosecutors, however, will convene weekly. A federal grand jury will be called. Witness testimony will point to three male suspects, members of the paramilitary exile group, Omega 7, facing extradition to Mexico for the attempted kidnapping of a Cuban diplomat. A few hours before the five-year statute of limitations will expire, the US attorney will manage to obtain a four-count indictment against the three suspects.

La Cubanísima will make known the plight of the three suspects. Other exile radio stations, television programs, and newspapers will follow suit. *El exilio* will set up a defense fund. Donations will pour in at breakneck speed. Despite the indictments, the three suspects will never be arrested or prosecuted. For reasons that remain unknown, the incoming US attorney, appointed by newly elected president Ronald Reagan, will dismiss the indictments against all three.

———

At the Palace of the Revolution, I don't think about the news director whose legs were blown off near my home in Miami. Or about those murdered execution-style after meeting Fidel at a conference in Havana like the one I had just attended. The twenty-five-year-old father of two shot in Puerto Rico by Comando Zero militants two blocks from his mother's house, then left alive as he hung trapped in his overturned car, or the father of a twelve-year-old shot in New Jersey by Omega 7 commandos as he was getting into his car and his son watched from the back seat.

I see, hear, read about such things, but such things happen to others. They don't happen to anyone I love, and they don't happen to me: wife, lawyer, mother of five. Cuban-born daughter of parents who in 1961 joined the mass exodus of the Cuban privileged shortly after the 1959 rise of the revolution.

For years, my parents called themselves *exiliados*. Called the United States, where we settled, *el exilio*. Our stay in this strange country with its strange language and strange people who looked at us as if *we* were strange would be short-lived. Of course we'd be back—¡*Claro que sí!*— my father at the Sugar Kings baseball stadium, a handful of secretaries and underlings at his disposal; my mother riding in his new '59 Impala, teaching arts and crafts half days to overcrowded classrooms of illiterate children; my sister, Maty, and I catching purple-and-orange crabs by the riverbed of el rio Almendares and roller-coasting our Niagara bikes at full speed over the neighborhood's hills, the Malecón sea breeze cooling our skin.

Maybe Fidel was a bit smarter, and okay, much more charismatic, but he was still just another fly-by-night in a long string of puppet presidents. *This one* had fled into exile in a plane full of gold, weapons, and friends still in their pajamas; *that one* took off in the early morning darkness of January 1, 1959, in a plane full of the same essential amenities with the exception that the men wore tuxedoes and women evening gowns from the New Year's Eve celebration hours before. All had much in common: brutality, repression, corruption, and the full support of the United States.

That one is Fulgencio Batista, who Fidel—as a law student at the University of Havana, organizer of the 1953 attack on Batista's Moncada barracks, political prisoner in the Isle of Pines, exile in Mexico, fundraiser in Miami and New York, and guerrilla fighter in the Sierra Maestra—ousted with his army of long-haired men and long-rifled women, then marched down the Sierra Maestra to the cheers and chants of ¡*Cuba, sí, Yankee, no! ¡Fidel, esta es tu casa! ¡Viva la Revolución!* of street vendors and homemakers and professionals alike.

After many failed efforts of the US and *el exilio*—the Bay of Pigs invasion, an economic embargo that would turn into one of the longest and most combative in history, thirty-plus assassination attempts against Fidel—reality hit. Fidel was here to stay, and when the world and *el exilio* knew this, most, like my parents, gave up their dreams of returning.

Thirty-three years later, I am a recent Democratic candidate for Congress, a US-educated member of the Florida bar, and sole owner and founder of one of the largest immigration law firms in the state, made up entirely of women.

Thirty-three years later, I stand at the Palace of the Revolution waiting for what I believe will be my once-in-a-lifetime chance to meet Fidel Castro Ruz.

I stand in a long line that snakes twice amid golden doors, tropical plants, and big white lights hanging low from a black ceiling. I stand with hundreds of other Cuban émigrés from dozens of other countries, all of us invited by Cuba's revolutionary government to the Conferencia la Nación y la Emigración, designed to mend the wounds, bridge the chasm between those who opposed the revolution and left and those who remain faithful and stayed.

I am neither. I was dragged like a pull toy through the Havana airport, down the runway, up the stairs, and into that Pan Am plane. We left quickly—my mother, sister, and I; my father soon to follow—thanks to tourist visas issued with the wink of an eye by the US Embassy in Havana. It was obvious to the US, to almost everyone, that the mass exodus by the upper classes was not to visit the Statue of Liberty but to stay temporarily until the CIA got rid of Fidel, the same way it had gotten rid of leaders of other sovereign nations who were a bit too liberal for the US's liking.

I was eight; I knew nothing of this. But I did know that before the revolution, a thin, frail woman holding a baby would trudge up the long entrance stairway to our home, hold out the pink of her palm, and my mother would give her nothing but a can of Pet Evaporated Milk. My mother, who grew up poor in a small town outside Havana. What good would a can of milk do the woman? How could she walk up the long flights of stairs of the homes in our neighborhood and hold her baby plus the added weight of a can of milk? Why did my mother scoff at that voice on Radio Rebelde broadcast from the Sierra Maestra? That voice that cracked with a certain sadness, an impatience. Or at the man with the funny Argentinian accent who talked about little children who died of hunger and adults who couldn't read or write. *Reading is like eating*, Ché said, again and again. *¡Animales!* Mami said, again and again. *That's what these people are. Savages! Living in the mountains like that.*

That wasn't like my mother. She wasn't like my father or his family. She didn't think of herself as "high class," as my father's family said of themselves—in English. She walked around our house barefoot; none of the other mothers in the neighborhood walked around barefoot. She hid black pennies and bright red apples and fat brown cigars for her Afro-Cuban rituals. From broomsticks, she made Maty and me tall, very tall stilts. She told us stories of *el indio* Hatuey, a chieftain of the Cuban natives. As Spanish colonists burned Hatuey at the stake and priests offered him communion so he could go to heaven, Hatuey retorted, "If people like you are in heaven, I don't want to go there." So why did Mami treat the beggar woman in such a derisive manner? Why did she click off the radio when Fidel or Ché spoke of children who died of hunger and adults who couldn't read or write?

It wasn't that she'd married *up*, moved to the big city, smelled of Shalimar perfume, and, as the formerly poor are wont to do, cast a blind eye to the life she once led—that wasn't my mother. Shortly after the rise of the revolution, the CIA began transmitting *War of the Worlds*–like announcements throughout the island: food would soon be rationed; parents would lose all rights over children; the new communist state would send them to labor camps to cut sugarcane, and where they would be indoctrinated and abused, physically and sexually. Thousands of Cuban parents put their children, some as young as two, on planes to the US for destinations unknown in what became known as Operation Peter Pan, the brainchild of the CIA Father Bryan O. Walsh, a thirty-year-old Irish priest (soon to be promoted to Monsignor), who served as director of the Catholic Welfare Bureau in Miami and was given blanket power by the US government to issue visa waivers to Cuban children—highly irregular, given that as a non-government employee, he lacked the mandatory security clearance. Once in the US, many children were subject to physical and sexual abuse. Many siblings were separated, even though parents were assured that brother and sister would stay together. Some children didn't see their parents for years. Some never saw their parents at all.

And yet, it never occurred to my mother to send my sister and me off on a plane like that. Cuba is where she thrived, belonged. So why did she leave? "Because they said that you and your sister would go hungry," she would tell me years later.

I didn't know about the pressure and fear percolating in my mother. All I knew was that I wanted my mother to like Fidel. Why didn't my mother like Fidel? If she liked Fidel, maybe my father would come around and like Fidel too. Everyone liked Fidel, my *amiguitas* up the hill, their well-to-do parents, my second-grade teacher at the American-owned school Maty and I attended—everyone. Havana was noisy and wild with life. It may have been noisy and wild before, but this wasn't the noisy and wild of the American Mafia kingpins or the Batista corruptors and corruptees. That guardedness, that peculiar way adults communicated with each other under Batista—not with words but with a look, a gesture—was no more. When five years later I would cover every inch of wall of the Miami bedroom I shared with my sister with teen-magazine photos of John, Paul, George, and Ringo, that's what I would remember: the energy, the fervor that overtook the island. *Milicianos* riding high on open-air Jeeps, their long hair flowing behind them. How you could see their faces. How you could see *all* their faces, women's faces. No longer were women depicted as nothing more than big *tetas* and fat *culos* on Tropicana posters. Celia Sánchez, Vilma Espín, Aleida March, Haydée Santamaría, and many other *milicianas* who fought alongside the men had a voice in the new revolutionary government.

Some of the *milicianos* were stationed in our neighborhood in a house abandoned by a family who'd left shortly after the revolution. Translation: Batistianos. The closer to January 1, 1959, the departure, the higher the probability that they'd been closely aligned with Batista. When my *amiguitas* and I would spot the olive-clad, black-booted squad coming down the hill, we'd run up to them, march alongside: "¡*Uno, dos, tres, cuatro! ¡Comiendo mierda, rompiendo zapato!*" 1 2 3 4! Eating shit, tearing up boots! They'd laugh, play hide-and-seek with us.

Change came quickly. *La reforma agraria*: country folk, *guajiros*, were given title to a small tract of the land that for years they had cultivated and on which they lived in dilapidated quarters. *La campaña de alfabetización*: volunteers thirteen and older traveled to the countryside to teach *guajiros* to read and write. *El programa de urbanización*: city dwellers opened their homes so *guajiros* could attend trade school. One afternoon, my *amiguitas* pulled me by the hand to their house up the hill. They lifted their garage door. The musty, darkened room now had light and a sink and running water. A little man came downstairs from inside the house. He'd just had dinner with Dr. Lalo and Piedad, my friends' parents. The little man's wife and children were back in the mountains but would soon join him, he said, once he started technical school and had a job.

———

In our home was a little man too. But this little man did not speak to my *amiguitas*. In fact, my father told my Maty and me that we were not to bring our friends—anyone—into our home. My mother stood behind him, put a red-manicured hand up to her forehead. When she put it down, I noticed it was trembling.

The little man's name was Jesús, *Heh-seuss*, although sometimes when I said *Jesús*—in a whisper, always a whisper—he forgot to answer. He sat in the innermost room of the house: small, white, cube-shaped, a room with no windows. Was it a closet? From the doorway, I would see his profile, only his profile. It was a rather long profile, and the chin too was long and pointy. At the corner of the mouth, I could see a dark, thin line of mustache so thin it looked like you could peel it off. The hair was black and inky. Had he overdone the Brylcreem? *A little dab'll do ya* went the American TV jingle, but the little man had more than a little dabbed.

All day he sat in silence, unmoving almost; his legs were so skinny that when crossed, the top one almost reached the floor. He sat, his ear bent to the radio or his eyeballs opened wide, staring at the TV screen. I would tell him, "It's bad for you, to sit so close." If I forgot and left a door open, he would rise quickly and close it quietly, very quietly. He sucked on Lucky Strikes that sparked red-orange with each inhale and threw the lit cigarettes on our terrazzo floor—one cigarette, then another, on and on.

To my sister and me, my mother said, "If the *milicianos* come and take me away, jump the wall and ask Esperanza," our next-door neighbor, "to call your aunt." Her sister, our Aunt Tíita, my godmother. My mother said this time and time again, each time without flinching. Then she'd scrape the red polish off her fingernails.

Then one day, Jesús was gone, just like that. My sister and I were relieved. She didn't say it, but I felt it. Then he came back. From the front porch, we watched as he walked down the hill to our home. And I felt it, the same fear in her as was inside me.

Not long after, I woke so early it was still dark out. *¡Que mierda!* That new room air conditioner, brand new, and already broken. Godawful cold metal box stuck in our bedroom window, blocking the sea wind like that, groaning, sputtering then *T-t-t-t*—knock! Knock again! The knocking, it came louder, faster.

It was six weeks after my eighth birthday. April 17, 1961. And the Bay of Pigs invasion.

Cuban exiles trained in Central America by the CIA but untrained nonetheless had set sail from Nicaragua four days earlier. Waving at the pier was General Somoza, who asked exile members of the Brigada de Asalto 2506—so named after the ID number of an exile trainee who at the CIA camp in Guatemala stumbled and fell from a mountain—to bring him back some hairs from Fidel's beard. Under a moonless sky, some 1,500 *brigadistas*, comprised mostly of ex-Batista officers and sons of upper-crust families, disembarked at a mosquito-laden swamp, the site that after much debate with the CIA and other top advisors, Kennedy had settled on. Virtually unpopulated, it would be thinly defended, if at all. It did take a small band of *milicianos* who spotted the first landing more than an hour to get to a radio telephone. Paul Revere–like, through marsh and swampland, came not *The British* but *The Yankees are coming!* of the people. Battalions of *milicianos*, not waiting for orders, dispersed to the beach.

Unbeknownst to us, Fidel was ten blocks from our home at a modern midcentury house typical of the neighborhood, where he spent nights awake at his emergency command post known as *Punto Uno*. That an attack was imminent was no secret, in part due to Cuba's highly efficient intelligence network, but also the *lenguas sueltas* of exile recruits that got the community talking, prompting the *Nation* and *New York Times* to report on the upcoming invasion. Besides, Kennedy's too frequent assurances that US forces would not intervene in Cuba led Fidel to the conclusion that Kennedy would not make a point of excluding US participation unless the island was on the brink of attack.

At 3:15 AM up the hill from our house, Fidel's telephone rang.

––––––––

The Bay of Pigs was a failure, says the CIA, because Kennedy canceled air support at the last minute. Thirty-three years later, *exiliados* are still furious with Kennedy and in overwhelming numbers vote a straight Republican ticket. But US aircraft did attack. Cuban pilots, who on Fidel's orders had stayed up all night, were able to take complete control of the air. That—and the *lenguas sueltas* of exile recruits—may have won the Bay of Pigs for Cuba.

Fidel's assessment differs. *Los imperialistas*, he says, focused only on logistics and firepower. The revolution, however, had from the very beginning prioritized the *bienestar* of the people. One of the revolution's first projects was—well, to drain the swamp. Residents of the swampy peninsula, with no transportation in or out other than a small train that often derailed, were some of the poorest on the island. After the revolution, roads were built, co-ops were established, and the now famous Zapata Swamp was stocked with American flamingoes and Cuban crocodiles. Despite warnings to Kennedy from both British intelligence and the US Embassy in Havana that the island was filled with overwhelming support for the revolution, the CIA had assured the president that the people would take up arms against the revolution in a mass insurrection. The *brigadistas* waited for it, but it never came. What came instead were townspeople who ran to guard the town's fuel and water tanks and its electric power and radio relay stations, and those who took up arms against the *brigadistas*.

After nearly seventy-two hours on the front line, Fidel spent the day on the beach inspecting enemy positions and asking questions of the captured men. There were so many of them that many stood around Fidel, one brigade member told me, weapons still in hand. At first, he said, they feared immediate execution but instead were taken to Havana's naval hospital. President Kennedy assured the international community that the US was not involved. It was, he said time and again, Cubans fighting Cubans.

In Cuba, trials of the captured men were televised. Nearly all were sentenced to thirty years' imprisonment. After twenty months of negotiations, Cuba released the men in exchange for payment from the United States of $53 million, not in cash but in food and medicine, to the Cuban people. Admirable, you could say—certainly. But Fidel had—and will have to the end—a way of making a point. Thumbing his nose at the US. Sticking it to them, as my kids would say. And that, in my estimation, is the reason the US has made up with North Vietnam, is buddies with China, but won't let go of its obsession with Cuba, despite the fact that the Cold War is over—long over.

Years later, when Donald Trump makes *Make America Great Again* the rallying cry of his campaign, I will wonder, don't the people know he took it from Ronald Reagan? But when he makes *Drain the Swamp* another slogan, that's when I stop dead in my tracks. Might Trump have taken it from none other than Fidel?

———————

The morning after the invasion, I played jacks on our front porch with my *amiguita* and her sister from up the hill.

My *amiguita* said, "The *gusanos* and the Yankee imperialists came in the middle of the night and attacked us." Already I knew that *gusanos* meant more than the worms we caught in our yard. *Gusanos* now were counterrevolutionaries, traitors—coined by the new revolutionary government and readily adopted by the people. Her sister said, "And Fidel fought them. From his *tanque de verde oliva*, he fought them, all night long." My *amiguita* said, "Fidel doesn't sleep." Her sister said, "Fidel never sleeps." My sister puckered her lips at me in *shh* motion.

In the living room, my father stood facing the television screen. Not stretched back in his recliner, looking far away and dreamily listening to Johnny Mathis, but standing stiff, like a soldier, the same way he stood in church clutching a rosary and mouthing endless *Ave Marías*. The bluish light of the TV screen cast a weird glow on his face, on our entire living room.

On the television, men in white T-shirts were led into what looked like a courtroom, like the ones on *Perry Mason*. The men's wrists were bound by big silver bracelets and chains. Handcuffs, like they said on *Perry Mason*. They walked in a straight line the same way our second-grade teacher said we had to walk, *obedientemente*. And their heads were bent as if they had just gotten into a lot of trouble. They looked up only as each name was called. Another line of men sat behind a long wooden desk that was raised high like the judge's on *Perry Mason*. But here, it wasn't one judge but a row of them, and the men behind the high desks wore uniforms like the ones Fidel, Ché, and the *milicianas* wore. And the men standing before them with their bent heads and wrists bound in chains looked worried—and tired. "What did you think you were doing?" Fidel asked them. I drew in a sharp breath. My father turned around. "*¿Que tu haces aquí?*" And he shooed me away.

In a matter of days, my mother, sister, and I were on a Pan Am plane, destination Miami. My father stayed behind a few more months. He had a few more jobs to wrap up for the CIA.

I didn't know about my father's involvement. I only know the story he told and retold months later, sitting in the tiny nook of our Miami Beach efficiency. He spent his last night on the homeland driven through the streets of Havana by his friend, *el jefe de la policía*. Whether my father's driver was one of Batista's ex-chiefs of police carrying out underground missions—burning and bombing hotels, major department stores, cane and tobacco fields—or a new chief of police named by the new revolutionary government who was really a double agent, who knows? Who knows if *el jefe de la policía* was ever taken to *el paredón*, the Wall—the firing-squad wall—and executed by the new revolutionary government, or if he's walking the streets of Miami. All night, my father rode through the streets of Havana crouched in the back seat of the police chief's car until dawn, at which time he was given another name, handed another passport, escorted into the private office of a Pan Am flight captain, and sneaked onto the plane seconds before takeoff. My father was a hero.

My father hid that man at our home, I later realized, in preparation for the coming invasion. Jesús and his cohorts would reinforce the land troops once the invaders made it past the beachhead. Then they would march on to victory. The US would win; the US always won.

From my father, I learned that the man he hid in our home was *fusilado*, executed by firing squad. To this day, my father speaks of him. "You think that's right?" he asks me. Except he forgets *Jesús*, and says *Mingo* instead. "Mingo, Mingo was *fusilado*."

My father hid that man in our home, and my mother acquiesced. How could she have embarked on such an *atrevimiento*, put our lives in danger like that? My mother could have been sentenced to who knows how long an imprisonment, my father *fusilado*. What would have become of my sister and me? *Jump the wall.* What were the chances Maty and I would have mustered the courage or moved quickly enough to jump the wall? Risk leaving the other behind? Or that Esperanza would have called our aunt? Assuming her neighborly friendship with my mother would have trumped her support of the revolution, what were the chances that Esperanza would have risked her own *pellejo* and that of her husband and son Jaimito? Certainly, the new revolutionary government wouldn't have executed my sister and me—this wasn't the Bolsheviks and we weren't the Romanov children—but we could have been killed in an exchange of gunfire or taken, where? To the orphanage across el Malecón where giant ocean waves crash against a wall of sea rock?

Thirty-three years later, I stand at the Palace of the Revolution and think about such things: What were my parents thinking—my mother, especially—putting all our lives in danger like that?

I don't think, How could I put all our lives in danger like that?

———

At the Palace of the Revolution, I stand in a line that's not really a line, but an *arroz con mango* of my compatriots, heads bobbing up-down, hands slicing the air—everything blocking my view. Move to the right, move to the left, and still I can't catch sight of him. But I hear it, that throaty, raspy voice with tinges of sadness, impatience; the same sadness and impatience from those days long ago of the Sierra Maestra, of Radio Rebelde, and of the beggar woman standing silent at the front door of our Havana home.

I rise on my toes and take a little jump. Then I see him. The famed profile. The long Castilian nose. The once-black beard.

Simulating the Sierra Maestra, light-filled green spaces of mountain rock and tropical foliage are scattered throughout. Cameras—video, photographic—are everywhere. *Shlick* at our smiles and waves. *TkTkTkTk* at the moving images of Fidel shaking hands with the men, kissing the women on the cheek as they're shuffled quickly through the receiving line. On the bus ride to the palace, a Cuban government official had told us that the reception would be videotaped and photographed, but only by their people and only for historical archives. My friend Eddie Levy had yelled across the bus, "What he's really saying is that all you *pobrecitos* who live in Miami needn't worry," and we laughed. Eddie is a Miami Cuban, like most of us here at the conference.

The line is at a standstill. Then it's not. It moves fast, faster. Now I am second in line, *batter-batter on deck*, like the Havana Sugar Kings ballplayers my father managed in those days of long ago.

An artificial stream with cascading water separates me from Fidel. To get to him, I must step across a small half-moon bridge such as one would find in a garden.

A mustached man in traditional dress shirt, a long-sleeved, white linen *guayabera*, motions at me to step forward. *Adelante.* He does this with an odd mix of graciousness and caution—protectiveness, for the president of the Republic of Cuba, the secretary-general of the Communist Party, the commander-in-chief of the armed forces, a few steps away.

I smile, keeping a cool front, as law professor Hausler taught me twenty years back: onward, when grappling with a demanding client, a hanging judge, or stone-faced jury. But this isn't a client, a judge, or jury. This is the major leagues.

I cross the half-moon bridge, the rush of water drowning out everything. *¡Pa'lante, mi'ja, pa'lante!* as my mother would say. But not *¡pa'lante!* if she knew I was seconds away from meeting Fidel.

———

I speak first: "*Comandante.*" From behind, a drop microphone is lowered to my mouth. "*Comandante,*" I say again, nearing closer. I'd never heard

Fidel referred to as *Comandante*, but that's how I heard other conference participants refer to him the past three days.

I hold out my hand first. Our palms meet—a steady, precise handshake, my left hand cupping the union of the two. I look up. Never have I seen such a tall Cuban. Fidel has more than a foot on me, making him well over six feet. To see him, I must stretch my neck so far back that I think I'm going to fall backward, cause quite the spectacle.

An embroidered white star and olive branch adorn the epaulet of Fidel's military uniform of olive green. He stands surprisingly fit—trim. Recently, I'd heard Fidel referred to on the floor of the US Congress as an old, fat dictator by an old, fat congressman considered by his congressional peers too liberal on Cuba.

Fidel bends to me for the traditional kiss-on-the-cheek greeting. I lift my face, his lips light on my cheek, my mouth puckered at empty space. He smells groomed—soapy. I step back, look up, continuing still to grasp his hand, as if for support.

He asks where I am from. I tell him my old Havana neighborhood of Nuevo Vedado, minutes away. There's Vedado where *la clase superior* of the turn-of-the-twentieth century built their splendid houses with big balconies and winding staircases and there's Nuevo Vedado where, midcentury, *la clase superior* rebuilt their splendid houses with big balconies and winding staircases when *la clase inferior* crossed the line into their territory.

"Ah," says Fidel, "Nuevo Vedado." An *O* puckers his mouth. Several *compañeros* stand semicircled around him. Just as I am about to say, *Where are the* compañeras?—women after all had been, were still, supposed to be a big part of the revolution—one of the *compañeros* leans into Fidel and whispers. Fidel opens his eyes wide. "Magda!" he says, as if the realization was his own. Instantly, I know. The *compañero* told him I am Magda Montiel, the same Magda Montiel who not long ago ran an unprecedented—in exile circles, a most controversial—campaign against my congresswoman who quickly gained distinction for becoming the first Cuban American elected to Congress. Predictably, I lost. But the word among political circles was that I had a future in the unpredictable world of politics. Try and try again and eventually I would topple the popular congresswoman. Her fans would be dead by then and the rest would stop hating me.

I did garnish 33 percent of the vote—a victory, considering my scandalous platform on Cuba: food and medicine should be exempted from the US embargo. But what I wanted to say is that the embargo should be lifted not because for the past thirty-three years it hadn't worked and would never work—the usual "liberal" argument—but because the US should leave Cuba alone, respect her sovereignty. But the experts—political consultants and my husband, Ira—said, *Not yet*. And I felt like a fraud, taking only baby steps, not coming out, not shouting out: *Cut the bullshit*. Pre-revolutionary Cuba was not the utopia you make it out to be. The revolution has done lots of good, for lots of people. That woman who used to come to the front door of our Havana home, hold out the pink-white of her hand, hold a baby with the other, after the revolution, I never saw that woman or anyone like her again. In 1981, when I began dating Ira and he took me to the island—my first trip back after twenty years—I didn't see people sprawled on the streets as I'd seen throughout Latin America, and in the US. I didn't hear about the African American woman whose cancerous tumor burst inside her breast because she couldn't afford medical care, as I had recently read in the *Miami Herald*. On the streets of Old Havana, I saw a shiny brown man with a wide smile of missing teeth who told me in the old days before the revolution, he lived in the mountains in huts made of mud with roofs covered only by palm leaves and now his children were *universitarios*. Not absolute, I know. Not all *fusilados* executed by firing squad were Batista henchmen or conspirators in the Bay of Pigs committing acts of sabotage that killed thousands, like the man my parents hid in our home, maybe even like my father. But what government can profess that the innocent are not at times convicted? What revolution can profess no killing? So cut the bullshit. George Washington may have not told a lie, but he sure shot plenty of bullets.

Fidel's dark brown eyes crinkle—he seems amused. "I heard you talking this morning—"

For a second, I'm baffled, but I glide over it, thinking, *He means one of my many news appearances the last few days*. Instantly, I conjure images of Fidel watching television, olive-clad legs long, outstretched; black-booted feet sprawled atop a coffee table. The word among exile circles is that Fidel attended the conference incognito, parroting all I heard growing up, hear still: Fidel watches all, hears all—every single transnational and international telephone call into and out of the island.

"*Pero ¿no te lo explicaron?*" His fingers are long, and his fingernails too, I notice, shaped in perfect ovals, reminding me of my father's hands, not from vanity though but practicality, left over perhaps from the days of the Sierra Maestra, when he and the rebel army had to suck on sugarcane, skin a pig.

Explain what? I missed half of what he just said, so busy was I envisioning him watching television and looking at his fingernails. A little laugh escapes from me. I shake my head no.

"Let me explain it to you." Each word is enunciated in careful, precise Spanish, unlike the way we speak *cubano*, running our words together, swallowing our *s*'s, though I imagine that when in nondiplomatic circles, he belts out a good Cuban *¡Coño!* and *¡Carajo!* and *¡Pinga!* and *¡Pendejo!* too. "They should have explained it to you." He looks to his right, to his left, in clear admonition of the *compañeros* about him. The lower lid of Fidel's eye trembles.

"Yes," I say. "Someday you will have to explain it to me," at a loss as to what *it* is, assuming he means, *I would like to explain it to you someday*, not now, not when a long line of conference participants stands behind me patiently waiting for their once-in-a-lifetime chance to meet *el Comandante*. So I end it, say what I planned to say as I'd stood in line.

"Fidel, I want to tell you something. Thank you for what you have done for my people. You have been a great teacher to me."

There is silence.

I turn to leave.

Fidel grips my forearm, pulls me back. The lower lid of his eye trembles again. "I want you to run for US Congress again." He Uncle Sam–points his index finger at me.

I do an about-face, inwardly smirk. The *alboroto* my exile compatriots would cause were they to get their hands on what Fidel just said. Their incessant campaign attacks resurfacing: *Didn't I tell you? That desconocia springing out of nowhere, traitor, spy! sent by Fidel to unseat our beloved congresswoman.*

I open the exit door to the smell of fried plantains and *frijoles negros*.

I don't think, This is the end of my life as I know it.

2

YOU'RE EITHER ON THE BUS
OR OFF THE BUS

———

I am first on the bus. I sit plush and air-conditioned, next to other attendees. Well, most attendees. Some decided not to take *el Comandante* up on his invitation to tonight's reception—*Muchas gracias*, but no—celebrating the end of our three-day conference. A success, government officials declared, and most of us agreed, this first step toward reconciliation. The old-guard hardliners, no, but word has it that younger generations of Cuban Americans are coming around.

White marble steps grace the entrance to the Palace of the Revolution, white columns stretch across the top. The royal palms are like bursts of stars around the monumental figure of José Martí. Like waiting brides, wrote Martí, are the royal palms.

But somewhere near, beyond the walls of the palace, a transaction is underway. Seven hundred US dollars exchanges hands. Or maybe four hundred. Media reports will be sketchy.

———

We whisk past a cemetery with thick walls of faded gold paint; around the Karl Marx Theatre, its sleek seventies façade in juxtaposition to the grey cast concrete of what was, until the recent fall of the Berlin Wall, the Soviet Embassy. Overhead, a Spanish colonial cathedral looms large, its chalky white cross rising high into the black of the Havana sky. I jerk with each thrust of the stick shift, the potholed road bumpy under my butt. A sharp turn onto the circular driveway of Hotel Comodoro with its coconut palms, yellow-speckled crotons, and hot pink bougainvillea. Below me, reporters mill about. I stay seated, wait for everyone to exit. When finally I appear, reporters scamper to my side.

"*El Comandante*, tell us about your meeting with *el Comandante*."

"I have here with me Magda Montiel Davis, former Democratic nominee for US Congress in Florida's District 18."

My mouth hurts from smiling so long at the Palace of the Revolution. My feet hurt from standing so long. I'm hungry.

Michael Putney from Miami's ABC affiliate bends over me, stiff-sprayed hair coiffed just so, plastic credentials dangling loosely from his neck. "Is there any truth—*any truth*—to the rumor coming out of Miami that Fidel Castro is dead?" His gaze sinks into mine.

I quip a Mark Twainish comeback: "The reports of Fidel's death are premature."

He looks at me expressionless. Bad joke? Dumb ears? I scurry to pull away. I'm hungry. My feet hurt.

3

SPY

———

I wake at daybreak. All night, haunted, exhausted sleep. I couldn't stop thinking about Ive—Ivelisse, but since we were three, she's been Ive (Ee-veh) to me. I called her the minute I arrived. The fleshy film over her eye that I noticed my last trip here last December is now larger, thicker. I pulled out a family photo of Chanukah. But when I handed it to her, she said she couldn't see, and put on a pair of old glasses that didn't look as if they belonged to her. I assumed it was the reaching-forty syndrome. Now I wonder if it's much more. She didn't know how to take a picture with my disposable camera and laughed at herself. "*Somos subdesarrollados.*"

I decide a hot bath will make me feel better. Not a shower; a bath, like the wild, splashy baths she and I took in the backyard sink. But the bathroom smell nauseates me. I thought it was the plumbing, sewer slush perhaps, dumped too close to shore. But maybe it's the hotel soap, tiny white tablets that split into pieces when I try to peel them open. I grab one of the Dial soap bars I brought to give away to friends, hotel workers—anyone, really. Ah, the warm, soapy smell of the terry cloth on my face; that, too, reminiscent of those days of long ago. I stretch back, place my still aching feet under the steady stream of hot water. But the smell, it comes and goes.

I give up, wrap a towel around me, exit. I stop, dead in my tracks. The door to my room is open. Slightly ajar, but open still. How can that be? Was it open a few minutes ago when I grabbed the soap bar? When I woke? Could I have been so tired last night that I forgot to lock—even close— the door? My bags are intact and so is my money. Was it done to give me a message, a sign? If so, by whom? The *real Cubans in Cuba*—as a Clinton-appointed official told me not long ago, then tried to wave away the faux pas—or an exile militant group?

Maybe they—whoever *they* might be—think I'm another Mrs. Ames, the wife of the accused Soviet spy, just accused herself. Maybe I'm getting paranoid. Fear begets paranoia, and I don't want to get paranoid. It starts with mild warnings from family and friends, and then a threat of military action from Alpha 66 appears in your mailbox.

––––––––

Two months ago—and my forty-first birthday. I stood outside our home waiting for the building contractor. For over a year we had not lived in our home, such was the devastation from Hurricane Andrew. Our house, two blocks from the beach, had taken a direct hit; water surge, sewage spill. The contractor was coming to assess the damage. And I'd come to assess him. Might he turn out to be yet another unknowing unknown flocking to South Florida professing honesty and prestige?—*tremendo paquete*, as my mom would say. But given the countywide destruction and shortage of reputable contractors, we decided to stay in the house despite sodden walls and rotten smells. A week later, the roof of our three-year-old son's bedroom collapsed, flattening his bunk bed—minutes after he'd gotten out of bed.

I looked at my watch, paced the courtyard, past our purple tiger orchids working hard to come back to life. My client had a deportation hearing at the immigration building behind the Pink Pussy Cat. If late, the immigration judge could very well, would most likely, deport my client. Ten minutes, I thought, and I leave; meanwhile, might as well do something productive. So I headed to our mailbox, a one-legged flamingo of pink plaster. I opened the bird's mouth, a little trap door under its beak, looked through the mail for a plain white envelope from the Cuban Interests Section in Washington, DC; "Interests Section," not "Embassy," because sixteen days before he left office in 1961, Eisenhower severed diplomatic relations with Cuba. For years, there was no embassy, no interests section, *nada*, until Jimmy Carter let the US travel ban lapse. Each country opened an interests section in the other country. Reinstatement of diplomatic relations seemed probable during Carter's second term. But a second term was not to be. Instead, newly elected Reagan reinstated the travel ban. So, in the "interest" of my safety and that of other Cuba activists, the envelope I was to receive would, I knew, be plain white with no Cuban Interests Section anywhere, no Cuban anything anywhere.

Inside would be an invitation to a conference in Havana to be held in two months. No invitation was in store for me that day, but I smiled at the prospect. Havana. Giant ocean waves drenching *enamorados* kissing and rubbing along the Malecón seawall. Boys pulling in their fishing lines. The singsong *pregones* of street vendors, the smell of warm roasted peanuts filling the salt air.

Back to the stack of mail, *flip flip* the bills, catalogues, junk ads. Then I stopped: ALPHA 66 / P.O. BOX 420067 / MIAMI, FL. 33142 ink-stamped in bright red at the top left of another white envelope. My name, written the Cuban way: MAGDA MONTIEL, without the inclusion of Davis, from my teenage marriage to high school boyfriend Paul. The font was that of a long-ago typewriter, a Corona, maybe. And strange: a period after my name, after our street address, after Key Biscayne, FL., after the zip code, even. Were the periods some interterrorist message? Or just poor typing?

The first few paragraphs contained the usual: "This is the final hour for Alpha 66 to deliver upon our suffering homeland its most annihilated democracy. Our Commandos, full of valor and tenacity, are ready to accomplish their glorious mission. Those who choose to ignore our mandate shall tremble with fear . . ." Why am I being sent this? I thought. Then, four paragraphs down, there it was: "Anyone who travels to Cuba . . . dialogues . . . shall suffer *acción militar.*"

Never had I come face-to-face, much less touched, a real live threat before. During my congressional race, a man in a truck did stop at a major Calle Ocho intersection. "*¡Comunista!* Look at her," he addressed the crowd, "she's even wearing red!" He revved the motor, opened the door. I stood unmoving. Maybe because it seemed so unreal. Or maybe because of my years of going to court with clients where so much depends on feigning confidence. But the light turned green and the man moved on. Some threats were also called in to the campaign office, but I got them second-hand, reported to me by Ira or volunteers. But not this, never like this.

How, I wondered, did these people get our home address? When Ira and I began dating, already he'd been threatened by the Klan and other white nationalist groups for suing the government for discriminatory treatment of Haitian refugees: en masse deportation, indefinite detention at remote locations where lawyers couldn't get to them, suicides by hanging, children separated from parents, brothers from sisters. And threatened as well after exile radio announced that he was communist; worse yet, a communist Jew, Fidel Castro's lawyer. Why? Ira had represented a couple in Cuba who wanted their fourteen-year-old daughter back. She'd run away to Miami on a raft with her eighteen-year-old boyfriend. While arguing

Ha llegado la hora de las decisiones para el enfrentamiento final. La ASamblea Nacional
en Campaña, Celebrada el los dias 27 y 28 de Marzo de 1993, adoptó acuerdos concretos
a fin de lograr, en el menor tiempo posible, la victoria definitiva que lleve la tan
anhelada libertad y democracia a nuestra sufrida Patria.

Una organización como **Alpha 66** que tiene racimos de mártires y héroes, toma siempre
decisiones concretas y las cumple. Eso ha creado mística de la liberación y la confianza
del pueblo.

En esta importante y trascendente reunión hemos reafirmado la tesis de la organización,
ratificado los principios ideológicos y se han adoptado acuerdos para la liberación
de Cuba.

Uno de los acuerdos históricos fue hacer un llamado a todas las personalidades
extranjeras, turistas o industriales, que visitan Cuba para que dejaran de hacerlo antes
de Noviembre 27 de 1993 ya que ello no solo otorga reconocimiento al régimen
totalistarista cubano sino, lo mas grave, oxigena la economía cubana lo que retardara
la caida del tirano, sumando mas dolor y pena a nuestro pueblo.

Conscientes de que somos los abanderados del valor y al tenacidad, Proclamamos hoy, que
todas aquellas personas que visiten Cuba, dialoguen o apoyen directa o indirectamente
al desgobierno que oprime a nuestro pueblo, independientemente de su nacionalidad y
naturaleza, será declarado objetivo militar y sufrirá las consecuencias dentro o fuera
de Cuba. Nuestros Comandos estan listos para cumplir las gloriosas misiones que exige
la Patria. Como se dijo en la Asamblea Nacional. ¡Estamos en Campaña.¡Estamos en campaña
heroica y decisiva. No pararemos hasta lograr la victoria.

Aquellos que osen ignorar nuestro nuevo llamamiento temblaran de miedo ante la violencia
de nuestras acciones. No estableceremos distingos innecesarios e injustificados.

Es bochornoso y aberrante presenciar como mandatarios y personalidades de gobierno,
miembros de Congresos y Parlamentos elegidos en un sistema democrático, funcionarios
y empleados de institutos, organizaciones, etc., intelectuales, científicos, periodistas
y hasta religiosos le han hecho y le estan haciendo el juego al Castrato.

La organizacion comprende el alto precio que tiene que pagar para lograr el objetivo
central. No vamos a parar nada y sufriremos las consecuencias.

En la etapa denominada **"Punto Final"** del Plan Máximo Gómez, Alpha 66 asume con todo
su poder, de su larga historia y de su ascendencia en el pueblo ese honroso titulo de
vanguardia de la libertad de Cuba. Reiteramos nuevamente que "Vale mas Fracasar por
tratar de Triunfar, que dejar de Triunfar por temor a Fracasar".

Que nadie se llame a engaños, recientemente la Corte Federal de Cayo Hueso reconoció
la beligerancia y el derecho del pueblo cubano en el exilio a luchar por la libertad
de Cuba, con su sentencia adsolutoria a los 9 Alphistas que habian sido detenidos
injustamente cuando salian para una DE las miles de acciones militares que se realizan
contra el régimen de la isla y que continuaremos hasta la caída definitiva de Fidel
Castro y su camarilla.

Nos mantendremos en la vanguardia por la libaertad.

Andres Nazario Sargen   Diego Medina MD.   Hugo Gascon Congora
Sec. General   Sec. de Prensa   Sec. de Finanzas

First threat from Alpha 66, the oldest and one of the largest paramilitary, exile
terrorist organizations. The *Miami Herald* reported that "even before Havana
released a partial list of invitees earlier this month, a number of the expected participants received a letter from the anti-Castro group Alpha 66 warning they could
become 'military targets' if they traveled to Cuba. Alpha 66 leaders acknowledged
drafting the letter, but deny mailing it to anyone" ("Havana Conference: To Go or
Not to Go," April 19, 1994). The threat, postmarked February 26, 1994, was delivered
to my South Florida home on my forty-first birthday. The FBI claimed to be investi-
gating but never made an arrest, despite the clear identity of the perpetrators.

before a federal judge to reunite the girl with her parents, outside on a park bench, Immigration handed the girl a green card. So Ira only used his office address. When we married eight years later, he told me to do the same.

————

The contractor—finally arrived—was massive and muscular and referred to most everything as *sweet*. Real sweet, mighty sweet. "Wouldn't a recessed ceiling look sweet here in the dining room?"

Alpha 66 threat in hand, I curled, uncurled its edges. *Curl, uncurl.*

"And the purples. Is lilac still okay?"

I folded the threat 1 2 3 4 times but succeeded only in making it too fat to fit back inside the envelope.

"Your husband was making all these comments: 'Doesn't my wife know any color in the spectrum besides purple?'" A big smile of loose dentures. "Very funny guy, your husband."

And so, amid our mildewed walls and rotten sewer smells and warped hardwood floors and ruined family photos curled closed and giving the building contractor instructions to, yes, go ahead and paint the area below the chair railing a shade darker—"No! It's not lavender," he said, "it's creamy plum"—I wanted to say: *You don't understand! I am the subject of military action.*

Six weeks later came the plain white envelope and the invitation, in bulk—not fine linen—paper, in the form of a letter, its letterhead typed, not engraved; its ink faded. In an attempt to give it an invitation-like feel, its text, in typewriter cursive, was nevertheless formal. "We transmit to you, by means of this letter, an invitation extended by the organizing commission for the 'NATION AND EMIGRATION' conference on April 22, 23, and 24 at the Palace of Conventions of Havana, Cuba." Special round-trip fare of 256.00 USD and, at no additional charge, the processing of all travel documents, even 5 extra kilograms of baggage.

Guess which letter I readily accepted and which I chose to ignore?

————

I run. Sun-dappled banyan trees. Shirtless boys swinging from one vine to another, then tumbling to the ground, as did Ive and I, as my kids have never done. A couple on a bicycle come by, she perched on the handlebars

EMBASSY OF SWITZERLAND
CUBAN INTERESTS SECTION
2630 16th Street, NW
Washington, D.C. 20009

Washington, D.C., 4 de abril de 1994

Sra. Magda Montiel Davis
Miami, Florida

Estimado señor (a) :

Por instrucciones del Ministro de Relaciones Exteriores de Cuba,
Roberto Robaina Gonzalez, trasladamos a usted, a traves de esta
carta, la invitacion formulada por la Comision Organizadora de la
Conferencia "LA NACION Y LA EMIGRACION", a fin de que participe en
las sesiones que tendran lugar durante los dias 22, 23 y 24 de
abril en el Palacio de las Convenciones de La Habana, Cuba.

Le rogamos acuse recibo de esta comunicacion.

Atenta...

A... P...z
Jefe Seccion de Intereses de Cuba
en ... D.C.

if

Invitation to the Havana conference signed by Cuba's foreign minister,
Roberto Robaina Gonzalez, sent to me on April 4, 1994, by the Cuban
Interests Section in Washington, DC. For security reasons, it was sent
in a plain white envelope with no return name or address.

while he pedals. "*Montate,* and we'll take you for a little ride." Someone
yells, "*¡Quema la grasa!*" *Grasa?* What *grasa?* Oh God. Cellulite? I laugh,
run on.

I call home. Katy, home for spring break, answers. But I can hardly hear.
A distanced "Mom!" that sounds like Maggie. "Ira said he lost weight." Now

Paula, definitely Paula. "What'd he do? Get a nose job?" I hear Ira's "Why am I not laughing?" The three older girls are from my first marriage, but I've never heard Ira say "stepdaughters." And though the girls call him Ira, they refer to him as "my dad."

"Hey guys," I say after a while. "Can I speak to your grandmother?"

"*¡Abuela!*" they yell in unison. She's either outside smoking or tending to her Afro-Cuban rituals in her bedroom. Mami has always lived with me, even when I was married to Paul.

"*¡No esta!*" Mami says, until they tell her it's me on the line. "Hah-lo?"

"Mami?"

"*¡Chi chi! ¿Como éstas?*" And when I reciprocate, "*Aquí,*" she says. I've never understood this. How are you? I'm . . . *here.*

"Beba." *Babygirl*, my childhood nickname, what Mami always calls me. "Is it true Fidel—"

"No, Mami, Fidel is not dead."

A fluttery—a nervous?—chuckle. "*¡Ay! ése Radio Mambi*—"

"Mami, how can you listen to that shit? That's all you do."

"*Bueno*, it's in *el Miami Herald* too."

"Oh, that's a reliable source. And no, Fidel is *not* dead. Maybe Mas Canosa"—Jorge Mas Canosa, the very wealthy chairman of the most powerful anti-Cuba lobby who spreads rumors Fidel is dead, then names himself President of Cuba—"got him confused him with Richard Nixon." Who now is.

4

FLYING WITH YOUR WINGS CUT

———

squeeze through the hotel doors just as they're about to close on me. Ive and sister Susy wait for me in the lobby. Our ritual: right before my trip home, I give them most of the cash I have left. "*Coño, carajo*, I'm sorry." I lean over, give Susy a kiss, lift Ive off her feet. "I didn't know it was going to take so long."

"You go to the conference, run like a madwoman all over Havana, have a rendezvous with *tu tío*"—uncle, one of the many ways Cubans refer to Fidel.

"That was last night," I say. "And it was a reception. Full of people."

"*No importa.* I sat my fat *culo* here on this cushy sofa . . ."

I rummage through my backpack, feigning calm as Ive chatters on but I can't do the math. Airport departure tax tomorrow: Is it twenty dollars? Or twenty-five? Breakfast, included in the hotel package? And my long-distance calls home, so expensive.

"*Oye, qué pena me da*," Susy says in a small voice.

"Why?" I look up. "If it was the other way around, you'd do the same for me."

"Yes." She taps her head on my shoulder. "The same for you."

"*Bueno, ya*," Ive says, "don't talk so much shit."

Back in Miami, Channel 7, the local Fox station.

RICK SANCHEZ: For four days, there were rumors that he may be dead. But take a look at this. Tonight proves that Fidel is alive and well. And we have the video just in from Havana to prove it. The images you see—of Fidel with hundreds of conference attendees in Havana last night—fly in the face of what the exile community has been saying, that the entire conference was nothing more than propaganda orchestrated by the Cuban government.

I sink into a sofa, Ive into a huge wicker arm chair. She plunks one, two meaty calves on a coffee table, throws back her head, simulating deep sucking on a cigarette holder. "Here. Take my picture." Then, in thick MGM melodrama, "Sarita Montiel in *El Último Cuplé*"—the glamorous Spanish star of fifties musical film puffing long breaths of Pall Mall smoke over her prizefighter matador, just mangled by a bull.

"Instead of looking for *fula*"—US dollars, in Cuban lingo—"in that crazy bag of yours, get your camera out and take my picture so you can take it back to *La Yuma*"—local slang for the US, taken from the fifties western *3:10 to Yuma*—"and say to all the *gusanos*"—a high-pitched, aristocratic voice—"'*This* is where my best friend in Cuba lives.'" A hearty laugh. "Like when they come here, show us phony pictures and say, 'This is the mansion where I live, and here are my vacation homes, and all the *automóviles* I drive, and yachts I sail.'"

Susy rolls her eyes, turns to kiss me. "*Bueno, un besito.*"

"No, don't go. Stay, please." I pull them by the wrists toward a steady burst of sounds.

Eddie Levy, blind eyes behind black sunglasses, sings at the piano bar along with wife Xiomara and other conference attendees. Discordant sounds coupled with chirrupy, velvety sounds. A chorus of socialists.

I hop on the half-moon stage with Francisco Aruca (*Aruca* to us), owner of Marazul, the first Cuba-travel charter company that Ira incorporated for him, then friended. We sing *Nosotros*. Aruca and I harmonize. He's drunk; I'm not. I hear Xiomara's high-pitched vibrato, Eddie's Pavarotti-like antics. I hear the rasp of my breathing, my own absence of tone.

Michael Putney from Miami's ABC affiliate is interviewed
by competing CBS news anchors.

MICHAEL PUTNEY: It is ironic that these are the people that as they were going down to the island, told us, 'Well, we're not really there to be Castro's puppets. We're not being manipulated.' But, by gosh . . . As I said, we couldn't attend the reception last night, and then Cuban officials sold us this videotape. They tried to sell it for a hefty sum. We got them down a bit, but, ah, when they finally saw Castro last night, they were like, ah . . . it was hero worship, that's what it was.

DIANE MAGNUM, CHANNEL 4: Did something change? Was the tape manip—

MICHAEL PUTNEY: No. I'm sure the tape was not manipulated. This is the way it was.

ELIOT RODRIGUEZ, CHANNEL 4: He has that effect on people, doesn't he, Michael?

Ive and I merengue out the piano bar, our hands on each other's hips, one two, one two. We head for the restaurant, merengueing still, *Tú me hicistes brujería* playing behind us.

"You know they say Fidel has a great *brujero*," Ive says.

"I can't hear you."

"How do you think he won this great revolution? And got all these people to follow him, got all these women"—she juts her chin at me—"to be enamored with him?"

"*¡Ay, Ive, por Dios!*" Susy says.

"*Sí, Ive, por Dios*," I say.

Tú me hicistes ¿qué? ¡Brujería! I get caught up in the wanna-dance rhythm of the bongo drums, the horns, the piano.

Miami, Univisión, Noticias 23.

Video clip of female conference attendees on the receiving line.

CONFERENCE ATTENDEE 1: You look *muy bien, muy bien.*

FIDEL: *Muchas gracias.*

He leans down, kisses her on the cheek.

CONFERENCE ATTENDEE 2: *Mucho gusto, y una larga vida para siempre.*

Fidel leans down, kisses her on the cheek.

CONFERENCE ATTENDEE 3: This has been the dream of my life always, to extend my hand—(Her voice breaks.)

Xiomara waves from across the lobby, her eclectic ensemble of bright geometric print flowing behind her as she walks to us, Eddie's hand on her shoulder, taking short, careful steps. After introductions to Susy and Ive, "*Oye, Magdita*," says Eddie. "Xiomara and I were standing behind you in line when you met Fidel."

"Yes," says Xiomara, "and we were wondering why didn't you let him answer you."

"Answer me, what?"

"*¿Como qué?* 'Answer me what?'" says Eddie. "About the *fusilados*, that's what."

"The question, *querida*, that you asked," says Xiomara. "At the conference. About the firing squads."

"Never before," says Eddie, "had Fidel offered to explain in open forum, to the whole world, about the *fusilados*."

"You mean that's what Fidel meant when he said, 'Let me explain it to you'?" My eyes, wide open. "I didn't even know what he was talking about. I assumed he meant he'd seen me on TV, at an interview. But I've said so much, I didn't know what he was talking about. So I just smiled and said, 'Okay. Someday you're going to have to explain it to me.' I just . . . assumed."

"*Ay, Magdita*," says Eddie. "You missed the opportunity."

"Oh, well," says Ive. "Such is life. Missed opportunities."

Telemundo, Noticiero 51.

VIDEO CLIP: Fidel pats Aruca's arm heartily. Aruca tries to move away.

FIDEL: "*Bueno, ¿los problemas se siguen*"—continue—"*resolviendo, verdad?*"

Aruca "*Sí, sí*," nods, keeps moving away.

Then, "Magda!" Fidel turns his cheek to the side for the hello kiss.

"I heard you talking this morning [inaudible] *los fusilados*."

I lean in.

FIDEL: "They didn't explain it to you?"

"*Bueno, vámonos, Eddie*," Xiomara tugs his arm.

"Can they make the music any louder?" says Eddie. "Soon I'll be both deaf *and* blind."

Xiomara turns to me. "I might not see you tomorrow. We're visiting *mi mamá* in—"

I nod and smile. I can't hear her over the bongos, the maracas, the sweet-sad plucky sound of the Spanish guitar. Kisses for Eddie and Xiomara, kisses all around, Eddie's hand back on Xiomara's shoulder, and off they go, Xiomara's caftan making little waves behind her.

"That's the blind guy you told us about?" says Ive, and when I nod, "*¡Coño!* The Yankees make it so even the blind don't look blind?"

Miami, ABC's Eyewitness News.

FIELD REPORTER: "Good evening. What began as a small gathering for Earth Day ended in a heated protest. Demonstrators took to the streets. Hundreds of cars draped with Cuban flags drove from South Dade to Little Havana." Newsreel of pickup trucks and motorcycles, Cadillacs and Jaguars. "They say the conference attendees are puppets for Cuba's propaganda." Bullhorns and pumped fists. Giant Cuban and US flags wave side-by-side.

CONGRESSWOMAN ILEANA ROS-LEHTINEN: "These people down in Cuba aren't denouncing human rights violations. They're not denouncing the lack of freedom or lack of rights. They're just there to be good students, listening to this . . . monologue. This is not a dialogue."

The smell of *criollo*: olive oil, singed garlic, sizzling onions. "*Tengo hambre*," I say.

"Ah-ah," Susy says, a twang of friendly sarcasm. "Now you know what it's like."

I walk Susy and Ive to the restaurant in the far back of the lobby.

"*¿Una langostica?*" offers the young fellow at the take-out counter.

"Oh, God, no, no lobster," I say. Right before I left, our own Chairman Mas was once again on TV, saying that we were coming to Havana to eat lobster and drink champagne with Fidel. So no, no lobster, lest I be caught red-handed eating lobster with Fidel by Mas Canosa spies.

"*Tres pizzas*," I tell the fellow. "Takeout."

"Three pizzas?" he says *en inglés*. "Boy, can you eat."

"*Ay, ay, ay*," Ive says. "Don't tell her that. Now she won't eat for a week." She squeezes my waist. "*Como el pesquezo de un guanajo*." The size of a turkey neck.

Miami, Telemundo, Noticiero 51.

FIELD REPORTER: The radio stations and the people on the streets of Little Havana are *ardiendo*.

SPEAKER 1: It's been the *descaro mas grande del mundo, mas grande del mundo, mas grande del mundo*, all those people hugging Fidel. After he kicks them out, how can they . . . *no lo comprendo*.

SPEAKER 2: *¡Las expresiónes eran de idolatría!*

SPEAKER 3: Good for nothing, that's what they are. *No sirven para nada*.

[None interviewed mention a particular conference participant, when suddenly the reporter declares: "Interviews are over."]

FIELD REPORTER: Well, you've heard their reactions. By far, all the astonishment and indignation is directed at Magda Montiel Davis, who recently ran against our *congresista*, Ileana Ros-Lehtinen.

I give one pizza to Susy, another to Ive, keep the third for myself. "Wait," I turn back to the counter. "Milk, you have any milk?" give a cup each to Susy and Ive for their children—"No, no lid," says the fellow, "and no straw either"—and arms intertwined, walk them outside. Slapping US dollars onto their hands, "*Uno, dos, y tres*," I try to make light of the moment.

"If you don't have enough *dolares* when you get to the airport to get back to *La Yuma*"—every time Ive says this, I envision vision Van Heflin trying to get Glenn Ford's ass on the 3:10 train to Yuma—"come back to my place and I'll make you *frijoles negros*, just the way you like them." She holds her hand over her mouth, pretend-whispers to Susy: "With sprinkled sugar. But don't tell our *amiguita* here, or she'll never eat my *frijoles* again."

I grin. Then I take a breath. I ask them finally what I have wanted to know for thirteen years now, since Ira first brought me back. "If you could immigrate to the US, would you? I'm an immigration lawyer," I remind them. "I can process the necessary papers for you."

Susy shakes her head no. I'm surprised when Ive joins in assent.

"Not without my father, and he won't go." Susy looks down, her sandals making little circles on the pebbled ground. Their father, a medical doctor, is one of the few who was faithful to the revolution and stayed. "Papi feels he sacrificed for the revolution, worked so hard, so long. He's got the family home that he built, what? over forty years ago, patients he still attends to—the children of babies he once delivered—even a little farm—"

"Yeah, a little farm with nothing left on it," says Ive. "Even his favorite horse got stolen." Susy's mouth downturns into a sad smile. "Mami tells us we have young children to look out for and if we want to leave, we should. I cry and I tell her, 'How can you say that?'" She looks away. "No. We'll all die here, together."

"I told you," says Ive. "Missed opportunities. And now, our children, missed opportunities too."

The hotel porter opens the door of the turistaxi, a Mercedes. I prepay their cab fare. Susy and Ive smile their good-byes at me through the closed window. Ive balances her unlidded cup of milk, raises it as if clinking a toast.

Funny, I think on my walk back to my little bungalow through the dark hotel grounds, I never eat pizza at home (but it tastes so much better here). I hear a wolf whistle. I shake my head, ready to take on Mister—Señor—Macho. But it's not Macho Man. It's the hotel's parrot. "Very funny." I smirk at the bird. He looks at me, drops his head to the side. *What do you want from me?* he seems to say. *I'm just another* comemierda *here, perched on the same limb day in, day out*, jodio *as hell. Ever tried flying with your wings cut?*

Miami, Telemundo, Noticiero 51.

NEWS ANCHOR: The scene was akin to fanaticism. And *el Comandante* signing autographs as if he were a Hollywood star, and not the dictator that he is.

WOMAN IN LITTLE HAVANA: Magda Montiel Davis? It's unbelievable—exasperating—to all of us Cubans *en los Estados Unidos* that she told Fidel Castro that he was her maestro.

VIDEO CLIP: I look up at Fidel. "*Has sido un gran maestro para mi.*" I nod as I say it.

A close-up of Fidel's face, his profile.

And again: "*Has sido un gran maestro para mi.*"

Skirting through curlicues of walkways, I skip over any broken or missing tiles. *Step on a crack / break your mother's back.* I balance on the rim of a lagoon-shaped aquamarine pool, its surface reflecting the shimmer of the Havana stars, its depths a dark blue, almost black. Storybook bridges connect man-made waterfalls, hot tubs, and cozy wading pools.

"*Muy hermosa usted.*" A deep, low voice. Jolted, I take a look, then loosen. Just a young black guy. And from his rhythm of speech, I can tell he's Cuban. I return his smile, then smirk inwardly. Miami. Miami, where my high school friend's son walks in a jewelry store with his white friends, and the minute the sales clerk sees him—the black of his skin, he said—she goes behind the counter. "Close to the emergency alarm button," he said. "Ju-uhst in case."

Hmm, I say to myself, good-looking yourself, and tall and muscular too, but me, beautiful? I keep walking, throw back my head at him and quiver a laugh, my cheeks burning. Then I hear, "*A pesar de los años.*"

"No, really," he says, "don't take it as a lack of respect. I can see you once were—"

Once were *what*? Let's see what that physique looks like, buddy, when you're forty-one. I pass the 800-numbered buildings, 800 this, 800 that and now I'm at—how can that be?—the 500-plus buildings. Bad sense of direction. Always, since childhood, bad sense of direction.

Where is 672? My bungalow. A second-floor studio walk-up, but here at Hotel Comodoro, with its storybook bridges and cozy wading pools, they're called bungalows. I plop onto a small Caribbean-white bench, its panes warped, its sides rusting, but I have more pressing matters to worry about. My stomach. *Ay!* It's the *café con leche* I had this morning. The milk here, it's too thick. Tastes damn good, but whoa, sheesh, ough—I run for a bathroom. Where's the bathroom? *Compañeros.* The first bathroom I find. But no matter. I run in anyway. No door. No door on the stall. And no toilet paper. Shit! Again I forgot to throw toilet paper in my bag. Don't leave home without it when in Havana. When I asked Ive what she needed me to bring back on my next trip—"Toilet paper?"—she said: *"Ay, mi'ja,* I gave up those habits years ago." They use old towels that they wring in the bathroom or kitchen sink. "The Yankees continue to tighten the embargo because that's what the Cubans in Miami say will topple Fidel, *¿y nosotros los cubanos?* We continue to wipe our asses. Just find another way to do it."

Now the toilet doesn't flush. I hold down the lever with my foot. I hold it for a few long seconds, turn the rusty lever this way and that. Flush, damn it! I don't want a poor hotel worker who was faithful to the revolution and stayed to have to face my unflushed toilet. I hold the lever for a long time and—yes!—it flushes. How many would do that for the revolution?

I walk past lemon-yellow townhouses and pink-orange ones. I walk past snow-queen hibiscus like the one in my childhood home minutes away. And past French-doored terraces like the one in my Miami home. Minutes away too, if airplane rides count: forty-three minutes HAV–MIA.

Finally, 672. I climb the stairs. God, they're steep. God, they're narrow. God, I'm tired. I reach for the banister, but it wobbles like a loose tooth. Thrusting the key into the keyhole, I fling open the door. Unlatching the windows with a happy fury, I unbutton my sundress, let its bright, deep purple fall to the floor. Necklace, wedding ring, everything off. I stand at the window. Ah, the smells, the sounds, the feels of my country. Its curious contradictions.

I don my soft, cottony nightshirt with tiny prints of baby pink and baby blue kitty cats that Katy, Paula, and Maggie, and sometimes little Sadie like to wear, that prompts Paula to tease her brother: *Benny, would you like to wear Mommy's clothes too?* as he stands, utterly dumbfounded, white belly protruding from his three-foot frame.

Cross-legged on the bed, I hear my stomach chuck a complaint, eat the pizza anyway. I look at the telephone on my night table, or rather, it looks at me. *Pick me up*, it says. *Pick me up and call home.*

No need. By this time tomorrow, I'll be home. *Ay coño*, but Ira. Already he was annoyed because I postponed my flight home. By half a day. But I needed the extra time to talk to the Cuban official about the exit visas for my clients here on the island.

"Okay, I'll call," I say aloud. Ira *did* say to call home at whatever time I got in. "Just wanna make sure you're all right." I reach for my journal, eating pizza still, and jot down some notes as to how I'll respond. (Just because he's so smart and unless I'm fully prepared, he'll get the best of me):

1. It's only half a day. In the grand scheme of things, what difference does it make?—given the difference I can make in my clients' lives. Or

2. I had a very productive stay (this I will say if he starts out asking me how my day was) not the least of which was getting the Cuban government officials to grant the exit visas to my clients. (Well, they haven't yet but with Ira, you have to embellish.) Or

3. What about you? You're gone all the time, to Haiti, or DC. (But this won't work with him.)

Okay, I am prepared. After meeting Fidel, talking to a parrot and fighting with a toilet, I'm ready for anything. And maybe it won't be so bad. Maybe Ira will have that voice that is so transparent, so obviously happy to hear from me: "Sweetie?" he'll say, and if it's *sweetie* and not *Magda*, I'll know there's room to negotiate.

I lift the telephone from its cradle, hear the distant *beep beep* indicating the rusty-wired connection has been made.

"Mom?" It's Maggie, daughter no. 3.

"What." An emphatic *What*. What is she still doing up? What shenanigans now? And by which one of the five of them?

"Mom!" she says in that little voice she uses to warn her siblings they're in big trouble. "You were on TV kissing Fidel, and all these people keep calling here saying they want to kill you."

PART TWO

———

ATOLONDRAMIENTO

5

GET AHOLD OF YOURSELF

———

Okay, Magda, get ahold of yourself. I press the pen hard on the page, my handwriting large, frantic. *Thank God you called*, and I forget to spell God *G—d* like I was taught when I converted to Judaism.

This way, you'll have . . . what? Springing out of bed, I flip the contents of my backpack: Marazul Charters, HAV-MIA 26April94, 11am. I count with my fingers. 10 11 12 . . . *Thirteen hours to prepare.*

I pace. Not the length of the room. Short paces, 1 2 3 about-face. I scribble as I walk. *But there's no one to talk to. Not even Xiomara.*

Where did she and Eddie say they were going? To visit her mother. Where? I don't remember. Some small village. But I don't know those small villages.

———

WHAT is Ira thinking? SAFETY. *Do I need to call home again? (Shouldn't he be home by now?) Ask him if it's okay for me to go home alone from the airport?*

Will he yell? Is there a slight chance he'll be proud of me?

And the kids. Oh my God. The kids.

I just wish I knew the consequences and could get it over with.

Okay, Magda, just keep writing. The answers, they will come to you.

Okay. I'll pack. I pack with a quiet mania. I pack the files I brought with me with good intentions to work on but didn't. I pack the letters from Cubans here on the island filled with problems for me to solve. They heard of me, they write; they know I can help them.

And who's going to help me?

I run across the photograph I tried to show Ive, or rather, it runs across me. It's of the family, last Chanukah: Ira's schnozzy profile, bent over the prayer book, reading a blessing in unintelligible Hebrew; Maggie lighting the eighth candle of the menorah, trying hard, in all the awkwardness of adolescence, to get it right; Sadie sporting a wide, anticipatory grin of loosely splayed baby teeth, Chanukah presents abound; Ben in his favorite T-Rex pajamas cut off at the knee, curls frizzing wildly; Paula trying to put a red Santa hat on Goblin, the pink of his tongue stark against the black of his fur. I have a spontaneous, open-wide laugh that looks like it just escaped from me; Mami looks heartened, amused. She'd asked if this was *las Navidades judías*, then let out one of her signature heh-heh-hehs; Katy, home for winter break, standing solemn, as if passing judgment, probably on me.

My unfinished article—I hold it in my hands. It's about women. Women here, women there, two very different political systems, but the same juggling, the same negotiating, the psychological tugs of war. Maybe tomorrow I can make the corrections. I'll get to the airport early, finish it there—

Who am I kidding, finish it there?

But now I see the stone, the stone from the rivers of the Sierra Maestra that a Cuban official gave me at last night's reception. The stone, tossed among my still sweaty jogging bras and shorts. I pack it carefully. I knead my ring finger. I call home.

Here's what happens when I call home: Mom, it's okay.

It's Paula. Sweet, vulnerable Paula, who still evokes nightmares in me that she's drowning and I can't save her.

A mother who never learned to swim.

It's okay, Mommy, Paula says again.

I draw the phone to me, press my lips. Almost a smile.

Ira takes the phone from her. He says hullo. That throaty hullo.

I say Ira.

Then there's silence.

I take a breath. Is it safe for me to go home alone? I ask. From the airport, I mean.

Do you, uh, want me to?

Never mind, I say.

An echoey *beep, beep, beep*. How much time left before we're cut off?

No, he says. I'll pick you up. And take you home. He says this sweetly.

My articles, I say after a few silent seconds.

They were published, he says. Your articles were published.

I wait.

They were good, he says.

I . . . was working on an article. Women here, women there. I thrust my head forward. You think I could still write it?

Yeah. He laughs. They'll be more likely to print it now. His voice seems too loud.

I take a step back.

That *beep, beep* again.

I'm losing you, I say. The connection, I mean.

Look, he says finally. It's like—here I think I see him shrugging—it's like George McGovern having ice cream with Fidel. You know, when the press made such a big deal and kept playing it for days. And here I think I see his lips tighten. And then it blew over, he says.

Communist. Supposed to be a bad word. When that woman at the confer-ence, that medical doctor who lives in Puerto Rico, stood and said, Yo soy comunista, *it shocked, even me.*

This must be how gays feel when they come out, or are "found out."

Like McGovern having ice cream with Fidel, Ira said. Three to five days, he said. Then it'll blow over.

And I think of Jane Fonda—

Damn! But what's so wrong about all this? I didn't cheat or steal or kill. I'm a moral person. Oh God now I sound like Richard Nixon.

————

Did the Cuban officials set me up? "Hail Mary, full of grace, the Lord is with you." I say it in my head, I say it out loud.

Could they prohibit me from leaving? Separated from Sadie and Ben? Katy, Paula, and Maggie? Forever? Ira? My mom? Hail Mary, full of grace, I say it fast, in a frenzy, not enunciating the words but letting them rise, fall, in crazed musicality.

Could the Cubans here try to hurt me, kill me, to pin it on the Cubans there? HolyMaryMotherofGod, I run the words together, alternating my birth language, adopted language. Birth country, adopted country. *Santa María, madre de Dios.* Mary, Motherland, Mami. The three of them.

The Cubans here. *I hope they know, I will not denounce them.*

6

EMERGE IN THE SINGULAR

———

The cabbie, he knows to let me be. I feel sorry for him, his look of concern, my quiet dismissal of him. Finally, *"Un video,"* I say. *"De una recepción. Con el Comandante."*

We ride through Quinta Avenida, former mansions converted into embassies of the Americas, Europe, Asia; the US nowhere. Was I at *la conferencia*? he asks.

"Sí." Then, *"Vivo en Miami."* I needn't say more.

"Ay, mi'ja, now you're going to leave me worried." His eyes, narrow through the rectangle of rearview mirror, are like a surgeon's—eyeballs moving right, left, mouth fully masked, and you're sure something has gone dreadfully wrong but can't bring yourself to ask. Like when I was about to give birth to Paula and the anesthesiologist couldn't get the needle in my spine at the right angle and then this and that specialist was called in and then another and *Arch your back!* they'd say, *Like a cat!* until finally, *I don't have a cat!* I yelled, and they had to put me under and I didn't get to witness her birth as I had with Katy and as I would with the next three.

———

AEROPUERTO INTERNACIONAL JOSÉ MARTÍ, the sign is bright blue. The Arrival/Departure board is reminiscent of old *Family Feud* reruns. Rows of plastic slates snap open, snap closed. Flights are alphanumeric, departures listed in military time. *Destination Miami: On time.*

To my left, the ticket counter. Women mingle in tightly packed Capri pants. Wrinkled *viejitos* adjust their dentures, *viejitas* clutch sacks of plastic flowers. Except for the men with the open-button shirts and big gold medallions, there's no distinguishing who will soon play dominoes along Havana's seawall or in Little Havana's Calle Ocho.

At the edge of the crowd stands Max Castro, conference attendee and sociology research fellow at the University of Miami, writing such things as *The Politics of Language*. Soon after declaring my congressional candidacy, we thought about making him my campaign manager. "Cuban American, progressive on Cuba," said the local chair of the Democratic Party. "Hard to find." And Ira and the two or three Cuban Americans progressive on Cuba sitting with us agreed. "But maybe not," the chairman quipped—I thought quipped. "His last name is Castro." So we ditched the Cuban American progressive on Cuba with last name Castro for campaign manager. But that was two, three days into the campaign, when we thought we had the luxury of choice. After a long search, we found no one in Miami willing to be my campaign manager. And it had to be someone from Miami because no one outside Miami would be privy to the ways of exile politics. Invariably, those we asked—the two or three who agreed to meet with us—would raise eyebrows. "*¿Estas loca? ¿Contra Ileana Ros-Lehtinen?*" Taking on Ileana & Co was *puro suicidio*. Politically, socially, professionally—*puro suicidio*. "Plus, I have little children," one said. After a silence, "Have *you* thought about the danger?"

Already I'd come into the race with one big strike: Ira. Because of his legal representation of El Banco Nacional de Cuba, I was linked to Fidel Castro. Out of options, Ira asked Max Castro. Max said no.

I touch Max's arm now. "The video. Of Sunday night. It's been released."

I think I hear a little shriek coming from his insides. I think I see his body take a jump back, like a character in an action film blown several feet in the air then plopped back down, only Max's are smaller, stunted motions. "But they *assured* us any filming, photos were . . . they were for historical archives only." Now he composes himself. "I have nothing to worry about." He mumbles something about standing up to Fidel.

Yeah, right.

He lost his US passport, he says; the Cubans here stole it from him. Not Cubans as in *la gente del pueblo*. Cubans as in El Centro de Investigaciónes de la Seguridad del Estado.

I think (or do I say?), "Why would they do that?" calling up the open door of my hotel room, its sliver of bright light, how it blackened everything around it.

He says, coincidentally, or maybe in answer to my question, "Just to *bother* me."

I say, "I hope you will support me."

He is silent.

I nudge my way through the crowd, *"Permiso, permiso,"* pay the twenty-dollar departure tax. *"¿Usted ésta,"* I wave my hands at a woman, white handkerchief at her eyes, *"en linea?"*

But there is no line. Husbands, wives, sons and daughters, lovers. Brothers and sisters. They bid each other good-bye; wave heartily—or weakly. *"Adiós,"* Stoic smiles, pretend-happy faces. Fractured hearts, broken souls. Kisses blown—like soap bubbles popping midair.

Overhead, *Control de Seguridad.* Trying to erase last night's fears—might I not be let out of the country?—I step forward. The passageway is narrow; no exit, just a locked, wooden door to my left. Two rectangular mirrors look down on me, one aimed at my back, the other at my face. The young woman in olive green studies for what seems to be a long time the photos on both my passports. My true-blue US passport, my grey Cuban one smelling of cheap vinyl. She examines my forehead, nose, chin. My eyes. Should I toss her a friendly grin? Don a mug-shot expression? She smiles breezily, buzzes open the door, waves me through.

I lift my backpack onto the conveyor belt. "Can I keep this with me?" I call across to security. "They're just papers." Just my article, my unfinished piece. I hold it to me.

"No," he says. "That goes too."

Two Miami TV newscasters stand at the foot of the metal detector. No sooner than I step through to the other side than: "Can we interview you, Magda?"

Do I nod?

"We need to wait for permission from the Cuban authorities here at the airport."

Smile?

"If not, we'll interview you on the plane."

Where? Squeezed in the aisle? In the back by the smelly bathrooms? I picture myself midair, trying to balance amid turbulence, tossed to one side, then the other; newscaster stumbling to keep the tip of the microphone at my mouth.

Blue, everything is blue. Blue plastic chairs, clamped into rows. Blue Etecsa pay phones. Even the walls, blue. "Continental Flight Number 4881 to Miami will be departing in a few minutes." The intercom is loud, crackles with static.

A small television mounted high on a wall blasts promotional videos of Cayo Coco, colonial Trinidad, Santiago, Camagüey. For as long as I remember, I've yearned to know the whole of Cuba; take a slow car trip to all her provinces and villages; soak in her beaches, breathe her mountain air. To her highest peak, Pico Turquino, in the Sierra Maestra. "Seashells," my mom told me when I was a child, "were found at its summit."

"You mean Cuba once lived under water?" And I wanted desperately to go to the Sierra, climb El Pico Turquino and find those seashells. When my *tía* Tíita planned a car trip throughout the island with Husband Number One, I thought, Here is my chance. Even though their destination was the shrine to La Caridad del Cobre—*La Virgencita*, Cuba's patron saint—somehow I'd work my way from the Virgin of Charity to the high mountain top and find those seashells. Have my picture taken with olive-clad, rifled *milicianos* along the way.

But, no, it was a small car with only room for one of us. My older sister. "*Tu hermana mayor.*" Always, *tu hermana mayor.* "But she doesn't even want to *see*," I protested, but got only a shrug and a promise of *next time.* But next time never came. What came instead was a Pan Am flight.

I go up the blue stairs, 1 2 3 4 5 6 7 8 9 count the steps to the landing, stop, breathy, 10 11 12 13 14 15 16 17 18. I make it to the top. "Coffee Shop," it reads in English. The air conditioner rattles behind me. "*Una colada de café cubano,*" I tell the woman at the counter.

She hands me a Styrofoam cup brimming with thick, amber-frothed *café* along with the customary stack of white, tiny paper cups to share with others.

I gulp down the entire cup like a shot of hot whisky.

Her eyes widen.

"*Dos, por favor.*" Back downstairs, I wander aimlessly and I laugh, that nervous laugh sitting next to my father at Sunday Mass. Atop the steep hill, the tiny chapel of Nuestra Señora de Perpetuo Socorro. Perpetual Help. The more I'd laugh, the more my father would give me that *impetuous child!* look.

Perpetual Help, bring it on.

The male newscaster walks to me from across the terminal. From afar, I see it, a smile. A sweet, tender smile, like Ira's. Then I realize, it's Kerry Sanders. He did a piece on me during the campaign and didn't attack. So maybe I'm safe, after all.

The blonde newscaster unfurls a triumphant smirk. "We got it. The okay from the Cubans here at the airport."

That waxy smile on my face again. I face the camera. A tiny red light flashes.

The woman starts with the usual warm-up questions. She thinks she will catch me off guard: Ted Kennedy, Gary Hart, Bill Clinton, unzipped pants down to ankles; Nixon's eighteen minutes of silent tape. But I'm ready for her.

When I hear her say "maestro . . . Fidel . . . your words of Sunday night," I stay calm. Seemingly calm. I jump in before she finishes. "I have been friendly with other political figures," I say, recalling my congressional race, "who sign death warrants, even though I am staunchly against capital punishment." Except instead of *shaken*, as in: *I have shaken Florida Governor Lawton Chiles's hand*, I say *shooken; I have shooken*. No matter. Whitman made up words: *compassionating*, and more. Stephen King too.

Kerry Sanders says thank you. The woman says, "*Sí, muchas gracias*," in that funny way non-Spanish-speaking Anglos try to talk Spanish.

"Marazul Charter Flight 4881 is now boarding," comes the loudspeaker, heavy with feedback.

I am first on the runway. Enrique Sacerio-Garí, professor of Latin American literature at Bryn Mawr College and conference attendee, catches up to me, cradles my elbow. We pass a small bust of José Martí, his head painted and repainted a chalky white, a crack zigzagging his forehead. High above Martí, the single white star of the Cuban flag plays in the wind. For a moment, the flag gentles, lies almost perfectly still, then begins to stir. It spreads suddenly, a sweeping wash of color against the blue of the Havana sky. We draw closer to the plane, the whirling of the engines getting louder and louder, gusts of hot air blowing the hair over my eyes. I head up the metal stairs, full of resolve and full of coffee.

Enrique sits next to me on the plane. "*No me lo explico*," he leans in and whispers. "On the bus ride to the reception, we were told, 'Nothing to worry about.'" Historical archives, yes; we know. He doesn't say what we both know: he will not be in the news; Miami will have no interest in a professor from Bryn Mawr. And if he is, *So what?*, Bryn Mawr will say.

Index finger to mouth, eyes shut, "A sound bite," he says. "You need a good sound bite before you arrive." He coaches me in precise, measured speech: "*El significado de las palabras surge del contexto*."

"*El significado de las palabras surgen—*"

"No." He smiles patiently. "Not *surgen*, in the plural. *Surge*." *Emerge*, in the singular.

"Right. The significance. Of words. Emerge from . . ." But what does *contexto* have to do with my words to Fidel? *Contexto, nada. Contexto* means taking a coward's way out. It means lying. Renouncing. It means joining the conga line of Julio Iglesias and Jon Secada and Jose Feliciano and all those other *comemierdas* who said a word or two not unequivocally negative about Cuba. At the risk of losing adulation, *dolares*, they backpedaled. *Oh, no, I never . . . Oh, no, I didn't mean . . .* And so, *contexto*, what? The only thing I can do is stand by my words.

"Flight attendants," comes the commanding voice of the pilot, "prepare for departure. Flying time to Miami: forty-two minutes."

On the frontage of one of the terminals: *Patria es Humanidad.* No need to attribute words to the author, we Cubans know it's José Martí. We taxi through the runway, away from the royal palms he eulogized, away from who I am.

To nothing, maybe to nothing. Maybe the plane will take me to nothing. All I need is to get through today, just today. This moment, the next few hours. Then everything will be all right.

I close my eyes what I believe to be momentarily and open them suddenly with a startling sensation of being pulled down. I see grey, grey waters, grey sky, the grey congested concrete of Miami. The grey aura of the Freedom Tower, which reputedly Mas Canosa will soon own. Where my mom, sister and I were processed for our Cuban refugee cards. *El Refugio*, we Cubans called it, and in we went and out we went, armfuls of powdered milk and eggs, dogfood-looking meat, huge tin cans of . . . what was this? Back at our one-room efficiency, I took a can opener to it, lifted its silvery lid, stared. Brown goo. I poked my finger into it, licked it, poked again. In no time, I was sliding my finger around the jagged-edged, almost empty can. Peanut butter, a taste of the US. I was going to like this. I couldn't eat peanut butter again for decades.

"Will those who attended the conference on La Nación y la Emigración please stand?" the flight attendant announces the instant the plane comes to a complete stop. There is a nervous quiver to her voice.

I and my fellow conference attendees stand.

And then, "Will Magda Montiel Davis step forward?"

7

BIENVENIDOS A MIAMI

———

It's only me now, standing up. *Would Magda Montiel Davis step forward?* and it's only me now, standing up. All eyes are on me as I squeeze through the aisle and walk to the front of the plane. A TV camera pops up from a row up ahead. On a newscaster's shoulder, its elongated lens follows me. I stare straight ahead. I don't look down and I don't look back when the newscaster calls out: "Magda!" as if reuniting with a long-lost friend.

As I step onto the jet bridge, a police officer approaches. He loosens my fingers, takes my bag. I start to turn in the direction of the EXIT signs.

"No." He motions with a stretch of a red goose-bumpy neck. "This way." He pivots the opposite way. A quick backward glance my way. "You thought about hiring a bodyguard?"

"You think I need one?" I say, immediately feeling stupid.

Wordlessly, we walk the long corridors. At the foot of an escalator, my own private US immigration and customs inspector. "Nothing to declare?" he asks, and smiles a genuine smile. "Nothing *more* to declare, I hope."

The police officer thrusts a big key into a grey metal door, cold and damp and lettered in red and white: RESTRICTED ONLY / VIOLATORS WILL BE PROSECUTED. He leads me down industrial-type stairs that clang hollowly with each step. Exiting to baggage claim, several conference attendees stand around the carousel of bags, their backs to me.

Alfonso Fraga, chief of the Cuban Interests Section in DC and Fidel's friend, calls me over. "Magda, ¿que pasa?" His face is round and stubby, and now, perplexed looking.

"*No sé.* A video, it looks like a video, of me and Fidel last night—"

"*Pero, ¿como pasó eso?*" He looks behind him for a chair, drags it over, its metal legs scraping the floor. Slowly, very slowly, he sits, rubs a beefy thumb across his forehead, shakes his hairless head side to side, slower still.

I walk to the suitcases banging and coursing their way on the baggage carousel. A tall man with ropy arms I faintly recognize as a conference attendee takes my suitcase and carries it for me. I look up at him and half smile, feeling a sense of appreciation so overwhelming that in my other life would have surprised me.

Police escort our conference group outside. The overhang is low, lower than I remember it, dark; the drop-off lane and the one next to it and the one after that, narrow. Harried drivers come at us like meteors on the loose. *OaaaOaaa*, roars of shouting come from the terminal upstairs, like the Orange Bowl ruckus heard as you zoom past on the Dolphin Expressway. The policeman looks down at me. "Your welcoming committee." A fast rub of the palms in *step into my parlor* motion. "Just waiting for you to make an appearance."

A bus spews a burnt diesel smell that nauseates me. It pulls up directly in front of me, snaps open its doors. I climb, count 1 2 3 steps. Sit. Airport employees clad in grey uniformed jumpsuits stand behind us at the curb. They hold white handkerchiefs over their noses, pinch their nostrils, fan their faces. We stink. Can they storm inside? Turn the bus over? The conference attendee sitting next to me, an elderly Cuban American doctor from Philadelphia, crosses his legs. "I'm glad I don't live here." He uncrosses then crosses them again.

The bus motor *waaauhs* as if talking to me, *waaauh, waaauh*, the sights below passing me as would a silent movie screen. Haitian drivers in fat yellow cabs. A mural of hot-pink flamingoes, *Bienvenidos a Miami*. And then I remember Ira. "I'll meet you at the gate," he said last night. Ira, amid that crowd. I walk to the police officer, the moving bus wagging me this way and that. The milky brown of the officer's sleeve, I stare at it, tug at it. "My husband."

"Don't worry." But the officer's voice cracks thin. "Your husband called this morning, worked everything out with airport security." He jiggles something in his pocket; keys maybe, coins. "You're to meet him at the other end of the airport, by the Delta counter."

The bus draws near the end of its horseshoe path, makes a sharp turn. Brakes. We lunge forward then back. The engine gurgles, stops.

I step off the bus and see, from afar, the too wide forehead, the loose belt circling the bottom of his belly. I walk, then run to my husband. We hug; for a long time, we hug. His cheek is baby smooth, this morning's splashing of Homme filling me. "It's like a scene from the movie *Reds*," I whisper, recalling Warren Beatty and Diane Keaton's frantic embrace at a train station.

"Appropriate title," he says.

———

Ira takes my hand. Usually we walk, arms swinging in rhythm with our steps, but today, he holds my hand steadily. We go up the black asphalt ramp to his Chevy with the purple and teal *MAGDA!* campaign sticker still affixed to the Caprice's fat upturned butt.

"I can't believe you knew to make all these changes." I speak fast. "Where to meet you . . . The police told me you were on the phone with them all morning, directing—"

"What do you think I am? Just a pretty face?"

I begin by recounting all the minutiae of the day, as if describing them in great detail will free me from them, make me understand them, like my *Dear Diary* entries as a kid, like my frantic journaling last night. "And then on the other side of security, there were these newscasters, Kerry Sanders and this blonde with these huge tits and lizard lips and—"

"You spoke to the media?"

I turn my head, my entire self at him.

"You should have spoken to Michael Putney first." A combination hiss-sigh. "He called this morning. I told him he could come to our house and interview you." His lips are squeezed thin; mine hang open. And as the car goes around the convoluted ramp of MIA parking garage, so do we, go around in circles.

"How was I supposed to know that? That you told Michael Putney I would talk to him first?" Except we're both talking at the same time.

"He's a friend, Magda. Michael's a friend," he says, unresponsive. "I've known him for years. He helped you during your campaign, covered all your press conferences. Or did you forget that already?"

"What difference does it make?" I shout. "At this point?"

He continues talking down to me; I don't *understand* the seriousness of the situation. "Calls and threats until 3 AM And that's only 'cause I finally ripped the phone off the wall."

His knuckles are white on the steering wheel. "And get ready. You're gunna be attacked by both the right—"

I cross my arms over my abdomen, double over in the front seat.

"—and the left."

8

STRANGER THAN FICTION

———

It's funny, in an odd sort of way. When the car swerves onto our driveway, the gardeners toil over the landscaping *como sí nada*. They bend, pull, squat, trim, and I wonder, Don't they *know*, listen to radio, watch TV? Or do they think it's nothing? Or they need the job? Maybe, just maybe, they're here in solidarity with me.

"Just in time," Ira singsongs as he brings the car to a screeching halt. "Juuuust in time." Our garden, the last phase of reconstruction after Hurricane Andrew. He clicks the motor dead, snaps the key from the ignition. "Perfect timing."

I start to step over, then skirt around the slab of concrete where—what? less than a week ago Sadie drew a heart with *Mom* next to it, Ben carved his name with a giant B and four-legged E, their tiny hands and feet imprinted deep in the concrete. The day I hurried to the car, destination Streetdance, office, airport—destination Havana. "Stop, Mommy!" Sadie yelled, "Come see," and I did. She jumped. *JumpJumpJump.* "Now you, Mom. You write my name." "I can't, Saduka," I said, "I'll get my hands dirty and I've got to go." I pecked kisses on each headful of curls, turned to leave, stopped. Then I looked back; I was relieved. Already they were back at their artistic concrete. Ben stood. "Mommy, when are you going to *play* with me?" He wiped his hands on his shorts. "When I get back, Benny." A keen awareness that I meant it but knowing full well that upon return I wouldn't. A this and a that would push and pull me—a client, staff, or money problem—and I would put the time promised them on the back burner.

I walk past our purple tiger orchids and yellow shrimp plants. Will we be able to stay in our house? my mind awhirl. The house I bought on my own shortly after I left Paul Davis, the high school boyfriend I'd married at nineteen. Katy was five; Paula, two and a half; Maggie, thirteen months.

The house where I struggled for years to meet the hefty mortgage payment; every month, three thousand, eight hundred and ninety-one dollars, give or take, depending on insurance and escrow and variable and usurious interest rates, and God almighty where am I going to get the money? Me, a mom alone, no help from Paul—I'd read in *Mademoiselle* to wait at least a year to sign any property settlement agreement, until the guilt passed. And I did, I waited an entire year, and still, no, no child support. Paul, you keep the marital home. I'm the one taking the kids from you and all you know, and love (but this I didn't say). I'm out of here with my mom and the dogs and the three girls to a rented two-bedroom townhouse in the island paradise of Key Biscayne that I couldn't afford; soon after, to this single-family, ranch-style, four-bedroom, two-bath home that I also couldn't afford, but it was eight minutes from Downtown Miami and two blocks from the Atlantic Ocean. And I was so thankful that Paul didn't disappear with the girls—back in '81, the media craze, horror stories of fathers absconding with children, mothers never to see them again—or that Paul, the more stay-at-home parent, didn't fight for custody or demand alimony for supporting me during my undergrad years and law school. So thankful that I handed him the marital home. So thankful that I waived child support. Federal legislation passed soon after: the right to support belongs to a child and may not be waived by a parent.

A few months into single motherhood I asked Paul for support, but none was forthcoming. So no help. No help from my daughters' father and, though I didn't ask, no help from my father, who with wife no. 3 was driving the streets of Miami Beach in his-and-hers Mercedes. But that too passed, and eight years later I married Ira—our bridesmaids and ushers were Katy, Paula, and Maggie and our nieces and nephews—and in this house, I sang *Nosotros* with my staff as Ira played his old drum set and we danced the horah, round and round with clasped hands and in circles we went. Ira and I held tightly to our chairs as our friends and his three older brothers lifted us, up, down, waving white cloth napkins. We aimed to peck a kiss on one another and later rubbed noses as we country two-stepped to *Could I have this dance / For the rest of my life*, Anne Murray's sweet rasp wafting through that April night in our pool-shimmering patio under the stars.

In this house we celebrated Ben's bris when he was eight days old. I leaned over his cradle, held my face to his as he wailed and the scissor-snipping mohel said, "Oh, don't worry, Mama. It's just cold he feels," and Ira said, "Yeah, right."

"A fun house," I once said to Ira. The magic and wonder of carnival fun houses. Opening the beveled glass door of our home to the smell of singed garlic and onions and fresh tomato puree, I hear the crinkly sizzle of the green peppers and olive oil that will soon go into the big pot of black beans I know my mother is making. I head straight to the big expanse of our combination family room / kitchen where I know she stands, fervently beating the first few drops of *café* with spoonfuls of sugar for the creamy brown froth that will surface like magic on each miniature espresso cup.

She hears me, I know she does, and sees me, but her head stays bent. Oh, God, she is angry. More than angry, *encabronada*. That's what Maggie said last night on the phone. *Yeah*, her voice lowering, *Abuela's really pissed*. And I thought, *Mami? Angry at me?* Maybe the news hadn't sunk in. Or maybe at that moment Mami took precedence over all else.

I sit on the family room couch, my body perpendicular to hers. Without moving my head, I turn my eyes far right. I watch her. After a few silent seconds, my mother lifts her face. She walks to me, slowly. Supporting her weight against the sofaback, she leans over, touches her cheek to mine, lifts herself back up, shuffles away. As if in afterthought, my mother looks back. Still, she says nothing.

I smile at her, heartened. She smiles, in weary acceptance.

———

Ira bolts into the kitchen, the Energizer Bunny missing only the marching drum. *He's late, he's late, for a very important date.* A court hearing, he says. Will I be all right? Am I sure? He turns and is gone.

I walk in the bathroom, take off everything: necklace, wedding ring, everything, pee, then pee again. A sense of dread as I step on the scale, recalling all I ate in Havana. Sliding the weight cylinder across the balance beam, I hold my breath, look down: 121 pounds. Not 128. Not even 124 . . . 121. I am strong. I am invincible. I am skinny. I can do this.

I walk to Ira's study, towel around me. I stay standing, pick up the telephone, dial.

"Law offices. May I—"

"I just want to know how all of you are."

"Oh, Ms. Davis." Miriam breathes in sharply. "Oh my God, Ms. Davis. Hold on." Miriam, with her insistence on calling me so stiffly proper, as if from another time, another life.

One by one, each of the women gets on the line. "You have no idea what it's like here." "Nonstop calls, threats, insults." "Very nasty, dirty things."

Yesterday, all was normal when I called the office from Havana at the end of the work day. The video hit the news last night. It's only midafternoon, and the threats and insults into the office have not stopped. Exile radio, I will learn, regularly reads out my home address, my office address, and every single one of my phone numbers: home, office, fax, pager. It's every listener's patriotic duty, it announces, to call and write to tell me what they think about me.

"It's so bad," says a paralegal, "that that new Brazilian executive called to say she was coming to make a payment and I told her 'No, don't come.'"

"You've got to stay calm." My voice comes out flat, hollow. "It's not going to do any good to alarm the clients." I hear the carillon of the front door, that familiar chime of Westminster Quarters in sets of four. "I'll be there tomorrow. We'll talk then."

———————

Through the beveled glass of our front door I see them, the parade of the press, a clumsily smeared mishmash of colors here only minutes after my arrival. "Just a second," I call out. What to wear? I yank a purple dress off the hanger, unlock my jewelry drawer for the pearl necklace Ira's mom gave me. No, not pearls. I'll look like a WASP from Massachusetts. But Salem, I think. Pearls it is.

A gust of hot air when I swing open the front door. As I lead the reporters through the courtyard, I see from the corner of my eye a cameraman hoisting a camera onto his shoulder. "No." I turn razor sharp, point at him. "You cannot film the house, any part of it." We skirt past the purple tiger orchids and bright yellow shrimp plants and battery-powered fountain Ira gave me last Mother's Day. "Or the street signs either."

Michael Putney first. He puts his arm around me in a gentlemanly way. "You know I would never do anything to hurt you. Or Ira."

"I know," and I do. I take him across the street to the corner where East meets Pacific. I stand facing our house, now back to its pink-peach color, its columns gleaming white.

The camera lens is all circles and squares, its glass iridescent. Turn this way and one color, turn that and another.

"Magda," says Michael, "on the video you were quoted as saying, 'Fidel, I want to tell you something.'" Every syllable is enunciated with clarity and precision. "'Thank you for what you have done for my people.' *What* did you mean?"

"The Cuban Revolution has made many significant advances in the area of health, education, and social justice." The sun, bright and hot, nearly blinds me.

"You also said to him, 'You have been a great teacher for me.' *What* did you mean?" A garbage truck backs up, a shrill of beeps. "*What* has he taught you? Why those words?"

I jump in, not a moment's pause: "Because in the face of constant pressure and aggression from the Number One World Power, Fidel Castro has stood up to the United States. Whether or not you agree with his ideology, you have to hand it to the guy. He stuck to his guns."

"By sending thousands of people to the—"

"To the *paredón*, Michael." I say *paredón* as he says *wall*. And again, "*Paredón*." I nod, once, in a *there!*, *bring it on* motion. "And I'm glad you brought that up, because I did ask about the *paredón* during the conference, and I did make a specific reference with respect to the *paredón* because it bothers me. Of course, it bothers me." A wind blows hot, and hard. "When I spoke to Fidel, I spoke clearly. And I spoke openly." I pull the hair off my face, wedge it behind my ear. "And the same thing I said to him there, I would say to him here."

I want to tell Michael Putney about the early teachings of Judaism: *When establishing a community, first build a hospital, then a school.* I want to ask him: How many young people in the US, as smart as our daughter Katy, can't go to a college like Wellesley, can't go to college at all?

And I want to recount what it was like growing up in a country that is supposedly so free, so advanced, the Number One World Power. What it was like being the only girl besides my sister who didn't sport freckles or have a name like Cathy or Kathy or Marilyn or Carolyn. What it was like in Jacksonville with its *Whites Only* bathrooms and water fountains to be pulled out of my third-grade classroom by my sister's fifth-grade teacher, precisely when my teacher had stepped out, facing that woman, that hate, knowing just enough English to understand I was being accused of stealing my classmate's money but not speaking it well enough to say it wasn't so.

And this too, I want to tell Michael: When Ira, *ese comunista*, took me back to Cuba, that's when I knew I'd been lied to, betrayed, all those years. I saw none of what I expected—the *favelas* of Brazil, the crumbling *ranchos* of Venezuela, the orange-haired children of Haiti. I want to say: *You were in Cuba too, Michael. Didn't you see it? Or it doesn't fit in with the storyline you know you'd better write?* But then, *He's a friend, Michael's a friend, Magda. Or did you forget that already?*

Next, the bouncy, pixie-haired woman. Angie Sandoval, she says, from Telemundo. I take her to the side of the house, the cool shade. "You can relax with me," Angie Sandoval says in thick Argentinian accent, "I'm not Cuban. I don't care about any of this," and lets out a little laugh. My heels sink into the dirt, sodden from recent torrential rains.

The same questions, repeatedly, despite my direct answers—*"Just a hello kiss . . . what was I to do? Stick out my tongue at him?"* And it is hot, so very hot. I wipe my eyelids, my mouth. Beads of sweat run down the string of pearls. *"Porque, Magda, porque?"* once, twice, three times. I walk away, my heels digging deeper into the mush of mud.

"¡Espere tanto!" a reporter whines; he waited this long and now I'm going back inside. When he sees he's getting nowhere with me, he starts in on the Telemundo woman; she went ahead of him, and he was there first. She took too long with me. He follows me into the courtyard. There is a pungent smell, and I don't know whether it's me or him or my shoes soggy with drain-field muck; maybe the decay of a dead animal. An iguana, maybe an iguana.

I close the front door on the man's face.

It is cool inside the house.

It is over.

Miami Herald

By Tuesday night reaction was even stronger as a seconds-long video of Sunday evening's reception with Fidel Castro at Havana's ornate Palace of the Revolution was repeatedly broadcast on television stations.

Over and over, Miamians saw lawyer Magda Montiel Davis kiss and chat amiably with Fidel Castro. Hundreds of angry people jammed the telephone switchboards of Spanish-language radio and television stations to voice their fury.

Montiel Davis said her comments to Castro were meant as praise for the revolution's achievements. She said, "He has had the courage to confront a world power and say what he has to say without caring about the consequences."

9

LET'S JUST GO

DAY 2 OF 3 (MAYBE 5)

———

Not yet 6 AM and the phone on Ira's nightstand rings. I spring out of bed, run to his study lest he wake, grope in the dark for the handset.

"Better realize people in this town can put a bomb up your behind," a man says.

But too late. Ira grabs the phone from me, listens for a second, slams down the phone.

I gape at Ira, still stupid from sleep. Or not sleep. "It was an Anglo man."

He nods. "With a Chicago accent." A long silence. "He wanted to know if my wife knew Fidel Castro bombed Pearl Harbor."

"It's so strange. It's all so strange."

"That's the way it's gunna be, baby." He walks away. "Every nut in Miami is gunna come out of the woodworks now." He stops, turns, lifts eyebrows in an *understand?* motion. "So it's not just the crazy Cubans we have to worry about."

I shower quickly, wash my hair, don my button-down, navy-blue dress. Elisa, my young associate, likes me in navy blue. She always said the only good thing about my race for Congress is that it taught me how to dress like a lady. But when I grab the keys to the station wagon, Ira, standing behind me, takes them from me.

"What? I can't drive now?"

"You have to be aware of your surroundings at all times." He jingles the keys at my face, a parent taking away a teenager's—worse, the little woman's—car privileges. "And you can't do that if you're driving."

I am silent. I hate the way Ira drives. I often tell him, "You drive like Fittipaldi," the race car champion, our neighbor here in Key Biscayne.

"Look at it this way, Davis. You'll get to spend more time with your husband." He L-bends his elbow, puts my arm through his. "Besides, that's the advantage of renting office space from me. We can drive in to work together." He opens the garden gate and then the car door for me—a first.

I slide in the front seat of his Chevy, wait for him, and when not a scintilla more of chivalry is forthcoming, close my own door. Three, five days, Ira said, is how long it would last.

I lean forward, fumble with his car radio. "How do you turn this thing on?"

"Here." He grabs my hand. "Turn this thing on."

I play-smack him.

"Davis, you can't figure out how to turn on a car radio?"

"I'm not good with gadgets—"

"That's not a gadget. It's a car radio. Watch."

"No news," I say, "not even NPR. So we can take our minds off everything."

"No, no news." We turn onto Crandon, the only road in or out of the island. "Okay, princess, what would you like?"

"Country."

He shakes his head, smiles a little bit. "I never went out with a Cuban woman who likes country music."

"It's the Jacksonville in me. And how many Cuban women did you go out with anyway?"

"Plenty, baby." He snaps his fingers. But as KISS 99 fiddles *The devil went down to Georgia / And he was looking for a soul to steal* and on Power 96 Jimi Hendrix asks if we're *Experienced* and Willie Chirino's salsa repertoire about all the damage Fidel has done to the homeland comes to an end, the deejay makes a crack about "meeting Magda in Havana." I gasp. Then I laugh.

"Keep laughing, Davis." But he laughs too. I love the way Ira laughs; a sweet, boyish laugh. We ride through US-1 to—well, to La Sagüesera, what Cubans call *southwest* Miami, situated not quite in the heart of but close enough to Little Havana, where in a flat-topped building that looks like it's two stories but is really three, my law firm enjoys the benefits of a long-term, overpriced lease from Ira and his older brother, Marvin—Ira, the baby of four brothers—for not a penny less than fair market value. No breaks for The Little Woman. But we—my army of women and I—are on the top floor, I like to jab Ira, one floor above his. The penthouse, of sorts. Very much of sorts.

The neighborhood abounds with rounded backsides of *viejas cubanas* as they lean over their laundry baskets and hang Papito's *calzoncillos* on the clothesline; *abuelos* smoking long brown cigars on creaking porch rockers; and tiny front lawns with life-sized statues of Santa Bárbara—or Changó, her Afro-Cuban equivalent—in glass-encased shrines of chalky white.

Veering a sharp left onto the hot, asphalted parking lot, Ira pulls into his spot. He walks to the trunk of the car—that bowlegged walk of his—lifts my boxful of files. Another first. "What?" I say. "A fear of dying taught you manners?"

"I'm not scared. Are *you* scared?" He struggles to open the lobby door, 8 CFR—the Code of Federal Regulations—under his chin, my box of files and his briefcase in one arm, using the pull of the key in the keyhole as leverage to open the door. "Why should I be scared?" He tries hard not to huff. "Married to Hurricane Magda."

I press the elevator button—"Your elevator is *slow*"—but when the door fumbles open to Ira's second-floor law office, he doesn't get out. Okay, I get it. My new life.

Unlocking the white-lacquered doors to my office, "How strange," I say, "Barbara's always here at seven." I turn off the alarm, its melodic chime. "Maybe her baby is sick again."

Ira doesn't say anything, just looks at me. "I'll be downstairs if you need me." He kisses my cheek and is gone.

I sit at my receptionist Miriam's desk, feeling cushioned, supported, back at my office, its purple walls, its pastels of pinks and greens.

Already the five phone lines flash a fiery red across the dial pad. Oh, no, it's Margarita Something-or-other, a client. She's calling to kvetch; to kvetch *again*. Janet, one of my paralegals—Colombian as well—says Margarita is a typical Bogotanian. But, no. Margarita is jealous, she says, she's always wanted to meet Fidel Castro. "Fidel is loved and admired in Latin America," she gushes, then lowers her voice. "Not like here."

Next, our ex-receptionist. How's her little boy? Her new job at the state attorney's? "How are *you*?" she cuts me off. She's worried about me. Do I need anything? A definite plus; two calls of support. I'll be sure to tell the staff. But it's already past nine. Where are they?

The back door creaks open. I smile. They're here. But it's not the staff. It's best friend Lazara. I stand, wait for her.

She walks to me, full hips swaying right left right. An awkward, loosely held hug.

My arms flop at my side. She feels empty to me.

"I don't agree with you." A barely audible whisper. "But I will support you." When she says this, she angers me. What does she know about Cuba? She doesn't even remember the homeland, left as a kid twenty-six years ago and never returned. And she doesn't even drink Cuban coffee; she drinks that American watered-down stuff: *agua sucia*, Mami calls it.

"Why are you whispering?" I say. "There's only two of us here."

She pulls up a chair, sits next to me, helps me with the calls. After a while, she turns to me. "Let's go," she says. "Let's just go."

"Go, where?"

"To Iowa," she says. "We'll pack up all the kids in my Bronco and go." Iowa, where Lazara just graduated law school and left a piece of her soul. She shares an office here with us.

"How can I"—I spread my arms a full semicircle around me—"just go? I can't walk away from all this, my practice."

The fax line rings. I take a little jump.

Lazara walks to the machine, rips the eerie-feeling, chemical-smelling paper off the roll, hands it to me. It's from Elisa, the young Cuban American I hired a few years ago, when she was fresh out of law school. She was Ira's top student and is the only other attorney in the office beside me, working *for* me, but I hate to say, think of it, like that.

Magda, begins her letter, not *MMD*, Elisa's pet name for me (and mine for her, *EMS*). She's tolerated a lot and has looked the other way. Why, she even supported me during my race for Congress despite my liberal platform on Cuba. But this time, I went too far.

I look up at Lazara. "She resigned." I wait a few long moments for Lazara, her cries of indignation, her reassurances, her show of camaraderie. But, nothing. "This was overdue in coming anyway." Feeling my leg shake under me, fisted hand under my chin, "It's all for the best. The one time she went to Mexico with me, you know, that time I took all those clients who were out of status to the US Consulate there—"

"Yes, Magda Davis, I remember. All those illegal aliens. When you took a truckful of them, all at once."

"—to get their visas, she made some comment about how her *husband* thought she should've been paid more money that week, for her time away from home and family. What about me? *My* time away from home? And family? Always slaving to bring money into the office, to pay *her*, to pay *all* their salaries. Anyway—"

Lazara opens her eyes immensely wide, flips her head at me, humoring, indulging me, annoying me.

"—we couldn't be at two more polarized extremes. You know what she said? That she *admired* Mas Canosa, how he'd worked his way up. Yeah, worked his way up all right. Mysteriously went from being a milkman in Cuba to amassing a g'zillion bucks from lucrative government contracts for his construction firm. Gee, I wonder how he did that?" A throttled grunt. "And then she said she was going to *join* the Cuban American National Foundation. The only thing she didn't do was tell me to cut her a firm check to pay her foundation dues." I shake my head fast, feel my cheeks Nixon-jiggle. "You know she's never even spit on a sidewalk? She told me. And she's never even put a mirror down *there*, even when she was little, or teen—"

"Or now. Now's the most fun time, and if you can have a guy do it for you . . ." A lop-sided grin. "*Don't* say it, Magda Davis. *Not* your Ikey. A guy with hair. Forget good looking. At least normal looking—"

"I've never even *seen* the woman's arms." I fold, unfold my arms. "When the entire office went to the Keys for the weekend—you know that client that let us stay at his resort for free in exchange for us doing his employees' visas?—she wouldn't even wear shorts, never mind a bathing suit. And our Christmas-card picture, just 'cause her knees were a bit too far apart, she had the photographer touch up the space between her legs, paint it . . . black!"

"Well, she *is* married to a Middle Eastern guy."

"You think he told her, 'Elisa, you must cover your black triangle—with a black triangle'? I *hate* the way he controls her. The way she *lets* him." A wry smile. "Oh, and when I was breast-feeding Sadie and Ben in the office, my God, you would've thought I brought in a live porno show. She'd wince, turn her head away."

"Well, Magda," she says, in slight Midwestern accent—*Meh-ag-da*—despite her short years in Iowa, "some people are funny about those things."

"What difference did it make? We were among women."

"Well, you did pull your tits out everywhere."

"To feed the babies. And look who's talking—pulling your tits out."

"That's right." Her nose is crooked, but she's beautiful. "Everybody's seen my tits." She tilts her head, turns back to the phones, looks back up at me. "But *my* tits are real."

———

Minutes, maybe an hour later, the back door opens again. This time, it *is* the staff.

"You scared me!" I say, relieved at the comfort of seeing them.

Barbara's big smile of braces that always seem to catch the light and, you could say, light up the room. Her legs wobbling in six-inch *tacones*, her big dark eyes curlicued with thick black eyeliner, Barbarita, as often we call her, is a child bride and new mom, striving hard to reach womanhood. She lost her mom while still a girl. When she gave birth to her little girl, she fell into a funk until one of us asked, "Barb, is it that having a baby of your own really brought out how much you *miss* your mom?" She didn't get it when we prodded her to eat bananas—"They're *good* for you"—but red did crawl up her neck when recently she said her braces would soon be removed and we told her Carlito, her husband, was going to be very happy.

Isabel's smiling cheeks that, despite bouts of volatility, seem to smile only at me, especially when we commiserate, I about Ira nudging me, she over heartbreaks—Sergio, Luis, Amador—but mostly sad, deeply sad, over her brother. Fraught with mental health issues, unable to afford insurance coverage, he set himself aflame and died.

Cary, the Latin yenta in the group (they're all Latinas, though not all Cubans), always revved to toss out / take in the latest gossip in that signature Nuyorican accent of hers; her tight curls stacked high on her head, sides of her head shaved—she laughs when I call her my miniature poodle—always ready to meet the next guy, always hopeful this is the one who will like her back.

Then there's Mily. I never know whether it's the real Mily or her role-playing the spacey blonde stereotype. Her hair, as yellow-orange as a slice of Velveeta, doesn't at all blend with her physicality. She sports obvious African features: the nose, the mouth, the warm brown skin—what Cuban doesn't? Well, some of us more than others, but for the rest of them, the black lineage is there, somewhere. *So what?* I want to tell her. *Flaunt it, enjoy it.*

Janet, recently arrived from Colombia, always stays late in try-harder, tackle-all immigrant mentality. But she'd assured me, during her job interview for a paralegal position, that she was bilingual, meaning that she was fluent in Spanish—that's a given—but also English. As it turned out, she didn't possess the English-language skills required of a paralegal. Finding legal staff proficient in English—even among the born-and-raised in Miami—is a rarity.

Miriam's hyper-vigilance about what others might be thinking or saying, a strict adherent to properness, Old World etiquette—preferably French, even though she's Ecuadorian.

Irma, who fled her small village in war-torn Guatemala, has an eighth-grade education and is among the sharpest and quickest of the group and makes me the best decaf.

Our collective man-watch: "Hunk alert!" Giggles and note-passing every time a good-looking guy struts in the office, which is not often. Our years together. The time we rented an RV and drove to Atlanta to see our client, a human circus, perform. They had just won an Emmy, they were on their way up—and so were we, on our way up, our very first corporate client. "Take care of my children," said Ira, as I lifted Sadie and Ben onto the RV, Katy, Paula, and Maggie in tow, and off we went with our children. Two in the morning and finally, Atlanta. "Park?" Isabel asked. "Or pull up to the hotel driveway?" I roused myself from sleep. "Pull up to the driveway," I said. "It's too cold. I don't like cold." The RV screeched to a furious halt, we jerked forward, fell back, all of us, cartoon characters bouncing in unison. Flurries of snowflakes, falling from the ceiling. No, not snowflakes. Fiberglass. Isabel pulled up into the driveway, all right. She crashed into the overhang. The driveway had a ten-foot clearance; the RV, a height of twelve. The night porter hopped into the RV, pointed at the hotel's fire sprinklers slicing through the RV ceiling. "Is this . . . yours?" Hand over his mouth, he stifled a laugh. "Or ours?" The sprinklers activated, drenching us all. When we finally checked into the hotel, I called Ira, as promised. "Did you get there?" he asked. "Yep," is all I said. "We got here."

So I'm happy. Happy at hearing their noises, the cadence of their steps, the trail of perfume they leave in their wake. I can always tell who's entering my office without even looking up. "For a moment there, I thought you weren't coming in." A little laugh.

They walk in single file. They want to talk to me, they say, and so I walk behind them and best friend Lazara into the kitchen.

10

KITCHEN DEBATE

———

What I notice first is their walk, how each individual style of my staff, my friends, has morphed into a Stepford Wives uniformity. The seven of them—and best friend Lazara—take their places around the kitchen table. And it's only me now, standing up.

They spoke last night on the phone, they say, and decided to meet for breakfast.

And decided to report late for work. I keep my face inexpressive.

I walk, four steps this way, four steps back. I look down, think as I walk. "Look," I say, "I can overcome this. But I can't do it without you. You guys are more than just my employees." I look up at each of their faces. "You're my friends."

Cary pulls me toward her; her grip is tight. She sobs a loud cry into my arm. "I had a bad feeling about this trip." The bend of her back rises, falls, with each shuddering inhalation. She lifts her head, wipes her eyes. "And I was going to say something."

"So why didn't you?"

"Would you have listened?"

"I wish you'd said something," I say. But all of us know the answer, and it's no.

Their families, she says, they're putting pressure on them. "Saying horrible things to us." Janet, her eyes in a squint, nods grimly. "And insulting us."

"I'll talk to your families," I offer, dreading it already.

"Okay, call a press conference." Isabel folds her arms. "And say we don't think like you."

I shake my head—"I can't do that"—knowing full well what comes with it: an acknowledgment I'm the bad one, the wrong one, to think as I do; and they, they're the lily-clean ones because they think like *them*, my exile compatriots.

"And Elisa quit," Mily says.

How does she know that? "So?" I say instead. "We can make it without her."

"And you'll go to all the immigration interviews and court hearings?" Isabel asks.

Now I see—Elisa was in on their conference call last night. "Yes," is all I say.

"And check all our work?" Janet.

"And manage the office? Return all the calls?" Mily again.

"Yes. Yes. All that." I look down, my navy-blue pumps tap-tapping mechanically in front of me, as if not connected to me. "Why not? Who do you think did it the first few years?" And when no answer: "Built up the practice. By myself."

Barbara sits up, shuffles her bottom side to side as if trying to find a comfort zone. *ShuffleShuffleStop.* "Carlito and I talked it over last night and we" (we = he) "decided I should leave." She says this as if she'd gone over it one, two, three times in front of the mirror.

"Carlito," I say, and turn away from her. I will not belittle myself, ask her to stay; I will not indulge her. I turn my attention to the others—Miriam's eyes nervously skirting the room, her shoulder to Irma's, both perfectly still, perfectly quiet. "Look, guys—"

"And I want to know about my vacation pay." Barbara's eyes are cold and hard. "I have three days of vacation pay coming to me."

"This is not the right time or place." I turn from her again, knowing from the skills I've learned as a lawyer to move on quickly, gloss over the weaknesses in a case, not let judge or jury hear more of the negatives than need be. And I have also learned—this from life experience—that the harshest insult is to ignore: *El major desprecio es no hacer aprecio.* Tell Barbara, through my silence, *You're nothing, nothing to me. Allow me, then, to dispose of you, the same way you have disposed of me.*

Irma slips a glance at me, her eyes steady. Miriam sits, hands clasped, silent as well.

"Magda, are you a communist?" asks Mily.

Lazara throws her arms in the air, her torso half lifted off the chair—

a Holy Roller in a Jesus moment. "*¡Niños*, Magda! Fidel Castro sends thirteen-year-olds off to minefields, with machine guns *this* big." She lifts her hand as far as it will go. "Bigger than them!"

I look at her, just look at her. What is *she* doing here? She's not even a staff member. I only gave her some office space—for free—so she could jump-start her own law practice for what? Her third or fourth job in just a year out of law school. And what is she talking about, Fidel sending kids off to minefields with machine guns bigger than them? My best friend, parroting the lies of the Little Havana radio stations. And of all the most inflammatory things she could say, at the worst possible moment, and in front of my staff.

"Look," Lazara says. "Why don't you just say you did it for a client, to get the Cuban government to issue those exit visas or return visas or whatever it is you're doing for them?"

"And do *what* with the clients? 'Oh, I'm sorry, I had to save my ass, so I picked *me* over you'? They're still there!" I pace again, long hard steps.

"You'll be a hero," she presses, "if you publicly denounce Fidel." She spreads her arms wide around her. "Everybody'll love you."

I am looking at her in disbelief.

"You could even run for Congress again. We could even start campaigning now, not like last time, when you jumped in the race *así como así* at the last minute. The election would be, what? It's around the corner, just a year and a half away."

"I'm / not / doing / that," I say. "And for your information, it's both exit visas *and* return visas I'm handling. Some Cubans, once they're here in the land of milk and honey, want to *return* to Cuba." I open my eyes wide in a *how about that?* motion. "So if things are so bad there—"

"And Fidel is so stupid," Isabel yells in a voice uncharacteristic for her, "that he doesn't even know the value of the video and sells it—for $700." And not $400?

"Magda, let me put it to you this way," Cary says. "Some man on the phone said, 'Look, *señorita*, the only thing your *jefa* didn't do was pull Fidel's pants down and suck his dick."

In my mind, I lean over, squeeze my gut until it hurts. But I keep myself ramrod straight.

"And when you called yesterday," Isabel says, "all you cared about were the clients."

I glare at Mily. Why does it not surprise me that's how Mily interpreted—

or chose to interpret—what I said to her on the telephone yesterday, to not alarm the clients?

"That's not so." I stop pacing, stand stock-still, my arms taut, my hands clenched at my sides. "The first thing I did when I got home yesterday was pick up the phone and call you, just to see how you all were." I look hard at each of their faces, but not at Barbara's, the ship jumper, the defector, and not at Lazara's, the—I don't know what anymore. I force my voice to untighten. "But there was no point in alarming the clients."

"Well." Mily leans back in her chair. "Not a single new client has called."

Oh, God, no, not the law practice I've worked so hard, so long, to build up, that is literally hand to mouth. Without new clients to stay afloat, how will we meet the ever-mounting expenses?

"And we haven't been able to get any work done," Cary says, "in two days." She holds up two acrylic rhinestone-studded fingernails. "Two days of nothing but threats and insults."

"Last night, when we all left and got in our cars," says Janet quietly, "we stopped and looked at each other before putting the keys in the ignition. We all knew what the other was thinking. And when the cars started," she squeezes her eyes shut, "I said, *Gracias Señor.* If something was to happen to me, who would take care of my baby? I'm all she has in the world." She presses her lips. "Me, just me, Magda. Not even my own mother would raise my little girl."

Sadie and Ben! A client called earlier: Margarita Ruiz said on her exile radio show, "What Magda Montiel deserves is for her kids to be kidnapped." It took this? Janet worrying about her little girl for me to react? I bolt from the kitchen, grab a phone, stab at dial buttons. The older girls—Katy, Paula, Maggie—they're all right. (Aren't they?) Katy, miles away; safe at Wellesley—no? Paula and Maggie just minutes away in PE or calculus right about now—or not, if they skipped classes. And Mami, where is Mami? Venturing out of the house trustingly, unknowingly, thinking it's all over, behind us? Chatting casually at the grocery checkout line? Making mental notes what she'll cook us for dinner, what time she'll pick up the kids?

"Shalom!" comes the principal's cheerfully recorded voice. "And thank you for calling the Gordon Schools at Beth David Congregation. We are very busy with your children at this time but your call is very important to us. *Para español, marque el uno.* For the Early Childhood Center, press 3. For the Upper School, press 4."

I press 3, I think.

"Shalom! And thank you for calling the Gordon Schools at Beth David Congregation."

Oh God.

"Please leave a message and we'll get back to you as soon as we can." A dead silence, then a beep.

"This is Magda Davis, Sadie and Ben's mom. Sadie and Ben Kurzban—"

"Gordon Day Schools." A human voice. "This is Rene speaking. May I—"

"Rene, this is Magda Davis. Kurzban. Magda Kurzban. Listen to me. This is very important. No one is to take Sadie or Ben out of school. Do you hear me? No one, except my husband Ira or my mom or me." Does she understand? I press her. Yes. "It's very important," I repeat. "Sadie and Ben Kurzban. It's a matter of life and death."

———

Back to the kitchen, voices inside. When I open the door, a certain quiet fills the room. Mily is the first to speak. "Magda, did you know my father was a political prisoner?" She drops her forehead onto her hand, shakes her head slowly.

"No, I didn't." Never once has Mily talked about a father, any father, much less a father who was a political prisoner. And Mily talks. About everything. Where did this phantom political-prisoner father come from? And why now? As a way of getting the upper hand—for herself, and the rest of the "lower level" employees—finally, the upper hand?

Suddenly, "I'll stay," Mily announces. "But only as long as I don't have to do any work for the CCD people."

At this, I laugh. The Cuban Committee for Democracy. Stuck-up lawyers, stiff-nosed intellectuals. "Agreed. No more CCD." Even if I am treasurer. Even if I am one of its founders.

Still, only Mily wants to stay, and she's not my first choice. She's not even my sixth choice, and there's only seven of them—but at least it's something, *someone*. I'd thought long and hard about letting her go—Janet too; Janet's English skills are . . . there are no skills and she's a US citizen—but I couldn't. "They're single moms," I'd protest to Ira every time he would kvetch I wasn't making money. And he'd retort, "You're the owner, for god-sakes! You shouldn't be the one taking a pay cut, or worse, not collecting a salary at all to keep all these women on staff. You're like the federal government, hiring all these people." And if not the federal government: "You're worse than a welfare organization."

So Mily stays. And the rest? I study their faces, a PTA-mom carpool line sitting around our kitchen table. None clamor to join in but I can tell I'm making progress. I call up Elisa's words to me not long ago: "You know, there's a certain something about you that makes people rally around you, give so much of themselves." For a second, I thought, *She's complimenting me!* Not hitting me with yet another complaint. Then she said, "If you could just *package* it" and held her finger a millimeter from her thumb. "Then you could retire, make *all* the money in the world." Then I knew. Not a compliment. Not a compliment at all. I was a fraud, a Brooklyn Bridge salesman. And she'd once bought into it but was not going to buy into it anymore.

"Look," I say to staff, "let's all go back to work. And we'll talk again later." I try to keep the *please!* out of my voice.

One by one, they follow me out of the kitchen into their respective workstations. Barbara skirts past me, a knob-kneed, Playskool-stilts wobble. For a minute, she turns back and looks at me. For a second, our eyes meet. Her eyes are bright and clear, the Barbara I know. Mine feel sunk, lost in my face. A beckoning pause. Then we both turn and walk away from each other.

Janet pulls me aside. "Magda, you've been very good to me," she says in Spanish. Her hunter-green eyes squint paper-thin, penetrating mine. "When I first got here from Colombia and no one else would even interview me because I couldn't speak English, you did." *Yeah, interviewed you because your brother-in-law*—Ira's gofer—*told me you spoke English.*

"Well," Janet offers, "I still can't speak it so well." She tilts her head. "And when not even my own mother would cosign a car loan for me so I could get to work, you did."

Yeah, and when you defaulted on payments and the collection agency came after me, I had to give you overtime hours and wasted double *the time correcting your bad English.*

"I'll stay too, Magda," Janet says, her eyes thickened with tears. An inkling she wants me to squeal in exuberance but I'm shell-shocked, though I now have a clear sense of the reason the staff misinterpreted my monotone of yesterday as caring only about money, and clients.

Mr. Maza has been waiting to see me, Miriam tells me, so I tell her to let him in. Jose Maza had been in the office for a consultation shortly before

I left for the conference. Could I get his wife and daughter out of Cuba? There seemed to be something tripping up their departure. "It's not for *political* reasons that I want them out," he said, "I even sympathize with the system there, but I keep *mis sentimientos* here quiet." He chuckled. "I'm a security guard at Home Depot. If my coworkers, bosses found out—*¡mama mía!* They don't even know I *go* to Cuba." No money, I assumed, to pay my fees, so I didn't bother to discuss a reduction of fees or flexible payment plan. But sure, I told him, I'll take the case.

I escort him into my office. "How was Cuba?" he says, eyes shining. "Did you get a chance to see my wife? And daughter?" His brow furrows. "What do you think are the chances?"

"Looks good. But you know—" I sit back, loosen. This is what grounds me, my work; moving about so expertly in the office, being so in control. "I don't really think the hold-up is with the Cuban government—"

And then it happens, in one split second.

11

BEFORE IT GOES SILENT AND DIES

———

A sound I have never heard in my life before, a sound I will never in my life forget. The cry a wounded animal makes before it goes silent and dies. I run to Miriam, grip her shoulders as if trying to bring her to human form again.

"Everybody! Get out!" Miriam cries. "Leave! A bomb!" The telephone falls from her grip. Mily, Cary, Isabel, Janet, all of them, stampede past me in a swiftness I never thought possible. They push each other in confused entanglement. In an instant, they are gone.

I watch the telephone dangle from its cord. It makes tight, tiny circles to the right, opens widely to the left. My steps soft, measured, I head to the elevator, heed the warning by the elevator door. *Do not use in case of fire.* Nothing about a bomb. Pressing the *down* button, I step inside the tiny, encapsulated space. The elevator drops under me. The door opens. I expel air, long and hard, walk to Ira's office. Is it a bomb? Or a bomb scare? Ira will know.

I stand silent in the doorway.

He looks up from his desk, smiles big when he sees me.

I walk to him. And I tell him.

His smile fades.

I search his face. Is it a bomb? Or a bomb scare? Ira doesn't know.

He rises, scratches his ear, paces the length of his office. "I've been through this before, sweetie, representing the Haitians." He scratches again, *flick-flick* at the pink of his earlobe. "They cleared out the building three times when my office was on Brickell Avenue." *Niggah-lovah*, the callers would hiss during the widely publicized trials. There was Ira, all five feet and a half inches of him, standing small but large; the black Haitian boat people scattered scared about him. And there was the army of federal government lawyers with the Ronald Reagan and soon after the George H. W. Bush White House and Rudy Giuliani directing the combat zone. The FBI thought the death and bomb threats came from the southern tip of the county, where many of the early settlers migrated once Miami became the "Gateway to the Americas," when more and more bumper stickers read: WILL THE LAST AMERICAN LEAVING MIAMI PLEASE BRING THE FLAG?

And though presumably not directed at him, they also evacuated the building on Brickell Avenue when all the glass walls exploded at the Mexican Consulate on one of the top floors. The time bomb was planted in 1981, shortly before Ira and I began dating—*el exilio*'s way of expressing its discontent with Mexico's relations with Cuba. The next year, a bomb was planted at the Nicaraguan Consulate. The same night, a bomb exploded at the Venezuelan Consulate.

And there were the death threats three years ago that Ira received when he challenged the Miami City Commission's ruling denying permission to a Haitian group to use Bayfront Park for a celebration of the inauguration of President Jean-Bertrand Aristide unless it provided assurances that Fidel would not be invited to inaugural festivities in Haiti.

I feel my face, every bit of me asking Ira for more: *assuage me, assure me*.

He picks up on my signals. "If someone's gunna bomb your building, they don't call and tell you, 'I'm gunna put a bomb in your building.'"

"Shieeuuu!" I hold my open palm to my forehead, turn to leave.

"Usually."

I whip back around.

He shrugs. "What do you want me to tell you, sweetie? That some crazy Cuban's gunna say, '*Ah, sí*, Magda Montiel, she's a nice piece of ass, let's not blow *her* up'?"

Nice piece of ass. Okay, I'll buy that. I go downstairs to the lobby, push the glass doors open, descend the front steps, 1 2 3. A car fishtails, middle to the outside lane, takes the curb, up half the sidewalk, up almost to me. It *BeepBeepBeepBeeps* all the way down Twenty-seventh Avenue to US 1. Hmmm. The wolf whistle in Havana but that was the hotel parrot. The young, good-looking black guy guarding the hotel grounds, but his compliment fizzled with the *I can tell you once were* disclaimer. A good piece of ass, coming from Ira, but he's blind and in love—but okay, I'll buy into . . . OHMYGOD. MygodMygodMygod. They recognize me, those people in the car. They beep and swerve at me because they recognize me. But the car is gone and still, I hear it. No, not beeps. Squawks and squeals and shouts of

"*¡Perra!*" but there's no dog in sight. An onslaught of nonhuman noises. A crowd in front of the Vega Medical Building across the street. TV cameras circle them, bend to them, angle their lenses high at them. I keep walking.

A shadow approaches from behind, much like the paper cutouts marksmen use in shooting practice. I walk faster. The shadow catches up to me. It's my client, Mr. Maza. He takes my elbow, walks beside me. The air vibrates like a wild percussion of drumbeats, waves of shouting coming high and deep. And then, a stillness. For a minute, the street seems devoid of cars, of motion. But in the stillness in me, an acuity of perception, that fight-or-flight phenomena that gives adrenaline-charged prey extraordinary sensory powers, that allows me now, despite the throttle of school buses and ten wheelers and stink of diesel fuel and stickiness of polluted heat, to make out: "Are you going to *singar* the old man too?" And to Mr. Maza: "Stick your *pinga* up her *culo!*"

In rhythm to the shouts and insults of my *compatriotas*, I talk to Mr. Maza about his wife and daughter's case, steps taken, overall strategy. At the corner, we turn, walk to the back of the building—not that either of us know where we're going, or why. In the back parking lot, we stop. I look at his face, only his face, continue talking about the case *como si nada*.

A white van careens past us. A shirtless man in the driver's seat sticks his head, then his torso so far out the window, I think he will fall head first. He flails a fist. "*¡Comunista!*"

Mr. Maza draws closer. "If you want to go inside the building, I will stay with you."

I nod. "I feel more danger out in the street than inside the building."

———

Ira is in the lobby, boxy airless space encapsulated in glass. He paces, right left right—that funny splayed walk. The car phone is gripped to his ear. A three-way call with City of Miami police and bomb squad. He looks at me, his eyes a fierce blue. I try to take in a mental shot of his image, but it's as if he's blur, all the while thinking, Will the building blow up any minute?

We stand perpendicular to the main entrance, floor-to-ceiling glass walls, doors. It hasn't occurred to me, to Ira, not to stand here. It hasn't occurred to me, to Ira, to lock the doors. The bomb squad is upstairs presumably checking for bombs. Neither the police nor the bomb squad has told us, *Stay out of plain sight. Stay in one spot where we can find you.*

City of Miami police "stayed in the background" as Miguel González-

Pando, Bay of Pigs veteran, was "heckled . . . then rushed by a mob of people who attacked him" at the Bay of Pigs Monument in Little Havana after he called for dialogue, Americas Watch found in its 1992 investigative report, *Dangerous Dialogue: Attacks on Freedom of Expression in Miami's Cuban Exile Community*. Twelve years before, González-Pando had met with Fidel during the 1978 dialogue that resulted in deaths and attacks on many.

In that same report, Americas Watch found that City of Miami police stood by and did nothing when a mob of *exiliados* urinated on the plaque honoring Mexican singer Veronica Castro in Little Havana's Walk of Fame after she performed in Cuba. They did nothing when the mob hacked at it with hammers. The next day, the City of Miami Commission voted unanimously to prohibit replacement of the plaque without commission approval.

But I don't think about the mob at the Bay of Pigs Memorial attacking the Bay of Pigs veteran. Nor do I think about the mob urinating on or hacking the sidewalk plaque of the singer.

I don't think it possible that before the end of the year, Human Rights Watch will publish another investigative report, *Dangerous Dialogue Revisited: Threats to Freedom of Expression Continue in Miami's Cuban Exile Community*.

And I certainly don't think it possible that in this November 1994 report, I will be singled out by Human Rights Watch as the conference participant who "has borne the brunt" of the "essentially non-stop" attacks.

———

Mis empleadas, Mr. Maza tells me, have taken refuge in the corner liquor store. From a distance I see them, Janet, Cary, Mily, et al., standing stiffly in the adjacent lot. When Janet sees me, she pushes her thick, meaty breasts forward, waits for me to walk to her. "You know what would be really sad, Magda?" She squints, her eyes a fierce green. "If you were to lose this beautiful practice you worked so hard, so long for all these years." And it strikes me: what Janet wants is precisely that. I say nothing, leave.

From afar, a gangly, familiar figure exits the office building. It's Gabriela, the Russian American woman who works at the travel agency across the hall from us. She stops when our paths cross. "Why don't you leave the building?" Her hair weighs down the hard lines around her eyes and mouth. "It's true." She says this as if in response to the expression on my face. "Look at all the trouble you cause."

An acknowledgment prepariah Magda would have conjured up a quickwitted, spiffy comeback. In silence once again, I leave.

Ira is back in his office with a few immigration lawyers and others I don't recognize. He stands King Henry–ish at the front of the room, pretending he's taking in what the others are saying but ultimately calling the shots, getting his way. And I'm struck with a thought: How did he get them up here, sidestepping the pandemonium downstairs? When Elisa's husband sees me in the doorway, he pulls me gently aside. "Elisa quitting is nothing personal. And she feels very bad." He looks at me soberly, sincerely, says, "We'll always continue to be friends." I nod a *yeah let's get on with it* nod. "I have the greatest respect for—" I think he says *Ira*, just for Ira. I'm not sure I hear respect for me. I hear my *hmmph*, walk away.

Strange voices—muted, muffled ones—rise from Ira's reception. I edge closer, watch the sounds take shape: Marvin and Isabel, Ira's brother and partner, are at each other.

"You had no business alarming my staff," Marvin says, pushing a little too strongly.

"Next time, you come to me first and—"

"And what?" Isabel's cries implode as if from her gut. "Let everybody blow up?"

I block out the name-calling, press my hands over my ears, childlike. When I think the screaming is over, I say to Isabel, "It's safe now." I wrap my arms around her from behind, encircle her waist.

She cups her hands over mine.

"Everyone can come back up now." A pause. "The police found no—"

"I don't think anyone's coming back, Magda," she says in little whispers.

I nod slowly.

She turns around and is gone.

"That bitch," Marvin's secretary says. "That bitch called Marvin 'a fucking Jew.'"

I didn't hear it.

Isabel comes back.

I brighten up.

"I forgot to tell you. I went to the bank and took my name off as authorized signer on the account. And here are the office keys." She lifts my hand, drops the ring of keys on my palm.

Down I go again to the ground floor, not knowing where to go, what to do with myself. I press my mouth, forehead against the glass doors in the lobby. Good, the crowd, I've blurred them hazy now. I step back. The screaming, fist-shaking spring back to life. I burst into a loose hysterical laugh. What life? *This Is Your Life*, Magda Montiel Davis, that hokey TV show I watched when first we came to the US so I could learn English. I step back two, three steps, my reflected silhouette meshed with theirs, my *exiliado* compatriots. When they see me, the roaring intensifies. A presence now, at my left.

"Sweetie."

I whip around. Ira. With him is a somewhat-recognizable intellectual-looking English-gentleman type, neatly trimmed beard; long, pointy umbrella in hand. A Jewish Mary Poppins.

"Sweetie, you remember Alex Aleinikoff . . . holy shit!" Ira's eyes dart and widen, more than widen. His tiny lips flop open. "What the fuck is going on?"

"Wha-aht?" I say, shrug.

"Whaddya mean 'Wha-aht'? The flock of Cubans across the street, that's what. And what are they—oh, excuse me." He takes on an inexpressive face, looks at Alex Aleinikoff. "Pardon me, Alex. Just—just a little *household* matter to attend to, with my wife." He turns slowly to me, one foot, then the other. "Do you mind telling me what's going on?"

"I told you—"

"No, you *didn't* tell me. You *told* me there was a bomb scare. You didn't tell me half of Calle Ocho *and* all of Batista's army *and* the Cuban American National Foundation were protesting outside my building."

Alex Aleinikoff's head, his entire self is utterly immobile, save for his eyes, shooting like BB-gun pellets at me, at the crowd, at Ira, back at me.

"And what're you doing standing here?" Ira says to me. "What're you nuts?"

"*You* stood here."

"That was an hour ago, Magda."

"Well." Well, what? "Didn't you see them when you took all those attorneys up to your office?"

"No, dear. I guess your fans only rumba when they see you." He pulls Alex to us. "Well dear. As I was saying. Allow me to reintroduce Alex Aleinikoff. You remember him, the new general counsel of the Immigration and Naturalization Service. You know the INS, right, dear? The government agency we're always after to grant our cases and earn a living from?" A pause. "President Clinton just appointed Alex general counsel."

"Oh." I give it a tilt of the head.

Alex Aleinikoff gives me a nervous half smile. A cab swerves, stops short at the front of the building. Alex scurries down the steps amid the hurl of insults across the street, jumps in the cab. Ira flaps his hand at him in an attempted wave. Alex hammers his fist on the window lock, once, twice. The cab whisks him away.

I step into the elevator. "I'm going back upstairs. Sit at my desk, answer the phones."

Ira looks at me, assessing my, what? Reliability, dependability—lucidity?

"Business as usual." Upstairs, I glide past the Magda Montiel Davis, PA, purple lettering with magnificent swirls and step into my now empty law firm.

12

OUSTED

———

The police officers order a pizza.

I sit at the reception desk, the telephone clutched to my ear. "Law offices . . . I'm sorry, *la abogada*," I say about myself, "*no esta disponible*." Not available. Indisposed, of sorts.

The phone lights blink red, frantically. Which button to press next? The one at the far right, I decide, smiling to myself.

"—You sucked the asshole of the biggest son-of-a-bitch dictator."

"—Get ready, *negra de mierda*." Nigger bitch. "I'm gonna get you, and Ira too."

—*Click* after lesbian, degenerate, whore.

—*Click* after *TRRRRR-TRRRRR* machine-gun sounds.

A client calls. She just heard on WQBA "La Cubanísima" that my entire staff resigned.

"It's not true." Not all, I want to say. Just six. Two haven't jumped ship yet. And none would ever speak to the media like that and risk sending my clients into a panic, risk my losing the law practice I worked so hard, so long to build up.

A telling pause comes over the telephone, one that I have learned to recognize after so many years of clients in fear of deportation, so I beat my client to the punch. "Your immigration case is fine," I tell her, unsure.

"It's not about my case," she says. "It's about you."

I look up as City of Miami police officers stand around eating gooey triangles of pizza and wonder how the delivery boy was able to skirt past the frenzied crowd across the street. Miriam stands over me. A sudden role reversal, my receptionist watching me juggle the onslaught of calls.

She stares at me. Is she leaving? Is she staying? She looks at me, glazed, bewildered, like my grandmother the last time I saw her, a few hours before she died. I was her only visitor. She looked up at me from her hospital bed, her eyes steady but her look, stupefied. I gave her the same look back. I couldn't give her a look of comfort—only, the same look back.

"Ms. Davis," Miriam says, then stops midsentence.

"Miriam, call me Magda. How many times do I have to tell you? Call me Magda."

She gnaws at her skin of her nail bed. "Oh, no, Ms. Davis, I couldn't do that."

"Not even now?" I turn back to the phones.

"—I swear to you by God, when I catch up to you . . . giving him your ass like that."

Ira comes upstairs from his law office on the second floor. "Congratulations, dear. You managed to scare off *even* the mailman." He hands me three stacks of mail, the features of his face unreadable. "I told him I would bring these to you."

There is something different about the mail. Some, the usual: the US Department of Justice, Immigration and Naturalization Service, smacking of its denizen absurdities. But most, not. Not the usual at all. Plain white envelopes with no return addresses, handwritten in large, convoluted scroll. "Magda *jinetera*"—whore—reads one. Another is adorned with red swastikas and hammer and sickle. "Communist—you are a pig."

Ira takes an envelope from his pocket, this one, addressed to him. I lift its torn, gummy flap. YOUR WIFE, reads the folded paper. A big jagged arrow directs me to flip open the page.

"Oh my God!" A caricature of me on all fours, crawling in doggy position; ballooned breasts drooping in front of me; Fidel's penis pressed hard against my buttocks screwing me from behind; *"Ay maestro"* coming from my enlarged lips.

"And to think," says Ira, "I had to pay the mailman for it." And that perfectly timed pause. "Insufficient postage."

Back to the mail. "God will curse you and your children, for seven generations, [illegible] the Yoruba cult. All of you will die in pain and in hell."

"You have thrown your education, career, family away. Pick up and start over in Yugoslavia, Bosnia, or Herzegovina."

". . . the memory of your grandparents. How they must feel, you aligning yourself with Jews, faggots, and Satan."

Ira stands over me as I continue to squat on the floor, bent over the hate. How many in all? I have lost count. I am embarrassed reading them in his presence, as if his proximity will suck him into the vileness I now represent to so many.

He waits for me to finish, then, in silence, helps me up. "Keep a log," he says, "of all the incoming calls." Okay. Round 2. But the calls keep coming in: "*Cuidate.* Buy dark glasses and a blonde wig"—faster than I can trace them. "The walls of the firing squad will be stained with your blood"— the telephone shrilling and the lights on the dial pad flashing at me faster than I can zap them away. "I can't," I tell Ira.

"You can't, what?"

"Listen to the entire message, dial star 69, write down the phone number, the time—"

He says I must, I must record all that is said. "The FBI will want it that way."

"The FBI, oh my God, Ms. Davis." Miriam's mouth flops open.

"What was it?" I say.

"What was what, Ms. Davis?"

"What was it that the caller said?" Maybe if I shake her. "When you screamed, Miriam. The bomb threat."

"Well, you know, he said, '*Mire, señorita*, we have nothing against you,' and that . . . that we're just employees, you know, but that we'd better get out of the building. And then he said, '*¡Ahora mismo!*' Right now, Ms. Davis." Little shrieks burst from her again.

After a few silent seconds, I say, "So, Miriam," I try hard to sound casual, "are you leaving? Are you staying?" *Say yes.*

Finally, "I don't know. My husband says it's not safe for me to stay here." She chews at her fingers again. "But my father says I shouldn't abandon you."

From a distance, I hear Ira talking to the police officers. "Look." The words waft in and out, but his voice is firm. "Your job is to protect us, not *something something*. When . . . in front of the White House . . . does National Guard get the President out? No, *something something*. But . . . not gunna argue with you. Just get my wife out safe."

The *What* House?

The pizza the police officers eat is of the Miami-Cuban variety. My law office reeks of *lechón*, the stale grease of pork butt.

Cynthia Corzo from *el Nuevo Herald*, the Spanish-language version of the *Miami Herald*, calls. "Is Magda there?" Sure! Magda? *Mas o menos* there. And on a first-name basis too. Oprah, Cher, Madonna, . . . Magda.

"I'm sorry," I say in secretarial singsong. "Ms. Davis is not taking calls from the press."

"Just answer this question," she says, her voice high pitched, delectable with excitement. "Is it true she's fled the country?"

"She's closer than you think."

The air conditioner stops, a dying whine. It starts, it stops.

Coming back upstairs is Ira. He walks his receptionist to me. She will help me with the phones. But when she gives me the messages, I can't make out the names or numbers and some of the digits are missing. "No!" I say. "This is *not* how we do it."

But there is no *we* anymore. It is just me. I look about my office. Even Miriam is gone.

Just me and the police officers and Ira and the scrawny Xerox technician who continues to toil over the copier *como si nada*.

I walk to Ira, show him the messages from his receptionist. "She can't even take a number down right."

He says I'm ungrateful. He says I'm in no position to be picky.

———

"Time to go." A police officer extends his arm my way.

I remain seated, look away.

"If we wait much longer, we won't be able to get you out."

I look at the telephone, at my watch, at the stacks of files on my desk.

A second officer approaches. "I just looked out the window. The crowd's not across the street. They're in front of the building now." After a minute, he clears his throat. "And my backup downstairs just radioed me to get you out. In no uncertain terms, to get you out."

"It's only four o'clock," I say. "We don't turn the phones off till five-thirty." I turn to Ira. "Ikey." Ira is a lawyer with his own practice too; he'll understand. "What if a client gets through the phone lines and I'm not here? They'll think I've fled the country, taken their money." I try to keep my voice firm, "I can't lose my law practice," steady, "on top of everything else."

"Sweetie," he says. "We have to go. You heard the policemen. If we wait much longer, they won't be able to control the crowd." He stands over me, lays a weighted hand on my shoulder. I look up; his eyes, so blue. And then, that smile, that sweet, tender smile. He squeezes my shoulder, pulls me to him. I rest my head on his hip, coil my arm around his thigh. For a moment, he strokes my hair. Then he walks away.

I sit at Miriam's desk for how long? I don't know how long. Minutes, maybe an hour. I hear chants, bullhorns—conga drums?—outside.

A debate over which car to use. A police car? The windows are bullet proof. My station wagon—the White Hamster, the kids call it—so as not to draw attention?

"Here." The copier technician tosses his keys to Ira.

I am surprised when Ira, quick as a shortstop, catches them midair.

"Use my car." The copier tech is little and skinny and wears a wrinkled madras shirt. He looks like a recently arrived immigrant who scrounged barely enough to pay for a car.

It is cold, so very cold. I tremble. Someone rubs my upper back with quick, jerky strokes, much like I was taught in the Brownies when we lived in Jacksonville, when we first immigrated. *Rub two sticks to create fire.* I listen to my escape plan.

"Have her go down the elevator and exit the back door to the parking garage."

"No, because by the time the electronic gate opens, they'll maul her."

I am going to throw up. I go to the bathroom. I come back. I don't throw up.

"A change of plans." Now I'm to step out onto the fire escape, race down the three flights of stairs. Not the elevator. The elevator opens up to the main entrance, where the crowd now stands. Where the crowd will see me—it's nothing but glass.

The station wagon will be waiting for me in the back parking lot. With Ira, ready to go. Ira, driving the getaway car. Once inside the car, I am to crouch in the back seat. "Down, way down on the floor so no one can see you."

"Time to clear out, buddy," an officer says to the copier technician, still bent over the sputtering machine. Ira tosses the technician's keys back to him.

I tell myself to hold my head high.

I head to the emergency exit, try not to look out our wall of windows, but there's no avoiding it. Each frame is pretty much the same; the only difference is the angle from which I look—like riding on a train slowing to a complete stop. Except the sights are not of verdant countrysides or quaint rail stations. The sights are of people.

People unbarricaded and unimpeded by City of Miami police.

People pumping fists, posing for reporters.

People packing the streets.

People multiplied.

Mobs.

————

I am standing on the third floor, the emergency exit door before me. A police officer pries it open. It swings out with a gust of wind, slamming against the building wall. My first thought: this is what it must be like for a first-time skydiver to be pushed out of a plane.

Someone says not to look back. Not to hesitate. "Even if you think you won't make it."

I begin my descent. Through three flights of fire escape, my legs gain momentum with each step. When my feet hit the pavement, I sprint. But the station wagon, white and long and rodent-like, is far, so far away. Why didn't Ira park it closer? I am not going to make it.

They are turning the corner. They are coming at me, hordes of people, looks of fury on their faces. Women in tattered housecoats, pink foam rollers on their heads, open-toed *chancletas* on their feet. Raised armpits, fingers clutching rocks. Men in flimsy white undershirts—Maggie calls them "wife beaters"—18-carat gold medallions of San Lazaro around their wattled necks. Shirts emblazoned with the city's now defunct campaign: MIAMI, SEE IT LIKE A NATIVE / MIAMI, SEE IT LIKE A NATIVE / MIAMI, SEE IT LIKE A NATIVE. They are coming at me faster than I can make it.

Then I stop. I don't think about it, I just stop. I walk, fast, but I do not run. And I do not look down. I go for the front seat, next to Ira; fuck hiding in the back. I slide inside, just as I decipher two words in the muffled shouts: *Vende patria*. I sold out, betrayed the motherland.

They rock the car; right left right; front, back. They pound the roof and the hood. They kick the doors. They hit the windshield with sticks and snapped-off tree branches. Their fists punch at Ira's window; their open, pink-white palms slap at mine. A woman swings a broom at the car with the force of a baseball bat, the broomstick collapsing into an upside-down V, bristles everywhere. An umbrella springs open as if the Penguin was behind it. As if we were in Gotham.

A reporter knocks at my window. I stare ahead, forcing every muscle of my face to look relaxed. A long camera lens zooms in on me. *Shlick* goes the shutter, *ShlickShlickShlick.*

A big woman wearing big stripes blocks the car. Ira floors the gas pedal and I think, *He will hit her. He is going to hit her.* In a split instant, a police officer tosses the woman out of the path of the speeding car, the station wagon hauling ass through the parking lot, the White Hamster finally out of his cage.

The station wagon jerks us up, then *splat!*, down the curb. I lurch forward. Ira's arm, steady and strong, is at my chest, a crossbar. And as he makes a sharp turn out of the parking lot, he says, *como si nada,* "You all right?"

13

FULLY UNDER

———

Sarah Arizona sweater, loose and free and blankety. And leggings too. That's what I'll wear when I get home. The deep purple ones because purple looks pretty with any color and won't something pretty feel good on my eyes? I lean forward, flick off the air conditioner.

"Magda, what're you doing?" Ira brakes at the stop sign. "It must be ninety degrees outside." We're taking the long way home to avoid the red light, too long, too close to the office, too risky the mob will catch up to us.

The baby-pink wool socks too. I'll wear those. The ones I kept on my cold feet when I had Sadie. Funny, when I call up that image now, lying naked under those white sheets, the same way I'll be laid out in a plain coffin made of pine, because that's how Jews bury their dead, not in their Sunday best like Catholics, which seems silly anyway, all dressed up and nowhere to go.

It was night when I had Sadie. I opted for a spinal injection so I could stay awake; no general anesthesia for me. Ira stood by me in the operating room, held my hand. I retched and vomited and trembled uncontrollably and broke out into one Hail Mary, two, three Hail Marys, *Hail Mary full of grace, Hail Mary full of grace, Hail Mary full of grace.* Dr. Kalstone said, "What is she saying? I thought she was Jewish." And Ira said, "Don't ask." And I kept on, *Hail Mary full of grace*, between spurts of vomit, *Hail Mary full of grace.* And I was cold, so very cold. I'd been cold too with Katy and Paula and Maggie, but this was a different kind of cold, and I didn't know whether it was because of the below-freezing temperature in the operating room or from fright. Fright at the risk I took, at crossing the line, the *atrevimiento*. Then came Ben, the fifth cesarean. Three is the usual limit, Dr. Kalstone had said. Now I was beyond your usual *atrevimiento*.

In the recovery room, Ben tucked away in the nursery, *When can I go back to my room?* I could say the words in my head but I couldn't get them out. Back to my room so I could see Ira and my mom, Katy, Paula, and Maggie, and little Sadie, bopping about at fifteen months. So I could stop seeing the recovery room nurse, her masked mouth, her eyes shooting right left right as if something had gone dreadfully wrong. And to silence the pain of the patients next to me, across from me, everywhere in that vast, cold room. One o'clock, the nurse said, and held up one finger in an elementary way. A big white-faced clock with black letters moved its long hand half a click back, an entire click forward. A bit past one, I asked the nurse again. When I stopped bleeding, she said. Something about *blood pressure, down*. Again, the words in my head, I could say them. But couldn't get them out. Finally, "Blood pressure's down," I said, "Because. Of the pain." Isn't that how it worked? But she wouldn't listen. Why wouldn't she listen?

At 7 PM, finally back in my room, Dr. Kalstone dropped by; on his way out to dinner, he said, thought he'd check in on me. Pressing on my stomach, one long slow deep press, two quick ones, and *swoosh!* gushes of blood, dark and red across his face, silk tie, fine business suit. I heard *internal bleeding*. I heard *shock . . . in few minutes*. Bleeding, from where? No one knew. Back to the OR. And if they couldn't find the source of the bleeding? I heard Ira's *oh my god* and his breathing, I heard his breathing. I heard Dr. Kalstone call for a something or other unit. I heard Katy give Ira his brother Jerry's telephone number; Jerry, the doctor in the family. And Paula's *Mommy!* her voice breaking, I heard that too. I didn't know what to say to her. Instead, when the orderly ran in with a gurney, "So soon?" I kidded. He was burly and black and so gentle, and he covered me in sheets. "You're going to be all right, darling." Yes, that's what my mom said, and he started to wheel me out the door, but the baby, everyone forgot about the baby, I had to feed the baby. "Baby will be fine," the nurse said, my nutrients would sustain him and anyway, he'd be fed sugar water. Outside the doors of the OR, Ira stopped the anesthesiologist: How many surgeries had he performed? How many in the past year, month? Had charges ever been brought against him? License ever revoked? With each question, the anesthesiologist became increasingly exasperated. Then the anesthesiologist questioned me. "No," I said. "Not awake. Put me under. Fully under." But I didn't think I would die then, and I said my Hail Marys.

Three police car are angled wildly on our driveway. Ira stomps on the brakes. I'm jerked forward, then back. "Oh my God!" Ira slams the car door behind him. I stay seated. *Something has happened. To the children.* Then I move, slowly, a somnambulist ambling through our walkway.

Ira stands talking to police officers. The tall one turns to me. "Lieutenant Angulo." A strong handshake. "Key Biscayne police." His face is bronzed, his voice deep. "I was just telling your husband"—he nods at Ira— "there's going to be a demonstration here in Key Biscayne. On Friday."

"And the children?" I say.

"The children," he says, "are fine."

My heart paces back to normal.

Ira turns to me. "You know Key Biscayne, dear." He stands disheveled, thin strands of hair flying off his bald spot. "The vortex of political unrest. Last time there was anything political going on here was when Richard Nixon gave his hoodlum Cuban exile cronies the thumbs-up for the Watergate break-ins." He stands in frayed, wrinkled navy-blue blazer, his neck craned to almost 90-degree angle to Lieutenant Angulo, but he stands as if he were of even height, taller even.

"About the demonstration—," an officer says.

"Son of a bitches," Ira says. "They're just doing this to try to embarrass my wife, parading in our front yard, right under our noses. Son of a bitches," he says again. "You can't tell me Mas Canosa and Ileana Ros-Lehtinen and her crooked father and psycho husband aren't behind all this. They wanna make sure my wife doesn't run against *Ileanita* again." He pins down the lieutenant, as if cornering him on the witness stand, like the time he cross-examined Rudy Giuliani about the government's racially discriminatory treatment of Haitians and the federal judge made a finding that Giuliani's testimony was not credible. No, the demonstrators will not be permitted to cross Crandon Boulevard and come anywhere near our house. Yes, the lieutenant will personally see to it. Yes, there will be plenty of trained police on hand.

An officer glances my way. "Don't worry." Our PEACE TO ALL WHO ENTER HERE plaque with white high-flying doves hangs behind him. "They applied for a permit for one hundred," says another. "Which means fifty will show up," says Lieutenant Angulo.

I head to the bedroom, kick off my navy-blue pumps—though they did get me to the station wagon nicely—watch them somersault across the room. I throw on my Sarah Arizona sweater, squeeze into my purple leggings, and walk to my mother, who I know is in the kitchen making *arroz con leche*. Rhythmic, patient swirling of her milky rice pudding. Comfort food, for me.

But as I walk across the family room, I stop. A dead stop. There, on my left, on the bluish image of the TV screen, is my support staff. First Cary. And next to her, Janet, then Mily. Mily and bright yellow alpaca-fleece hair. "My father was a political prisoner!" Mily cries. And Isabel, oh my God, Isabel too stands in their circle, her face at an angle, her cheeks puffy in wide smile, their backs to my office building. Barbara makes an unintelligible announcement. The crowd hollers, frenetic fans in a sold-out rock concert. She steps forward in high-heeled feet, wraps her long arms around a little man in white *camiseta* undershirt.

Heads bop up and down in excitement. One face, then another appears before the camera lens, the way faces look avocado-like when too close to the camera. Says the newscaster, "All of Magda Montiel Davis's employees quit this afternoon in protest of her actions."

I fold over in *brace for impact* position, hold skin and guts between my fingers, squeeze. Isabel, my office manager, my trusted friend. And Barbara, who charmed her way into a job and my heart. Fresh out of high school, she came for an interview, garbed in grey business suit and heels so high they made me smile. "This," I said, "would be your . . . first job?" She unfurled a big smile, exposing a full set of braces. Her first day—grey business suit and heels again—she'd stand at my office door. When I'd look up—the girl was not going away—that big metal-braced smile. "How am I doing?" she'd ask, nodding enthusiastically.

When Barbara was on maternity leave, I discovered by chance that a lawyer on staff quit—while I was on vacation. She had taken our client list and was trying to lure away our clients. And she had taken a second lawyer and my then support staff. I called Barbara; the next day, she was at the office, bassinet with newborn in hand. Barbara and I took turns. If the baby cried and she was busy, I burped and rocked the baby, often with one hand so I could check cases with the other. And now she's gone. But it's *not* that she's gone. Although I was angry and disappointed, when earlier today she announced she was leaving, I think we both understood it wasn't final between us—the work relationship, yes, but not the closeness. But now, Barbara, all of them, to announce publicly news of the walkout, knowing the impact it will have on clients, colleagues, and immigration officers who decide our cases. Who's next? Elisa, the lawyer who this morning faxed her resignation? Will she now join the bandwagon, as it were? Miriam, Irma?

I sink into the family room sofa. What are the chances that at the precise moment I would step in front of the television and see Isabel, Barbara, Cary, the five of them, on television? But mostly, what are—*were*—the chances that they would have done such a thing? Now I understand the defector mentality, how quickly loyalty can turn, and in so cruel a manner. And now I understand this *identifying with the aggressor*; the oddity of it. You read of it with somewhat detached curiosity; hear of it with the high-profile Patty Hearst courtroom drama, but hadn't Mily, Isabel, Barbara, all of them, just a few hours ago been targets themselves?

In one scuddled jump, Sadie appears before me. "Wait, Mommy, wait!" She holds the baby pink of her hand out in a *halt!* motion, bolts out, comes back, wisps of dusty-blonde curls squiggling down her face. Arms akimbo, hands behind her back. "Pick one," she says.

A sob-laugh bursts from me. I tap one of her arms, making my selection: a small white gift box, the red-lettered script of *Lord and Taylor* logo angled across the top.

"Open it," she says. "Don't cry," she says.

I lift the fluffy cottony square from the box. Inside, a pair of my own earrings.

Maggie sits on one of our French country kitchen stools, legs astride, one knee hugged into her chest, the long lines of her body giving her a much older appearance than her fourteen years. She pulls at rubbery strings of melted cheese on two, three triangles of pizza as Goblin and Chaucer pant at her side and Paula watches a videotaped episode of *All My Children* and shrieks, "Erica Kane is getting married again?" and Maggie says, unimpressed, "I don't know why you're so excited, Paula. This is like the *eighth* time Erica Kane's getting married." And Maggie does all this as she bends over our vast expanse of kitchen counter, keeping a log of the hate and the threats against me. She sits lankily, stoop-shouldered, the telephone pressed to her ear, thick waves of chestnut-brown hair covering her face as she scripts unmargined columns in her left-handed, childish scrawl, 7:49, 7:52, 7:54, 7:57 PM and looks up at me, her brown eyes sinking small in her face, holding out a piece of paper to me that shakes in her hand and reads: "Is this the home of Magda Montiel Davis? Tell her I hope she dies."

———

Before the end of the day, Lincoln Díaz-Balart, once a Miami Legal Services lawyer, once a Democrat, now Republican congressman holding the distinction of becoming the second Cuban American elected to US Congress (behind Ileana Ros-Lehtinen, who I ran against), whose Aunt Mirta was Fidel's first wife and whose cousin Fidelito is Fidel's son, but you won't hear Rep. Lincoln say as much (Tía Mirta has never denounced Fidel, even let Fidelito return to Cuba to live with his father)—*that* Lincoln Díaz-Balart fires off a letter to Attorney General Janet Reno with a copy of the video demanding that under the Foreign Agents Registration Act of 1938 Attorney General Reno lists *some* of us conference attendees as agents of the Cuban government. With news alert to all major news sources.

14

FATHER ROSES

———

Everything," my father said to my mother. I sat outside their bedroom door playing solitary jacks. "They knew everything about us, where I work, where you teach, where the girls go to school." Who were *they*?

I threw the jacks on the floor, the ball in the air, but couldn't pick up the jacks in time to catch the ball.

"Why is your father spending so much time at the church?" said my *amiguita* Ive. I sat on our front porch playing jacks with a circle of friends.

"Father Juan works for the CIA," said her sister Susy.

"And so does your father," said Ive.

———

He stands on the other side of our front door, my father. I open it, step aside. In his hand, stalks of satin-ribboned roses, so red they're almost black.

"Two dozen," he says, pleased with himself, and extends the roses. From his wife, Bertha, he says, in an untiring attempt to rally me into acquiescence of his other family, told him to bring me flowers.

We walk in silence to the living room sofa, prettied and flowered in soft greens and lavender. He sits at one end, I at the other. One leg is folded under me, tightening the muscle of my hamstring, a hyperextension that feels good because it hurts. I sit, knowing I'm alone, my mom in the next room—in the kitchen, probably—close by, but not close enough.

I know my mom won't step into the living room; she hears my father, his familiar here-I-am whistle, the tread of his steps, though my father will stride into the kitchen before he leaves, sit high on one of our kitchen stools, and peel a banana in front of her. She will stand before the stove, and she will be barefoot, listening to the political "analyses," shall we say, of Radio Mambí, or "La Cubanísima," maybe watch the Weather Channel too if there is a hint of tropical storm that might just gather enough strength to turn into a hurricane, her sweat-soaked face looking up and gratified from the *casuela* of still warm *arroz con pollo*, stirring round and round patiently and lovingly, stirring. And maybe my father will even ask her to serve him, and she will. She will put a cloth placemat (never plastic) under his stoneware (never paper) plate and a glass of water with ice (always the ice), and she will do so in silent fury. The same silent fury when in Cuba he hid that *contrarevolucionario* in our home and she stood behind him in silence and said nothing.

I sit facing my father now, hoping my daughter Maggie will know not to show me the latest log of death threats. Not in front of him. Hoping hard my father won't ask why the telephone doesn't stop ringing, one ring atop another, on and on. Hoping hard my father doesn't come face-to-face with the rage and hate against his daughter.

We look at each other's silence. My father, a still handsome man of imposing height, who my mother likes to say looked sickly when she married him—so skinny, such a weakling was he. His doting aunts who raised him worried he was afflicted with liver disease, even though there never was a diagnosis. They watched *everything* he ate, overcompensating for the sudden loss of his mother when he was just a toddler of three—she died from a botched abortion in hyper-Catholic, prerevolutionary Cuba.

And when my mom met him, she was the pretty one then, but he managed to woo her and marry her, and she cooked *ajiaco* and *arroz con pollo* for him, and then he swallowed her whole.

Is my father now expecting me to say, "It's all a mix-up, Dad"? Or, "It's not what it seems"? "It's all a set-up"? Or has he resigned himself? Do I say "I'm sorry"? If I do, it's a different kind of "I'm sorry." I'm sorry for you, Dad. Sorry you never got a son to project your baseball aspirations on. Sorry you were too busy, too important to come to our birthday parties. Sorry I had to scrounge for the one thing I thought would bring you close to me, accept me: some smarts. Or at least pretend smarts. To stay in the ballgame. And I'm sorry I couldn't make you love my mother.

That Sunday night, when my sister walked out of our parents' bedroom, said, "Dad,"—no longer *Papín*, not *Papín* for a long time—"wants to talk to you. It's pretty important." She crisscrossed the living room into the bedroom we shared, my Miami Central cheerleading star and saddle shoes scattered throughout, her Miami Credit Bureau work suits hung neatly in the closet. She shut the door behind her. I scurried into the bedroom where I knew only he was, heart pounding, thinking, Oh my God, Dad found out I'm having sex with Paul. But no, it wasn't sex with Paul. Papín was leaving. "Don't you love her, Dad?" I offered him a way out that Sunday night. Just utter the protective parental lie: "Yes, but not in the way a man should love a woman" or even "Yes, but I'm not *in love* with her." But he lay in bed unmoving. And shook his head no. No, and the next morning, I went back to my inner city eleventh grade of academic nothingness, and then I married Paul.

He asks in silence now, my father. Sitting in my living room, prettied and flowered in soft greens and lavender, he asks. He asks with his eyes, not his mouth.

I nod.

After a while, and in futile attempt at self-comfort, he says, "That's a characteristic of the very intelligent, you know." His face, hopeful on mine. "They're very idealistic."

"No, Dad," I say, not even with a momentary impulse to lie. "There's nothing idealistic about the way I feel." I turn, face him squarely. "This is who I am. This is how I feel."

He bobs his head once. He tells me he loves me (loves me anyway?). "You are my daughter," he says, his voice breaking.

I don't feel the usual awkwardness around him today. For once, my father has been overshadowed by more pressing matters.

15

SHIT, SHERLOCK

DAY 3 OF 3 (MAYBE 5)

———

Ira bolts into the kitchen, his bowlegs forming a lopsided *O* under him.

Paula says, "Oh oh."

Mami heh-heh-hehs, taps 1 2 3 fingers on the kitchen island.

Maggie drops something into a skillet. "Ira, would you like to have breakfast with us?"

"And eat what? There's nothing to eat in this house." He thrusts open a drawer. "What is this? Magda, what are these? Birth control pills? Who's taking birth control pills?" He pulls out the entire drawer, its contents onto the floor.

"Obviously, not Mom," says Paula. "It's for the dog, to suppress her sexual urges."

Maggie walks to him, stretches her neck at the pills. "Ira, they're Mylanta."

"What are they doing in the battery drawer?" says Ira.

"They're in the 'B' drawer," says Paula. "Birth control pills, batteries."

"Did you study, wise guy?" says Ira. "I told you. At least two subjects each night."

"Okay then, lunch and PE."

He opens the pantry, slams it shut. "Davis, will you stop telling Gladys"—our housekeeper, of sorts, Mami's cousin—"to buy wheat matzo? Who eats wheat matzo?"

"Mommy does," Sadie says. "They're healthier than regular matzo, Daddy."

"Heaven forbid he should eat something healthy," says Maggie.

Spitting out her food on the paper plate, *"Aieech!"* says Sadie. "What is this?" Her chocolate croissant has some sort of Hamburger Helper–type meat inside.

"It's cow dick," says Maggie.

"Uh uh." Ben shakes his wild head of curls. "Cows don't have dicks. Bulls do."

"Sadie, just eat it."

"I don't eat meat, Paula."

"Then this one's a real delicacy. Eat it."

A rush of cold, bright light when Ira opens the refrigerator door. "*Look at this.*" On the top shelf, milk: fat-free, skim—it hasn't sunk in to Gladys that both are the same—2 percent low fat, A+ acidophilus low fat; whole—Mami won't drink fat-free, not even 2 percent; calls them *agua con leche.* "Ridiculous," says Ira. "I've never seen a refrigerator with no food. What is Gladys doing with grocery money?"

"Certainly not buying Lean Cuisine."

"The better question is, what is she doing with the groceries?"

"Not eating it herself. She's on Slim Fast this week."

"Unbelievable. Never seen a house that uses paper plates and plastic forks."

"There's too many of us, Daddy," says Sadie.

"No shit, Sherlock," says Maggie.

"Shit Sherlock, shit Sherlock." Ben runs frenzied little circles around the kitchen.

Mami holds up a lottery card to the light, bubbles in her selection for the week.

"Thank you, sweetie, for making me breakfast. You did a great job as usual." He slaps the counter. "Well, gotta go get dressed." He doesn't go. "Where are you going?"

"The fax line—"

"Jesus," says Ira. "Your mother has wolf ears."

"No," says Paula. "You're just going deaf."

"Yeah, well, this is what your mother has done to me. Before I met her, I was—"

"We know," says Paula. "Warren Beatty," say Paula and Maggie in unison.

I rip the incoming fax from the machine in Ira's study. "You are a disgrace to your nationality," writes Madelaine Gonzalez, Madelaine with an *a.*

"Let's go!" Ira's footsteps, *clomp clomp* our hardwood floor. "The bus is leaving. Everybody in the car!"

Plopping hollow on Ira's swivel chair, I skim the letter: "You are the

Biggest Hypocrite I have ever seen. The Cuban Community will never forget what you did."

"How did she get our fax number?" Talking to myself again.

"Last call! Mr. Mom here!" Ira walks into the study. "'Bye, sweetie!"

I jab at the paper. "*Biggest*, *hypocrite*, and *community* should *not* be capitalized."

"Uh, good time to obsess about grammar, sweetie." He kisses the top of my head. "Don't forget to call Sonnabend." Trying to slip on his wedding ring, "My finger is swollen," he says.

"Must be whatever disease you have this week," Paula calls out from the doorway.

"Yeah," Maggie calls back, "Ben and Jerry's Cherry Garcia."

"Daddy," Sadie says. "Let's go. Miss Mayle says I can't be late to school again."

"Oh my God," Maggie says. "Ira! *Look* at your clothes."

"What's the matter with my clothes?"

"It's a good thing we now have tinted windows," says Paula.

"Yeah," says Ira. "Thanks to your mother."

Clash clash, the slamming of our beveled glass door. I inhale big. I do as Ira said. I call Steve Sonnabend, owner of the Sonesta, the oceanfront hotel two blocks down. I can tell from his *Hello, Magda* that I needn't explain. "Do you think I might be able to um . . ." Gulp, swallow. "Use the Sonesta to meet with clients?" *Qué pena* if he says no.

"No problem," Sonnabend says. "I'll make arrangements so you can use an office, maybe a suite."

I thank him, over and over I thank him, lay the handset back on its cradle, lay my head on Ira's desktop, the cool of the emerald glass refreshing on my cheek. Suddenly, I'm in those days of long ago. My mom, after a night out at Tropicana with my father, would leave plastic drink stirrers in the shape of showgirls prettily fanned out on the black wrought-iron, skinny-legged bar of our Havana living room. Early morning, I would run from bed, climb a tall, very tall bar stool, and make the plastic showgirls with tiny waists and mango titties dance around the fat bottles of Bacardi rum, *clink clink clink*, the emerald green of the glass.

———

It's my open-mouthed drool on Ira's glass desktop that wakes me. I turn the other cheek. Then I see it. Janet. And Barbara. Working the phone lines at WQBA. In today's *Miami Herald*.

Scorned lawyer's ex-workers are offered cash, new jobs

DEZSO SZURI / Herald Staff

(TOP) *Miami Herald* headline, April 29, 1994. From the *Miami Herald*.
© 1994 McClatchy. All rights reserved. Used under license.

(BOTTOM) *Miami Herald* photograph, April 29, 1994. After the majority of my staff (and good friends) publicly announced their resignation before television cameras, newspaper reporters, and cheering crowds, the *Miami Herald* published an article about their guest appearance at WQBA-La Cubanísima radio station. One man, "overcome by emotion," heard them on his car radio and hand-delivered cash to the women. Others, including a wealthy community leader, called in three job offers. A local legislator invited them to apply for government positions. The photograph, by Dezso Szuri, *Herald* staff, shows two former employees, Barbara de la Gandara and Janet Thessen, taking telephone calls from supporters. From the *Miami Herald*.
© 1994 McClatchy. All rights reserved. Used under license.

The article is by Cynthia Corzo, on staff at *el Nuevo Herald*, but if style, content, and accuracy make the grade—scratch that, if sufficiently exaggerated, the *Herald* publishes it *en inglés*. The same Cynthia Corzo who minutes before I made my escape from the office the day before asked Magda-the-receptionist, "Is it true Magda fled the country?" to which she/I replied, "She's closer than you think." Cynthia Corzo who for years to come will be an ever-present specter in my life. Cynthia Corzo writes that my "five employees went on WQBA-La Cubanísima radio to explain their decision to leave [my] employ." Five. Barbara yes, Janet yes, Mily yes, Isabel yes. And the fifth? The fifth is Caridad Tremble. It takes me a minute: Caridad Tremble is Cary. Cary Sweiss. Now that Cary is on radio, television, newspaper, she's Caridad Tremble. "The sixth employee, Edward Trimiño, joined the radio show by phone." *¿Quien coño* is Edward Trimiño? Never have I heard of an Edward Trimiño, much less employ one.

There is mention of one Dr. Manuel Rico-Perez, a local physician, who phoned in two job offers. Who is in the process of losing his medical license for selling diet pills and/or other health products of questionable claims. "Miami Metro Commissioner Pedro Reboredo stopped by to praise the women. He invited them to apply for jobs with the county. 'Thank you for your patriotic and moral decision. It's an example many people should follow.'" In its upcoming November 1994 investigative report, *Dangerous Dialogue Revisited: Threats to Freedom of Expression Continue in Miami's Cuban Exile Community*, Human Rights Watch will underscore the "profound insensitivity to the rights of conference participants and others to freedom of expression and political belief" on the part of at least two elected officials: Commissioner Reboredo's calling the five employees heroes and offering them government positions, and Rep. Lincoln Díaz-Balart's writing a letter to Janet Reno, with a copy of the videotape, imploring her to make "certain conference participants" register as foreign agents. Following the letter came a press release to all major news sources. Díaz-Balart also issued a press release. "Jorge Mas Canosa, chairman of the Cuban American National Foundation, phoned in three job offers." *Chairman Mas*, son of a Batista big gun, who rose from milkman to maker of very lucrative City of Miami building contracts to leader of the most powerful anti-Cuba lobby on Capitol Hill to Cuban affairs advisor to Republican presidents Reagan, Bush the Father, and now to Democratic president Bill Clinton. Creator of rumors regarding Fidel's death, self-named president of Cuba, who I had recently written about in my conference articles for the *Sun Sentinel*. And financer of terrorist acts in and outside the island, among them the bombing of Cubana de Aviación flight 455.

"*Lo de Barbados*," Ive calls it, the worst day of her life. Even now, as she struggles to provide for her children amid Cuba's loss of trade with the now destroyed Eastern Bloc nations, the worst day of her life. Sitting with her sister, Susy, in the back seat of her husband's car, the three of them on their way to work as former gymnast champions, they turned on Radio Rebelde to the news.

16

CUBANA DE AVIACIÓN

———

The teenage girls, champions of Cuba's fencing team, carried their trainer in happy play after winning seven gold medals at the 1976 international fencing competition in Venezuela. They boarded Cubana de Aviación flight 455. Comprised of seventy-three passengers—all civilians, not all Cubans: brief stopover in Barbados; final destination, Havana. There, young athletic champions, coaches, and trainers would reunite with moms and dads, husband and wives, daughters and sons.

Ten minutes after takeoff from Barbados, one bomb exploded, then another. The pilot tried to turn back around but was unable to. So he flew far out into the ocean to save the lives of beachgoers below.

Luis Posada Carriles, often described as the US's "favorite terrorist" and chief suspect in the bombing, is a former CIA operative trained in Fort Benning. Convicted in Venezuela of the bombing—the first Western Hemisphere act of airline terrorism—he "escaped" from prison wearing a priest's garb. Soon to take part in a plot to kill Fidel, Posada Carriles will also take part in the Havana bombings of restaurants, discos, and hotels, killing an Italian tourist. He will then make an illegal entry into the US, and his deportation will be overturned by President George W. Bush. In Miami, Posada Carriles will take up oil painting and other things until he dies of natural causes at age ninety.

The brother of the Italian tourist killed in Havana will tell the *Miami Herald*: "It's like a New York resident who lost a relative on September 11, and the mastermind of this terrorist act lives in Canada. Wouldn't [the family] be furious at the Canadian government?"

———

The blowing up of Cubana de Aviación flight 455, such things happened years ago. So did the blowing up of the news director's car, the loss of both of his legs. Such things no longer happen in Miami. Nor do they happen in Puerto Rico, where the young father of two was shot, then shot again—mercy shot, the assassins called it—as he hung upside-down in his overturned car. Nor in New Jersey, where a twelve-year-old in the back seat of his father's car watched as ski-masked commandos gunned down his father.

Take Miami. Miami has changed. Hasn't Miami changed? To the extent that any of the foregoing may have been committed by any of the suspects, it's only one dark chapter of Miami history.

A dark chapter as was the House Un-American Activities Committee (now the Internal Security Committee): the electrocution of the Rosenbergs and the like; a dark chapter.

A dark chapter as was Salem. Bridget Bishop, the first sentenced to hang, made to ride backward on a horse-drawn cart for all the townspeople to see. Behind her, those once accused who had become accusers themselves.

––––––––

A moment of peace—not because of external factors. The calls, threats, and all else are still in full throttle. A moment of peace forced upon by me. I set it all aside and get to work. Sitting on the family room sofa, I slit open the office mail. What follows is but a random sample:

"*¡Bruja!* Take your broom, fly high, then descend to rock bottom with your maestro."

"May the devil continue to *acompañarte*. May he rip out your eyes."

"*Serpientes* slithered in hell. You and Judas sold out for the devil."

And then, the photo of me and Fidel that is now a fixture in South Florida households. Under it, this quote from Reinaldo Arenas's *Before Night Falls*: "All the pretentious people who dream of appearing on television shaking Fidel's hand should have more realistic dreams: they should envision the rope from which they will hang in Havana's Central Park."

17

GOOD FENCES, GOOD NEIGHBORS

———

After the bomb threat, mob attack, and office escape yesterday I called the clients I was to meet: "Instead of the office today, could you come here to my house, tomorrow?"

"*Claro que sí, doctora.*" They seemed to like that I was welcoming them into my home. But then I realized it was risky to have an uncontrolled flow of people in and out of our house, not knowing who was who, what was what.

Now I call clients a second time. "Can you meet me at the Sonesta Beach Hotel instead? Same directions, just a couple of blocks past our home. All the way down till you hit the beach."

———

Gladys wobbles herself into the kitchen. *Beba, perdona. Hay un carro . . . no sé.*" Tilting her head with a delicate shrug, a car, she says, it's circling our block. She's been watching it from Sadie's bedroom window. "Don't worry." I grin. "I have it all under control." I reach for the Pinkerton Security card, where yesterday Ricardo Martinez, account representative, had, with a light touch of his gold-plated fountain pen, written all his numbers: office, home, cell, fax, pager, PIN number even. "Anything you need, Ms. Davis." Had he bowed, Japanese style? "Anything at all. I'll spend the night patrolling the house, with a backup on call, just in case." When Ricardo Martinez and his men had inspected the exterior of our house and asked me to point out the children's bedrooms, I shivered and put on a second sweater.

I get a call back immediately. "See?" I tell Gladys. "True to their word." But it's not Ricardo Martinez, account representative, or even his second-string backup. It's Ira. "Sweetie," he says, in that soft-spoken way I so love but that he uses to break bad news to me. "The Pinkerton people just bowed out. They just called me. Apparently, there's some *cubanito* who is owner or part owner or a big client. Who knows? For political reasons, they said. Anyway, sweetie," he exhales, "we don't have any security tonight."

"How can that be?" I cry out. "Yesterday, they spent the better half of the day surveying the property. 'Whatever you need, Ms. Davis.' I should've known." Too suave, too polished, too much the Dale Carnegie type. But there's more to Pinkerton than meets the eye. It didn't register yesterday nor does it today that Pinkerton, with its century-old logo of a large open eye, is the same Pinkerton that made its name amassing big industrialist clients who paid Pinkerton to spy on unions, pose as guards and strike-breakers, and clash with striking workers. To use guns, bricks, and dynamite, and leave on a steel plant field dozens of dead and wounded striking workers.

"Call Rollins Alarm," Ira now says, but I can't get a line out. The calls, "*¡Prepara los funerales!*" and oh, no! Miguel Fernandez—again. Can he go over the questions on the nonimmigrant visa application with me? "The, ah"—here I hear him rustling through documents—"0-156 form." *I know the name of the form*, I want to scream, *and I already went through it with you, twenty times*! Camilo Betancourt: Where is his travel permit? He was to leave for Venezuela last Friday. His wedding ceremony, at the Saint Someone or Other Cathedral and five-hundred-guest reception, is this Saturday.

"Don't worry," I tell him. But *I'm* worried. How am I going to get his travel permit? I can't even go out into the street, much less to Immigration. Oh, God, the officers of Cuban descent. Mariano Faget: I'll never get an approval out of him again.

His father, Faget Sr., was a colonel in Batista's army, one of the few high-ranking officials who, immediately following the New Year's Eve celebration of 1958, fled on one of Batista's planes—and, it is said, with Batista himself. As head of Batista's BRAC, Buró para Represión de las Actividades Comunistas, he worked closely with the CIA, earning a stellar reputation for torture and brutality—the methods employed left no traces.

Ay Dios mío. In the name of the Father and of the Son. Now what? Ask Ira to sign off on my cases, file them as if his own; be the behind-the-scenes, the . . . *brains* of the outfit? (Okay, the brains-of-the-outfit part I'll skip.) Will the Florida Bar disbar me? Oh God, those three grueling years of law school. That tortuous, unintelligible bar exam; three hundred multiple choice questions—and that was just the first day. My dad drove *la niña* to the exam, waited outside. At every break, he was there. Two full days of this. He'd call Mami, his ex-wife (my mom): *la niña* was fine.

Some jittery months later, when my then boss popped his head inside my door, "I hate to interrupt you, dear"—I was meeting with new clients who were very British, very long winded and very neurotic—"but the bar results are in." After twenty more minutes of, "But what do you think? Go for the E-2 investor, L-1 executive visa? H-1 professional perhaps?" After a *Would you excuse me?* I bolted out the door, called the Florida Supreme Court. When the Southern-speaking young woman said, "You pissed"—passed—I doused her with *thee-ehnk-yoos*—she at least deserved I speak her native tongue. Never once did I, have I, told myself, *You're so smart.* Instead, *You're so lucky.*

Lieutenant Angulo walks through the arched doorway of our kitchen. Do I have all their numbers on my refrigerator? Yes. Key Biscayne, Miami-Dade County, City of Miami police? Yes. Bomb squad, FBI? Yes. He walks to the refrigerator door, gives it the once-over. Am I being careful? Yes Yes Yes.

"Then why is the front door unlocked? I came right in." He cranks shut the window above the sink. "And don't keep your windows open."

Scouring the pool area, "You don't know how these people are," he says. "What they're capable of." He looks down at Goblin and Chaucer, sprawled contentedly on the kitchen floor. "Maybe you should get a dog. A *real* one. And put a wall around the house. A big tall solid one. Not bushes. Bushes will take too long to grow." He turns to me. "And you have no time."

I stay calm, seemingly calm, still in a fog of disbelief.

Maybe fences *do* make good neighbors.

18

DARE

———

A demonstration," says Tía Tíita. "They're going to have a dem-onstration against Beba." My aunt waves a paper over her head. "Starting at *el puente*," the bridge. The toll-booth entrance to Key Biscayne, but Cubans call it *el puente*.

"How can that be?" says Paula. "People would have to walk for hours to get here."

"*Síii*," Tíita insists. "They're handing these flyers out at *el puente* to ev-eryone driving into Key Biscayne." She pulls her thin lips tightly, skimping on facial expression, lest it accentuate any existing lines or sprout new ones. While still in Havana, before any of us heard the word "plastic" used in the context of surgery, Tíita got herself a new under-the-knife nose; a thin, white woman's nose. The old nose, resembling my mom's and that of their four brothers, was a bit too wide, a bit too indicative of our black roots. When I moved to Key Biscayne with the girls and my mom in '81, Tíita warned Mami, "Magdalena, now that you live in Key Biscayne"—*Kee-ee Bee-eehs-kay-een*—"you can't talk with so much expression on your face."

"Okay, Mirta," Mami said, ventriloquist-like. "*No hay problema.* I'll talk like this."

Tíita ignored her. "Or go barefoot either. And you must wear these." She pulled out an assortment of muumuus from her beach bag.

"*Ay, Mirta, ¡por Dios!*" Mami said then.

"*Ay, Mirta, ¡por Dios!*" Mami says now. "*¡Bota esa mierda!*" Get rid of that shit. The flyer.

"Don't listen to her, Mom." Maggie drops a lanky arm on my shoulder. "She always gets her information wrong." Tíita likes to tell everyone she

A NUMEROUS GROUP OF CUBAN-AMERICAN RESIDENTS OF KEY BISCAYNE WILL MARCH FOR CUBA'S FREEDOM IN PROTEST TO THE RECENT PARTICIPATION OF CERTAIN INDIVIDUALS WHO WERE INVITED AS GUESTS OF THE CUBAN GOVERNMENT TO THE CONFERENCE WHICH UNDER THE THEME OF "LA NACION Y LA EMIGRACION" WAS HELD IN LA HABANA, CUBA.

THE MARCH WILL TAKE PLACE TOMORROW, FRIDAY, APRIL 29, 1994, AT 6:00 P.M. -- COMMENCING AT THE ENTRANCE OF THE CAPE FLORIDA STATE PARK (BILL BAGGS) LOCATED AT THE END OF CRANDON BOULEVARD, PROCEEDING ALONG SAID BOULEVARD, AND ENDING AT THE CHURCH OF ST AGNES, WHERE A MASS FOR CUBA'S FREEDOM AND CUBA'S MARTYRS WILL BE OFFICIATED AT 7:30 P.M.

PARTICIPANTS WILL WEAR BLACK AS A SIGN OF MOURNING, AND WILL CARRY A QUILT FROM THE ORGANIZATION OF HUMAN RIGHTS FOR CUBA, IN WHICH THE NAMES OF MORE THAN 5,000 CUBAN MARTYRS APPEAR -- CUBANS WHO HAVE DIED FIGHTING AGAINST CUBA'S REPRESSIVE SYSTEM: IN THE BAY OF PIGS INVASION, IN CUBA'S PRISONS, BEFORE FIRING SQUADS, VICTIMS OF ABUSES AND TORTURES, AND IN MAN-MADE "BALSAS" IN A DESPERATE ATTEMPT TO REACH OUR SHORES IN SEARCH OF FREEDOM.

Announcement of the demonstration to be held in my South Florida neighborhood of Key Biscayne on Saturday, April 30, 1994. The flyers were handed out for days before the demonstration to drivers at the toll entrance to the key and throughout the island.

speaks English, followed by her account of her years of teaching at Miami High. The second part is true.

Maggie takes the flyer from Tíita. Standing tippy-toe behind her, together we read it.

Lieutenant Angulo calls. The number of demonstrators is up to a thousand—"and counting."

Through the jewel-cut glass of our front door a figure paces, skewed out of focus. I swing open the door. Lieutenant Angulo would not be happy; I am not to open the door to anyone, not even to those I know, *pero bueno*. The man stops, smiles a tinge quivery. He's Felix Madera, he says with pride, General Manager of the Sonesta Beach Resort Hotel. "Steve Sonnabend . . ."

I block out Felix Madera's rambling, aware of what awaits me. "Our Cuban employees," I hear him say, "afraid . . . some trouble." He scratches behind his ear with the flick of a pinky-ringed finger. "Afraid some of them may see you, may, ah . . ." A shift of designer-clad feet. "If you, ah, *come* to the hotel . . . we don't want any problems." And he thinks for a minute. "For you too, you know."

"Oh, thank you," I say, but he doesn't catch on.

Taking a breath, he spills it out at rapid-fire pace: "I'm afraid it won't be possible for you to use the Sonesta," the features of pretty-boy face now relaxed.

I look at Madera in silence, hoping my stillness will impart some faint notion of my thoughts.

"But," he adds, "the people organizing the uh . . . they asked me to contribute to the cost of the, uh, but I told them no." He waves no. "Don't wanna get involved."

Almost, I shut the door on Felix Madera. Almost. But there, past our bird feeder and the battery-operated fountain Ira gave me for Mother's Day, stands television reporter Eliott Rodriguez, *GQ* persona in delightful juxtaposition to the squatting, sweat-drenched gardeners in my yard. "Magda!" Eliott waves frantically. "Magda! It's Eliott!"

The gardeners look up at him, look at each other, shake their heads, laugh. I walk to the refrigerator. Key Biscayne Police: 365-5555. "Ms. Davis?" I recognize the voice. "Officer Friendly?" She laughs. "Well, it's not Officer Friendly, really. That was my . . . *metaphorical* name with the kids." At DARE—Drug Abuse Resistance Education—when Katy, Paula, and Maggie attended Key Biscayne Elementary.

Do I want a unit sent out? Yes. Do I want the gentleman off my property? Yes.

Is it too late, Officer Friendly, for me to do drugs?

19

RINGO THE ROTTWEILER

————

Otto. My new bodyguard. Otto. At my front door. Otto. Stout and oily-faced, buzz military haircut and bulging muscles the size of Arnold Schwarzenegger's and the Incredible Hulk's combined. Otto, his wife Gretel—but neither is German, he says—at my front door, a purple-tongued, panting Rottweiler sitting obediently next to him, S&M-type collar with razor-edge spikes and baby blue flowered bandana around the dog's fat, throbbing neck.

"Otto," he says.

"Otto," I say in disbelief.

Otto swooshes past me, Ringo—that's the Rottweiler—next, wife Gretel after Ringo.

"*Buenas.*" She smiles demurely.

"*¿Eres cubana?*" I've never met a Cuban with red hair and freckles.

As if privy to my thoughts, Otto strokes her hair. "And it's real too." Otto is a member of the Antonio Maceo Brigade comprised of prorevolution activists, quite the anomaly in Miami. I met him at a brigade reception during my campaign for Congress. He offered me protection; for free, he said, from his one-man newly created enterprise, dedicated to the safety and security of underdog liberals. I had received some threats during the campaign but had shrugged them off, dismissing Otto and everyone else at the reception as left-wing paranoid, dramatic. Now with no Pinkerton security, no Rollins, Otto popped into my head. Even Ira was impressed.

Otto wets a stubby finger, flips the pages of Maggie's log of threats. "Any numbers appear over and over?"

"Several." I point. Then I stop. "Why? Is there a profile? A prototype?" My heart thumps hard. "What? Does it bring out . . . the frenetic, compulsive types? *Los locos?*" I press, calling up yesterday's early-morning call about Fidel bombing Pearl Harbor. Answer me! I want to scream. I want to know who my killer will be.

But Otto has no answers for me. I look at Gretel, her freckled face adoringly on her man. I look down at Ringo, a steady stream of saliva dripping onto our silk-stitched Persian rug, a wedding gift from one of Ira's clients.

Otto is not available tonight "on such short notice," he says, but he'll send Marcos—whoever that is—to patrol the house all night.

The *BeepBeep* of my pager startles me. Ringo whimpers, cowers toward the front door, the stub of his tail between his legs. I unfasten the pager from my waist; three numbers light up. I look up at Otto. "Somebody just beeped me to call 911." I blink. "Who would do such a thing?"

"Who has your beeper number?"

"Only those who are close to me. Family, friends." And staff. *Ex*-staff.

"Anybody else?"

"Reporters."

Back to the boxing ring. First on my list: call Lazara. Mily and some of the others told her they were willing to do cases from home, Lazara mentions. Hmm, I might just be able to pull this off, stay afloat, not be taken under by the wave of unfinished—unfinishable?—work. Then I get to the point. "Can you please ask the staff to stop going on TV and hopping radio to radio show?"—nudging, cueing, reminding my friend: *Take action, mobilize, as always you have for me; always, unconditionally.* "Every time the news is on, the calls here like, multiply. And if they're on the news, it's ten-times multiply. Already there's a demonstration—"

"Don't!" Lazara yells. "Don't try to turn me against them. Because what *you've* done—"

Some part of me listens to her screams, as if in an out-of-body experience, allowing me to remain bitchily calm.

"I have this pain," her pitch inflected in *Telemundo novela* drama. "This deep pain inside my chest, my heart—"

I can see her, pounding her chest in one of her extravagant gestures. I throw down the phone. Fuck her pain. Selfish, self-centered bitch. What about me, my pain?

I gravitate to the kitchen table where my files are haphazardly stacked. The familiarity of my color-coded system grounds me: blue files for family petitions; green, business visas; red—*oy vey!*—red is for deportation. I look for my appointment book. I had it, now I lost it again. I sort through each file, look at my watch: 4:20. I find Stanley Kuo's file but not his ledger; so how am I to know how much he's paid? José Restrepo's client card, but not his file. And where is Joya Santhiago's Brazilian passport? Her US citizen daughter's original birth certificate? I throw myself on the family room couch. I need order, that's all. I stand, sit, write:

1. *Cary/Mily: Work for me from home?*
2. *File cases under Ira's name?**on stand-by.*
3. *Move the office? (smaller, cheaper space).*

And then I see Irma. She walks through our courtyard, softly but surefooted over the bumps and dips of our S-shaped walkway. "I know I'm risking my life," she says quietly, "but I told my husband I couldn't leave you alone. And Mario said, 'Go. Go and help Magda.'"

I am like that character on *The Twilight Zone*—or was it *Alfred Hitchcock*? The shows that my sister and I watched shortly after we immigrated. The character whose five senses were intact but could not move. Left for dead, about to be buried, he could hear everything but could say nothing. Except that guy felt emotion—as in *horror*. I feel nothing. I should be appreciative, relieved that Irma is here. But I feel nothing and do nothing except stand back and let her take over, as she does when emergency strikes—*Quick! A client is detained, on the verge of being deported*—and we race against the clock to prepare, file, cajole Immigration to grant a motion to reopen and a stay of deportation. Irma takes over, making copies at supersonic speed, plucking out documents, this exhibit here, that one there. In a flash. Now, standing before me, she organizes the files, ledgers, client cards, and hands them to me in a tidy pile. And she smiles.

———

Irma, just a simple, country girl from a small village in Guatemala, but oh-so-smart. I met her when she was working in the old folks' home in which my grandmother was existing, the Little Havana version of a retirement home. Cuban American families take in *viejitos* and *viejitas* and tend to them in their homes, for affordable fees—and without the thought of a health or county license. Irma, having just fled the US-instigated civil war in her native Guatemala, was working 24/7 in one of these homes, tending to my *abuela* and others. One Sunday morning, I arrived for my regular visit earlier than usual and noticed rumpled sheets on the old living room couch. And it hit me: Irma was sleeping on that couch—with her three-year-old girl. So I asked her, could she take a bus and meet me at my office on Saturday and watch Little Sadie so I could get some work done? Lazara's mom watched Sadie at the office for me during the work week—I was still nursing Sadie and took her to work with me every day—but Saturdays were wasted days if I couldn't pump out more work. Just Saturdays, I promised myself, I'll have Irma come in Saturdays, in case she doesn't work out. Slowly, I gave her other tasks: Could she make a Xerox copy or two? Copy an entire L-1 visa packet? Label the exhibits? Once, the FedEx deliveryman trudged up the stairs: "Hey man, who's been sticking regular mail in the FedEx box downstairs?"

Irma looked at me, her dark eyes wide in frightened dismay. I convulsed in laughter, then she laughed too. Could she put in more days, work longer hours? I asked. When Sadie was seven months old and I found out I was pregnant with Ben, Irma got herself a full-time job. "Let's put your little girl in school," I told her. "Let's bring your son from Guatemala." Stricken with meningitis when a toddler, he wasn't getting the right treatment for severe developmental problems in war-torn, poverty-stricken Guatemala. And then, "Let's get your and your family's green cards. What the hell, I'll be both your lawyer *and* petitioning employer."

Standing now before the mirror, I smooth my hair with my hands, grab under-eye concealer for the sunken flesh around my eyes. "*Lista*," I say.

Irma drives me to criminal defense attorney Joe Beeler's office. She just passed her driving test; flashed me her driver's license and a big smile when she did. And she and husband Mario just bought their first car, a used Ford Escort. After my ouster from the office yesterday and the photos in the media of Ira driving the getaway car, my station wagon—my poor White Hamster—now ascended to celebrity status is too recognizable. So Ira parked it at the new strip mall across Crandon Boulevard. There it rests in peace.

I lie in the back seat of Irma's car.

"Yesterday, when I was at the corner parking lot," Irma says, "*las paralegales*"—she still speaks of them in reverence—"asked me if I wanted to speak to the reporters with them, to say I quit too. And I told them, '*Magda está con muchos problemas* and I have to stay by her side.'"

"Irma, who is this 'Edward' guy anyway?" And when she asks who, "Some guy named Edward Trimiño," I say. "Yesterday, the *Miami Herald* said the 'sixth employee' was unable to join the staff on the radio show—you know, when all the listeners called in offering *las ratas* money and jobs—and that he'd joined them by phone."

"Oh. That's that young kid who was typing an article for you. Janet's nephew."

"*That* kid? And he's my . . . *employee*? He worked, what? Five, ten hours in all? Jesus!"

"Magda, *las paralegals* were *embullandonos*," encouraging us, "to go on the radio with them. They called Miriam and she wouldn't come to the phone. They probably called him."

I stretch out on the back seat, lift my bare feet out the window, wiggle my toes. "Hey, Irma, you think I'm safe doing this?"

She looks back, laughs. "They may recognize your big toe. You'd better put them away, in case you need them to run again."

I watch the sky skirt past me, the way the power lines come together, then not, like when I was a kid, picking up my mom at the University of Havana from her postgraduate studies in pedagogy in my *abuelo*'s '56 Buick, my head nestled on my mother's lap the entire drive home, her hands long and graceful, her fingernails a fiery red, stroking the hair off my face. "Did you ever think you'd be chauffeuring a fugitive?" I ask Irma.

"In my Ford Escort." She reaches over to the back seat, hands me a bagel, my first meal of the day. Cinnamon raisin, my favorite. I can eat just two, three bites of it. "*Ay*, Magda," she says. "Thank God. Thank God your grandmother never lived to see this."

20

GUNS IN THE PLURAL

———

Criminal defense attorney Joe Beeler shows me how to work the digital burglar alarm. Me, who can't change the paper in the copier, who can't follow a Toll House cookie recipe. Who will choose an emergency exit seat for the extra leg room then lie to the flight attendant: Yes, in case of an emergency, I am able to open the emergency door latch. Yes, I tell Joe Beeler now, I understand how to turn on the alarm. Yes, I lie again, I'll be all right alone.

He leaves, swings back around. "Oh, and Magda?" He has a funny Midwestern curl to the tongue. "Every time you . . . dah, *meet* with a client"—he's full of dahs, but they are deep-thinking dahs—"pretend there's a microphone—a pretend microphone; you know, like the, dah, *hidden* microphone the media is saying Fidel was wearing when you met him." A chuckle. "A microphone with a, dah, *long*, invisible cord"—he strings two fingers at the air—"leading to the US Attorney's office. Better yet, the FBI. A microphone on your quote-unquote clients. Or, for all you know, in my office plants maybe. Or on me, right now. You, dah, *any* prudent lawyer should do that, but you, particularly, need to be extra, extra careful." He nods once. "Cautious." Chinning his white beard to his neck, he looks at me through the top rim of his glasses. "Paranoid. You don't know who's friend—or foe. Same thing I tell, dah, *all* my clients."

"But your clients are . . . criminals."

"You think, dah, *everyone* who is convicted is guilty?" His eyebrows shoot up. "How many serving life sentences—or those on death row—are innocent?"

I leave Joe and his universal truth, or else two more hours of talk and dahs. Aimlessly, I walk around the sparsely decorated, intellectual-looking office Joe Beeler shares with other criminal-defense attorneys—an office so unlike mine, with its purple walls and pastel prints and funny family photos and trinkets from clients from their home countries.

First is Stanley Kuo and I am happy he's here and on time. The slightest delay would have confirmed my fear that no one was coming. Stanley (his adopted name—in no time, most Asian clients morph themselves into Jeffs and Jessicas) offers a tiny book with a shiny red cover. Inside, black stick figures stand, lean forward, back, crisscross wildly across the page.

"For good luck," he says, in funny Asian-accented Venezuelan Spanish.

"But Stanley," I say, amusement in my voice, "it's written in Chinese."

"So is immigration law." He pats my back, 1 2 3. "Chinaman chance nothing happen to you. Look at me. From Taiwan to Venezuela to US like Wandering Jew in the desert."

"Well, hopefully, your green card won't take forty years, though with Immigration . . ." I spread Stanley's files on a long table, my hands moving deftly, automatically in front of me. I may never argue before the US Supreme Court as has Ira, but I have a cut-to-the-chase Cuban way of steering through the infamously understaffed, under-funded mess that is Immigration.

After Stanley comes a Glen Campbell–looking fellow fishing for free information, best possible service, lowest possible price. "If I marry my Peruvian girlfriend . . . she's illegal—"

"Out of status?"

"Yeah, whatever." Sitting back in attempted self-assurance, he crosses his blond-fuzzed, Bermuda-clad legs. "How can I be sure she won't leave me the minute she gets her green card? I heard they do that, you know. Get you to fall in love with them, use you, then kick you in the ass." He looks like first-husband Paul, and I think, oh God, I know what he looks like naked.

Then José Restrepo. "I was so scared for you, Magda. All those people yesterday, yelling, looking like they'd bolt upstairs any minute. I ran through them, past the police, three flights of stairs, just to make sure you were okay. I was so relieved when I finally saw you and—"

I look at him, dumbfounded.

"You don't you remember? You"—he pulls back his neck—"even answered me."

Ay Dios mío. Officer Friendly, where *are* those drugs?

Joya Santhiago—the client Mily warned not to go to the office to make a payment right before the first bomb threat—holds up a crystal obelisk dangling from a black string. "Wear it," she whispers, and scoops the crystal inside my blouse. It is soothing and cool between my breasts. "It's from the ancient mines of Brazil and will bring you protection."

And then, Gino Lascari. And his gun.

"Jesus, Gino, put that thing away."

"Who-oht?" He looks about him in *pretend the coast is clear* mode, flashes open his jacket, exposing a splendid gamut of shiny black pistols. His recently immigrated Irish bride scoots closer to him, runs her long fingernails through his gelled-back curls.

When I accompanied them to the I-130 marriage interview, Mariano Faget questioned them in different rooms. To disarm them, the easy questions first: When and where did they meet?

"Who-oht? Whot do you mean?" said Gino.

"At a party?" said Faget. "On a blind date?" No. Not at a party. Not on a blind date. Their answers matched perfectly. She was at work, each said.

"Oops!" Gino's bride put a hand over her mouth, looked over at me— "I wasn't supposed to say that, was I?"—then looked coquettishly, sheepishly at an unimpressed Faget.

"Where?" Faget said. "Where were you working?"

"Oh," she said. "Right here. Right behind you."

"Behind me?" Faget looked behind his chair.

"At the Pink Pussy Cat." The frequently raided strip club butt-to-butt with the Federal Building.

Gino was a bit more explicit about their first meeting. "Man, the minute I saw those tits, let me tell ya. It was love at first sight."

A loud grunt escaped from me.

"Whot? Whot?" Gino pivoted his 300-pound frame to me. "You told us to tell the truth."

"And what do *you* do for a living?" Faget asked Gino.

"Family business." Gino sat back proudly.

"Well," I said to Faget, "they *did* have the same answers."

And Faget smiled and shook his head. "*Ay*, Magda, Magda, Magda." Raising his approval stamp high, theatrically, he clicked *Approved*, red and inky and happy, on the I-130 visa petition.

"I'm here if you need me," Gino says now.

"Yes, Gino, I know. You and your gun."

"Guns, baby. In the plural."

———

I stay on task. Every half hour, I go downstairs, let out the last client, bring in the new one, keeping a discreet eye on the clock, careful not to let them see how delicate the balance is between an approval or denial—and deportation. How much their future really does hang by a string. Ah, *sprezzatura*—this I learned from a client—the art of making the difficult look easy.

But now, my next client is not there. I wait five, ten minutes, then go back upstairs, flip through flurries of While You Were Out messages, sort through a rumpled mess of mail.

I call an attorney who'd been Ira's student. "No great shakes," Ira said. "But you need somebody, fast. No way you can handle all these cases on your own."

Yes, she can be in Miami in a week, maybe ten days; she'll drive down from Boston. Agreed: five thousand dollars over the admittedly low salary I initially offered her, two weeks' vacation after one year, health insurance—and . . . will it will cover her fiancé once they marry? Fiancé? Jesus, that's all I need, a harried bride-to-be worrying more about her wedding gown and honeymoon specials in the Poconos—those geeky ads with blond-haired people in heart-shaped tubs—instead of worrying about cases and clients and putting in the fifteen-hour days the next months will surely demand of us.

Now she's asking about security—and it's not job security: What type? When? How often? I come this close, *this close* to telling her, No, I can't guarantee your ass won't be blown off, but I'm diplomatic instead. "Forget it," I say, and hang up.

And now, Enrique Teran. In he walks, in a finely cut European business suit, wife draped on his arm, done up and dolled up with her Maybelline-curled eyelashes giving Tammy Faye Baker a run for her money. *"Ay-yee,"* she cries. *"Gracias a Dios* you're here. We were *waiting* for you, downstairs." She huffs and puffs.

He wants his file, he says point-blank.

And they blow my house down.

I don't hide my annoyance. "I told your wife yesterday," I look sharply at her, "'If you want your file back, you don't need to come in for that.'" *Waste my time for that.*

"It's nothing personal," he says. "Nothing against you, nothing *political*. You have to understand," a pretend plea in his voice. "We've struggled so much, so many years, lawyers, and now that the case is finally *encaminado*, we can't take a chance."

Yeah, *encaminado*, because of me.

"And things are so bad in Venezuela," she moans, her tarantula lashes flapping at me.

"And getting worse," he says. "*Ese señor*"—how my upper-crust Venezuelan clients refer to Hugo Chávez—"already he . . ." His voice trails off when he realizes it's me he's talking to, *la comunista*. I laugh inwardly, calling up the ride in from Simón Bolívar Airport. The makeshift *ranchos* of the very poor down mountainsides, one atop another, making even the Three Little Pigs' straw house seem sturdy. This, in the oil-rich paradise of Venezuela.

Turning on my heels, I walk to his stack of files: the skinny ones of botched-up mess his earlier attorneys had created, the L-1 executive visa I got approved, his and the Missus's permanent residency cases I'd prepared so meticulously, carefully and *rats!* was on the verge of getting it approved. Holding out the files in an exaggerated way, I drop them in his arms. For a minute I wonder whether they've turned to Elisa to finish their permanent residency case.

"*Adiós*," he calls out. They wait; I ignore. *El major desprecio es no hacer aprecio.* After a few silent seconds, I hear the door close.

I sweat, my hands shake. A wave of fatigue, an insurmountable urge to lie down, sleep. Blood-sugar drop? Dehydration? I scrounge around for something, anything, find some vanilla-flavored powder in a torn Slim Fast packet inside an old portable refrigerator. Mixing it with someone's leftover half-and-half, I take tiny sips as I lie spread-eagled on the thinly carpeted floor. The ceiling tile looks black; everything, black. The ceiling at the Palace of the Revolution was black, a flat, muted black. Made to replicate the Sierra Maestra night sky.

Raising my arm to the conference room table, I pat blindly for the telephone until it falls. I catch it before it hits me. I call Xiomara.

"We just got back." She takes a breath. "Eddie and I were in the countryside, visiting my mother. We didn't know about any of this. Found out about it the minute we drove into Havana."

"Hav—"

"It's all over the news, *querida*. Everyone at MINREX, that's all they talk about—"

"MINREX." The Cuban Department of State.

"Yes. And they said Fidel is very concerned, very worried about you."

"Fidel."

"Robaina"—the foreign minister—"says Fidel calls him every day. 'How is she? Are you in touch with her? Are we showing her enough support?'"

"You know how Fidel is," Eddie, now on the other line. "About being grateful—"

"Showing solidarity," Xiomara says. "And did you see? What he said about you?" She doesn't wait for me to answer. "It was in the *Miami Herald*. Here, let me read it to you." A rustle of newspaper. "'A kiss is just a kiss,' according to Cuba dictator Fidel Castro, and he should be able to give and receive them without major consequences. It's common courtesy and 'not a political crime,' he said. 'I think it's been a very unjust reaction, negative, fascist.' Comments blah-blah made to Miami reporter blah-blah during interview in Barbados. 'I greeted many United Nations delegates today and kissed some of the female officials,' Fidel Castro said, 'I hope they won't want to throw them out of the United Nations because of that.'"

"And Hamlet," says Eddie, of Xiomara's son, "just called us from London. He said he was on his way to a club and saw you in the *London Times*."

"The *London Times*," I say.

"Yes, your picture, in the *London Times*. Well, you and Fidel." Xiomara giggles.

"When I called home and found out about the video," I say, "I had just said good-bye to you at the hotel. I remember I wrote in my diary: 'There's no one to talk to, not even Xiomara.' You'd said you were leaving, to see your mother. I had no way to reach you."

"*Ay*, Magda," Xiomara says. "*Lo que tu necesites*. Anything. *Incondicionalmente*."

"I don't know what, if anything, anyone can do." The back of my throat tightens. *Unconditionally*, she said. But I will myself not to cry.

———

I finish close to midnight. Through a smudgy glass door, I see Ira's Chevy, fat and jolly, parked in the back alley. I jump in. "Well, that was a first for you, Ikey."

"What? Picking my wife up at midnight in a dark alley on Biscayne Boulevard because she's being chased by the Cuban exile militia?" He looks about him. "We're safer here with all the pimps and the drug dealers than going back to Key Biscayne."

"No! A first, you being on time."

"For *my* wife . . ."

I ramble on about the cases and clients. "One client even came in to *start* a case."

"Did he pay?"

"No." I whack at his arm. "But he will. Jesus! Stop being so Jewish. Such a . . . downer." I don't tell him about the Venezuelan and Missus who asked for their files. "And everyone was so cooperative about postponing our trip to Mexico." My monthly trek to Ciudad Juarez to get clients visas, new lives, really. "'I just need a little bit more time,' I told the clients."

"Sweetie, if you were my lawyer, I'd say, 'Lady, you need a lot more than that.'"

"I even offered to reimburse them for the difference in airfare and not a single one took me up on it. So there. *And*"—I lean forward to the air vents—"Mily and some of the others may do cases for me from home."

"What?"

"Yeah. That's what Lazara said before she went bonkers on me."

"What're you thinking, sweetie? After what they've done?"

What *am* I thinking? Why is it not hitting home, what they've done? Is it that I think I have it coming to me?

"They were all on TV again tonight."

"Again?"

"Yes ma'am."

"Anybody can screw up, one big goof. But"—did Ira just shoot me a look?—"again?"

"Sweetie." He brakes at a stoplight, turns to look at me. "What's with you? This is more than a goof. Even yesterday was more than just a goof. Tonight, all of them, on TV. Again. What do I have to say to get it through to you?"

"Miriam?" I hold my breath. "And Irma too?"

"No. Not Miriam. Not Irma."

Through slices of inner-city "crime lights" I see his knuckles, white on the wheel.

"The five stars. On TV. Again. Guests of honor at Madrid Restaurant. Serenaded by Willy Chirino, that wannabee, never-will-be." His jawbone tightens. "Clinking glasses, receiving personal phone calls from Mas Canosa. And you know what he told them? *'Ustedes sí son cubanas,'*" he struggles in Yankee Doodle Spanish. "Cuban, my ass. There's nothing Cuban about those nincompoops you had working for you." Up the freeway ramp. "So while they were at Restaurant Madrid, being toasted to, slobbered over by Willy Chirino, and congratulated by Mas Canosa, I sat in front of the TV and prayed that my children wouldn't be blown up."

21

SWAT

DAY 4 OF 3 (MAYBE 5)

―――――

The Magda Parade is today. The demonstration. Ira said I had to leave "and leave early." His eyes are penetrating and exhausted. "While it's still dark out."

We sit outside Ben and Sadie's room in Ira's study, he at his desk, I on the floor, my back against the wall. Goblin lies on one side of me, Chaucer on the other, as if in requiem. It is a bit past 5 AM and there is a dead calm throughout the house.

Where to go? To Maty's in Fort Lauderdale? Or Key West? I hand Ira the fax from *un americano*, as Mami would say, whom I spoke with once, maybe twice in Havana, offering a week-long stay at his Key West condo, plus "a full house at your disposal with 24-hour guardhouse, VCR," plus "the facilities of my own house as well: two telephone lines, fax, computer, and (with certain immodesty) I'm an excellent cook!" Key West, where Ira and I honeymooned. Roosters flying across Duval Street. Three-toed kittens, descendants of Hemingway's cats. The very long pier with its too quick sunset. But I think of my mom. New territory is unsettling for her. At my sister's, she'll be *tranquila* (not that she ever lets on she isn't). I think of work. The second I arrive I have to transfer all the office calls. It will take me three, four hours to drive to Key West compared to forty-five minutes to get to my sister's from home. Still. Key West.

As if reading my thoughts, Ira stands, swoops me up, bringing me close. Even in early morning, his breath, all of him, smells warm, nurturing. "Sweetie, we'll go to Key West. In a few months, we'll go. Besides, it won't be the same without your husband."

I nod. "I'll go to Maty's. My mom will feel more comfortable there."

He steps back, looks at me in a *now that's a switch* gesture.

"What? I like my sister."

"I mean, your mom."

I dial, hear my nephew Jo-Jo's groggy *hullo*. "Mom just left this morning, for New York," he says. My sister is the owner of a day spa and very avant-garde clothing boutique in Hollywood, Florida, the antithesis of anything smacking of Tinseltown. "But sure, Aunt Beba, come on over."

————

Three men are at our door, hazy in the predawn light.

"I hired professionals," says Ira shaking the demonstration flyer Tíita brought yesterday.

The men, tall, corpulent, swoosh past us. One tips an invisible cap. "Mornin' ma'am."

I nudge Ira, mouth, "SWAT team?"

He tick-tocks his head in a more-or-less gesture.

The SWAT guys speak of their *glocks*, *glock* this, *glock* that. One bends. In a fluid, lithe swoop, he lifts his pant leg, looks up at me, and grins. "I do yoga."

"My wife does yoga too," Ira says.

"But I don't do guns," I say.

Houuu. A hearty laugh. He unstraps a leather holster from a milky white, sparsely haired shin. A grooved barrel, its pointy muzzle shiny, metallic, and grey.

Maggie staggers from her bedroom, hair matted in clumps of brown. "Mom," her voice thick with early morning hoarseness. "Can I spend to-night at Nacia's? Her dad offered. He thinks I'll be safer—" She stops at the sight of the guns. "Oh my God, Mom!"

I stand frozen.

"Let me bring you up to speed," Ira says to the SWAT guys. "These crazy terrorist—"

I hear the tinkling of wind chimes, the gentle rush of fountain water outside.

"—anti-Castro organizations, known to execute, blow up—"

"We know," says one of the men. "We live in Miami."

A plane roars overhead, a soft *rruu*, then a louder one almost immediately following.

"I'm worried that someone will try to use today's demonstration as a provocation," says Ira. "Firebomb the house." The first gleam of dawn casts a shadow across his face.

Maggie rubs her eyes with her side knuckles, reminding me of *The Three Little Kittens*. I know I should walk to her—at least that—but I stand immobile.

"What time are you all leaving?" asks one of the guys.

"My wife, children, and mother-in-law are leaving now."

"And you?"

"I'm staying right here."

They look at Ira in disbelief.

"No one's gunna run me out of my own house."

But nothing beats the look on their faces when Ira says, pointing, "Anyone tries to come inside our house, you shoot to kill."

———————

The sound of sparrows that come just before sunrise. "Nacia's dad just called," says Ira. "He'll be here soon to pick up Maggie." And as if reading my mind, "She'll be all right, sweetie."

My eye twitches.

"Paula," Ira says, imperiously, lovingly. "Help Abuela out to the car."

"*El desayuno*," my mother speaks as if straining for breath. "*El desayuno de los niños.*"

"*No, Abuela*," Ira says. "*Hoy no hay desayuno por los niños.*" No breakfast for the children today. Ben and Sadie are in deep sleep. Someone—the two of them?—pushed their twin beds together. They sleep, holding hands. Ira picks up Sadie, I pick up Ben. His breath is milky sweet, his curls snuggly on my neck.

Outside, a fresh, dewy smell. From a distance, the church bells toll, Westminster Quarters: 6:30 AM mass at St. Agnes, where thousands will walk *wearing black as a sign* (no shit) *of mourning for more than 5,000 martyrs who have died fighting Cuba's repressive system, in the Invasion of the Bay of Pigs . . . and in man-made balsas in desperate attempt to reach our shores in search of freedom*. We walk past the shrimp plants and tiger orchids and areca palms, but the garden is devoid of color, the morning fog penetrating everything. Mami's car slows to a dying whine, then springs back to life. It takes me a second to realize that Ira started the car for me. "Signora Corleone," I say to him, "good job."

I sit in the driver's seat, take roll call: 1 2 3 4. Mami to my right; Paula behind me huddled between Ben and Sadie sleeping limp and unaware. Ira leans in through the car window. "Call me. The minute you get there." His eyes don't leave my face. He stretches over, plugs his car phone into the cigarette lighter, punches at tiny buttons on its dial pad. "Here." He hands me the phone. "Just press 'Send' if anything happens." The number: 911. He walks to Mami, taps on her window. "Bye, Abuela." She lifts her hand in a motionless wave. "Bye-bye, Daddy." Foot on accelerator, gears in reverse, in the lingering darkness of morning, we leave.

"Mom."

I swing back my head at Paula.

She pulls out an earphone. "I told Dad I would stay over at his place."

"I don't mind driving you, honey." In my other life, I would have coaxed Ira into driving her; failing that, Gladys or Mami. Anything to avoid post-hurricane traffic.

"No, but . . ." She bites her lip in thought. "I don't know what to do." After a while, she says, "Maybe I should stay with you."

"We'll be all right, Paulie."

"I tried calling Dad to tell him I'd stay with you and, *Mom*, he sounded so excited. Said he'd just gotten back from the grocery store—"

"Yep. Bet he's cooking you a big ol' pot of black-eyed peas and country-fried steak."

For a minute, her face softens, then bunches into little puckers, and I can't gauge her: *I thought Mom needed me*—or worse—*I needed Mom, and she turned me away*. Maybe it's some incident at school, maybe even algebra she's thinking about. Or maybe she's amassing material for one of her one-liners, like the one right before I left for Havana: "Anytime somebody meets you, then Dad, they ask me what it was like for my mom to be married to my dad. And I say, 'Ethel Rosenberg meets Newt Gingrich.'" And when I shot her a look: "Just kidding, Mom"—a perfect comedic pause— "about Dad."

Our Paulichi, not just her early struggles with stuttering, but her escape into a world of Broadway tunes and a Paula way of thinking the absurd was normal, like donning panties on her head. A certain wounded innocence about her. "Mom?" she once asked. She was four, maybe five. "Is Papa still dead?" Paul's dad. And when I nodded yes, "Oh, man. I wanted him to take me fishin' again." But her face is colorless now, tiny beads of sweat dotting her nose. The comedian, silent today.

As the car angles up the big bridge, Sadie begins to stir. "I'm cold," she says woozily. "My feets are cold."

I untie my Sarah Arizona sweater from my waist, toss it to the back seat, my eyes on the road, my mom's eyes on me. "Paulie, could you please wrap Sadie's feet?"

Sadie, Kickkickkickkick. "Paula!" I reach behind me, tap her knee. "Earphones." And when they're off: "Can you *please* wrap Sadie's feet?"

"All *right*."

"Why did you wake me up?" A tremble in Sadie's voice. "Why am I in Abuela's car?" She looks around, the cherubic features of her face distorted. "Why is it still dark outside?" She looks down at her Little Mermaid nightshirt and screams, horrified, "And why do I still have my pajamas on?" She sobs, her head falling limp. "And no underwear, Mom, no underwear. You think I'm *you*, not wearing underwear?"

"Go, Sadie!" For this, Paula is earphone-free.

"What day is it?" Sadie says.

"Friday."

"I can't go to school in my pajamas!"

"You and Benny aren't going to school today." My voice comes out flat, hollow.

"But why, Mommy? Why? Our class has *something*." She weeps unconsolably. Then she says, "Where are my Queen Esther shoes?"

"Your Cinderella shoes?"

"No, Mommy. My Queen Esther shoes."

I don't know. I don't know what happened to her Queen Esther shoes. I didn't even know she had Queen Esther shoes. I don't know what happened to her Cinderella shoes either. Maybe they fell off when Ira carried her to the car.

"We have *something*, Mommy, for you today," she says between shuddering inhalations.

Oh God. She remembered. Queen Esther. The announcement of the Purim play, neatly folded in her backpack. Sadie, selected to play Queen Esther. Gladys made her a pink satin costume with a golden crown. She's been practicing, for days. How can I tell Sadie, "Mommy can't go out where people will see her"? I want to cry. "I'm sorry, Sadie." But I don't sound sorry. I don't sound motherly or loving either. "We can't go."

"But why, Mommy? Why can't we go?"

Traffic is unnerving. "We're going to Aunt Maty's."

"But why? I don't wanna go to Aunt Maty's. Why can't we go to our special Shabbat?" She cries, not a whiny, hoked-up cry but an *I've hurt myself badly* cry. "I wanna," she says between intermittent whimpers, "I wanna talk to Tata." Katy.

"Paulie?" I stretch my arm to the back seat, hand Ira's car phone to her. "Dial 1-617 . . ." Good, I'm able to call up Katy's number.

Paula shoves the phone back at me. "Wrong number, Mom."

"Are you sure? Oh wait. Katy's at—" At a new dorm and I don't know the name.

"Just forget it, Mom," Paula says. "And listen, when we get to Dad's, don't take a long time with him, okay? Don't *flirt* with him."

"Flirt with him? I never even flirted with him when I was *married* to him."

"That's nice, Mom," Paula says. "Talking shit about Dad."

I brake suddenly for the bright yellow bumper sticker on the upturned butt of the car in front of us: THE ONLY DIALOGUE WITH CASTRO: BLINDFOLD OR NOT?

———

Paul paces the parking lot of his apartment complex. His face opens up when he sees us. He leans into my car window, drums arrhythmically at the roof of the car. "Hey, there! Hey, Benny, hey, Sadie. *Hola, Abuela.* God, it's hot." He wipes his brow.

"*Hola*, Daddy," Mami says.

"Hey, Paula," Benny says. "How many daddies does Abuela have?"

"Shut-up, Ben," Paula says.

Paul's eyes dart about him, skirting my face. "A tenant in the building who works for Univision has been chasing me for an interview."

"Here's your chance to get even," I kid him.

"What? I'll talk to them." That old shaky smile. "I'll tell them I think you're right."

"Let's go, Daddy." Paula tugs at his arm.

I back up, start shifting forward.

"Beba!" Paul walks to the car. "You'll be all right." A quick squeeze on my shoulder.

Paula waves, childlike. "'Bye, Mommy." Her voice breaks.

My mother sucks on one of those honey-filled candies she always takes with her on car rides. *Viajes largos*, long car trips, she calls them, even though my sister's house is just the next county up. In my other life, her noises would have irked me. But not today.

Today I am gentle with my mother.

She stretches her neck, gapes at the gas gauge teetering on E. Today she doesn't nudge me: Why do I keep passing up exits to gas stations? And today I don't tell her it's because I need a full-service gas station. I don't tell her I can't get out of the car and pump the gas myself. "No matter what," Ira said. "Do *not* get out of the car."

She holds two gaudy ceramic roosters on her lap, splattered messily in ugly browns and muted greens and orange reds. The artist at the *botánica*— where she shops for her Afro-Cuban saints and twigs and all else—is not a believer in staying inside the lines. "*Los ki ki ri quis*," my mother calls the roosters. She tilts them at me, "For protection," smiles shyly, nervously, "for you and your sister."

I don't berate her for what the *botánica* must have charged her, the fair-game *vieja*, the minute they saw her shuffling through the door. "Forget ceramic roosters, Mami," I want to say. But I don't. I don't tease her that we're beyond that. I don't tease her that we need the real thing, live ones that we can offer as sacrifice to the gods.

Sadie has fallen asleep but sniff-sniffs little whoops of air, stops, then breathes out long, dolefully. Ben stares at cows grazing in the open pastures of Broward County. "Are cows descendants of dinosaurs, Mom? Just tell me, yes or no." And when I say, "I vote yes," he says, "Wrong, Mom. Wrong again." I smile, nod, reach for my paper-clipped messages, flip through a stack of tiny pink slips: *While You Were Out, While You Were Out, While You Were Out*, weave in and out of lanes.

Today, my mother doesn't complain that I drive just like my father.

———

A noise—I jump. Ira's car phone, it's ringing. It's Cathy. I smile. The third spoke in our Magda-Cathy-Lazara triangle—ex-triangle—of friendship. Seventeen years, the three of us. So many side-splitting laughs. Even in the worst of times, laughs, devotion. Unwavering support.

"How'd you get this number?" I shriek.

"I have my ways," Cathy says, with that matter-of-fact toughness of hers.

She's been trying to reach me, and "I just wanted to tell you"—a Cathy pause—"I love you."

I feel my heart swell. Then I take a breath, give her the lowdown on Lazara. "She sold out, Cathy. Just abandoned me."

"But Magda, you can't just let all those years of friendship and craziness go by the wayside. Need I remind you, my dear? You and Ira fooling around in the men's bathroom in his building, the two of you locked out of his office, him buck naked. And you called Lazara at two in the morning to bring you a pair of her brother's pants—"

"Yeah, well"—my words choppy with repressed laughs—"even *that's* not funny to me anymore."

"But you're laughing."

"I can't think about—"

"Magda." Her signature Magda reprimand.

"Cathy."

"We've always *known* Lazara is hysterical."

"Yeah, but she never used that hysteria against *me*."

"No." Cathy snickers. "Just on her men."

I smile, in spite of myself. The three of us would go to discos, and if the men were not to our liking, we would dance with each other to the astonishment of the '80s crowd. "If only Rey could see us now," Lazara would shout over the deafening sounds. Rey, Lazara's second husband, who last said to Lazara, "My friends think—not that *I* think—that Magda and Cathy are in love with you, that you're . . . a threesome and that's why they pushed you to leave me."

She would sit me and Cathy down, her attentive students, and rattle off the names she gave her men. There was Duracell and Tiparillo and Yahoo, who yahooed when he came. There were her anatomy lessons: "When I pulled down his zipper, I thought, 'Whoa! Does this thing come with a set of instructions?'" She sketched a big upside-down J in the air. "And then there was this other guy. I wanted to say, 'This is great, but where's the other half?' And there was the *last straw*, as she called it. "Finally, I get to go out with a black guy, and he's *white*—from the waist down. So I asked him, you know, about his heritage, the origins of his family name, blah blah. And he said his *grandmother* was German. *Aich!* Just my luck, man." Rapt smiles on our faces, as she would put one hand on her curvy hip and toss off one of her classics: "The only group sex I'm interested in is me and a group of men."

"We didn't know then," Cathy says, "that we wouldn't laugh like that the rest of our lives."

22

RADIO REBELDE

———

No sooner do I cut off the engine at my sister's than my brother-in-law, Joe, steps outside. "What took you so long? I was beginning to think you used me as a decoy." My nephew JoJo walks up behind him holding out a cordless phone. "It's Uncle Ira." And in a cautionary dip of the voice: "He sounds really pissed, Aunt Beba."

Before the phone is at my ear, "What's this about a Radio Rebelde interview?" Radio Rebelde, used by Fidel and the revolutionary army to broadcast messages from the Sierra Maestra. Listened to by Mami years ago, hands on knees, legs splayed open, cigarette dangling at mouth, face simultaneously opened and closed in half wonder, half scowl. "Did you speak to Radio Rebelde yesterday?"

Mami looks at me through the car window, the yellow-brown of her eyes unmoored.

"Yesterday," I say finally, "some woman named Zenaida *did* call. From Havana—"

"Is she a reporter?"

"I thought she was calling just to see how I was," I say in small voice.

"And did it occur to you, if she was a reporter, she would be *taping* you?"

I dig my nails into my palm of my hand.

"It's all over the news, Magda."

Mami tilts a bottle of Gerber's yogurt into Ben's mouth.

"I thought we'd decided you wouldn't talk to the media."

Ben sucks on his bottle, the corners of his eyes fixed on me.

"How many times have I told you?"

Sadie twists a wet ringlet of curl around her finger; twist, turn, pull.

"Do *not* talk to the media. Okay?"

I unclasp Ben and Sadie from their seat belts, walk into my sister's house, cross my arms over my stomach, double over, squeeze.

———

Our Man *not* in Havana but Little Havana calls. He's from Radio Mambi. And he's calling again. Calls every three minutes, as he said—as he promised—he would. "*La abogada* is not taking calls," I tell him every time.

"*¿Y porqué no?*" He slurs his words in garbled illiteracy. "*Pues,*" he says, except it's *pooh-eh,* "I will keep calling *cada tres minutos* till she talks to me. *Si ella puede podel*—"

"*Poder,*" I say with prim efficiency. *Poderrr,* an *r* at the end. The more agitated he becomes, the more I rev the hoked-up finesse.

No matter. "*Si ella puede podel.*" If she can talk to Radio Rebelde, she can talk to us.

A click, a droning of the dial tone, and on to the next call.

"We're gonna get you, *sweetie,*" from someone who knows Ira calls me "sweetie."

"Go with your teacher . . . fucking bitch."

"Do you need any employees?" The enthusiastic voice of a young Cuban woman, the same enthusiasm I once heard in Barbara.

"Yes!" I perk up.

"Oh, you're the woman who"—she laughs—"never mind!" and hangs up.

Like Chinese water torture, the calls do not stop. Drip, drip, drip. Like the death of a thousand cuts.

———

"Hold for Mr. Duran." It's Alfredo Duran's devoted secretary. Duran is the law colleague who sends me his very wealthy clients "in need" of a green card when fleeing white-collar charges in their country or "in want," as in: *In the US, I pay no taxes.* Along with me and a few others, he founded the Cuban Committee for Democracy last year. "Magda." His usual deep-voiced, alluring *Magda.* "*¿Como estás?*" The warm-up, referencing, shall we say, the Magda Affair.

I cut him off. "Will the Florida Bar disbar me?"

No, he thinks not. "When you're in politics, Magda," he knows just how low to pitch the tone, "every time you talk to someone, you have to use a bit of *picardia*." Craftiness. "And you don't have that in you. You're too direct to be in politics."

Good advice, I think, coming from the ex-Bay of Pigs invader, ex-chairman of Florida's Democratic Party; ex-son-in-law to ex-Cuban president Carlos Prío Socarrás; ex-Cuba advisor to ex-president Jimmy Carter. And the lawyer who fought to keep the fourteen-year-old girl—the one who sailed on a raft to Miami with her eighteen-year-old boyfriend—from reuniting with her parents in Cuba. Duran and the government won. And you would think, the girl. Except soon after, the girl cried to Ira, who represented the parents, to get her back home.

"Magda." And the pause. "The CCD is not a pro-Castro group—"

"If it's my resignation you want, you can have it."

But, oh no, he wants more. He wants it in *writing*.

"I'm not in the office."

In his silence, a discernible suspicion that I am lying. His devoted secretary did, after all, just dial my office number and got me on the line. I opt not to explain that all office calls were forwarded to my sister's phone. Instead, "Alfredo, I have no secretary, no typewriter. *Nada*."

"Then handwrite it."

"Okay. I'll put it in the mail."

"No. I need it today."

"I have no way of getting it to you."

"You can fax it."

"I have no fax machine." I am eroding, fading. "You don't understand," I say again.

But he's pressing, in that seemingly inoffensive tone he so extraordinarily uses.

Finally, "I will have the resignation over to you before the end of the day." JoJo, I think, my nephew. I'll have JoJo find a way to fax it to him. "All I ask is that when you speak to the press about me, you defend my freedom to speak."

———

David Berger calls, his law partner Jeff Bernstein on the other line. What war stories, the three of us, at Immigration. Alerting each other on the days one particular "good officer" was assigned to adjudicate cases. Refusing to snitch on each other after some *huele peo* lawyer overheard us call Supervisor Faget "the Gestapo" and told Faget.

"Yes!" I say to David and Jeff. "I *do* need help. I have a deportation hearing Monday, 9 AM." They don't do deportation work, they say, but sure, one of them will be there. "Just ask for a continuance," I say. "Buy me some time. It's Judge Solow presiding." Solow and his wife were at our wedding, they've been to our home. He has to know. "Just 'Your Honor' him to death. 'May I approach the bench? Kiss your ring?' and he'll be happy."

Ay Dios mío. Poor David; poor Jeff. I'm imagining Solow, that crimson red of his crawling up his neck, grilling my client on the stand. Oh God, Solow has to give me the continuance. At least that. "Oh, and David? Jeff? I have a client who was picked up by Border Patrol." A nervous silence at the other end. "No, I don't mean for you to go." Yes I do, but I can't do that to them. "Do you know of an attorney who can take over? For a fee, of course; I'll pay." Mary Kramer, they tell me.

I hang up the phone just right, a perfect millimeter between the threats and insults, and yes! a dial tone. But Mary Kramer can't take the case. Too busy? Too what? I don't hear the reason, only the no, and the client's aunt is on the line again. They found out about my *predicament*, she says—from my client. "But . . . he's detained." He saw me in the dining hall, on TV, she says, the other detainees started asking him, 'Hey, isn't that your lady lawyer?' I stare out the window. Doesn't Mary Kramer know what I'm going through?

Sadie comes into the room. "Mommy," her candy-green eyes on mine, "why are you so sad?" This time, I can't even hug her.

————

I pick up the phone quickly, before another threat, another insult comes in and amaze even myself that I'm able to recall the detention center number. Bounced from one extension to the next, I persist. Finally, the name of the deportation officer assigned to my client. "Mr. Ramlall." I swallow. "This is Magda Davis. I'm calling in the case of—"

"I know who you are," he says in Indian-inflected accent. I don't breathe; I don't move.

"Oh, honey," says Mr. Ramlall, "I feel so bad for you that I'm gonna go ahead and release your guy." I thank him, over and over I thank him. Then I throw myself on JoJo's waterbed. Maximum lapse time between calls: two minutes, tops. In between, I sleep; not a doze, a deep, albeit seconds-long sleep. At the sound of the next ring, my hand automatically reaches for the handset, as if not connected to me. Every few hours, there is a respite of a few seconds, and this is one of them.

I hear my Maty's "She's fighting for her life" and don't know if I'm in a dream. Stumbling out of JoJo's bedroom, I pick up the extension. "*Yo sé, mi vida.*" I know, my love, a man says to her. It's Bruno Rodríguez, calling from the Cuban mission to the UN in New York City. They have a letter they need to get to me, he says, but my sister won't tell Bruno my whereabouts.

"I thought you were coming back tomorrow?" I say when she hangs up.

A shrug. "Came back early." Her best friend Raysa comes up the walkway. I don't want to see her; don't want to hear her. Raysa, so Miami Cuban, so of that *Abajo Fidel* mentality. I squat back to JoJo's room, keep my head, my entire self low.

JoJo's clock: 7:10 PM, it reads. Ira hasn't called but he probably can't get through. Or maybe this is it. Maybe he'll call and say he can't take it—can't take me—anymore.

"Hope, and keep busy," Louisa May Alcott wrote. I resolve to do both. First, turn off the phones. I punch * and # and every button on the dial pad but can't transfer back the calls. *Ay Dios mío.* The entire weekend, nonstop calls to my sister's. I call Southern Bell. Every rep I'm put through to—Joyce, Nancy, Maggie Campos, Shirley Clark—know who I am. "Goodness," one says, "you received 181 calls, most of just one, two minutes' duration." Yep, that's how long it takes to hear *Cock-sucking bitch. You're una hija de puta*—son-of-a-bitch in the feminine; *daughter*-of a bitch, I suppose—*and your husband a maricón*"—faggot—or, *You're gonna get cancer of the rectum, Fidel stuck it so far up your ass.* And yes, I tell her, I answered all 181 calls myself. "Hold on, sweetheart. It'll be just one minute. . . . Okay, there you go. Done."

"Thank you," and "Thank you" again. I jot down her name. I jot down all their names. "I'm going to write a letter to Southern Bell." The ex-staff liked to tease me when I complained about—at times praised—something, someone. "Write a letter," they'd say. Because always I'd hand-scribble them but couldn't type. Afraid I wouldn't go to law school and would be secretary to a man, I never learned to type.

I wait until Maty's friend Raysa is in the kitchen, walk outside to the car, pick up my makeshift law office: files, ledgers, client cards, all sprawled on the car floor. Back in JoJo's room, I build my sandcastle. Cases to prepare, here; calls to return, there. I step back, look at my creation. Sorting through the next batch, I make neat little piles. Order, that's all I need. Then Ben bolts into the room. He karate-chops one stack. Client intakes, notices of action, all to the floor. He then goes for the messages, flinging them over his head, weightless pink slips floating through air. This Colombian birth certificate mixed in with that Brazilian divorce, Stanley Kuo's passport pictures staring up at me with *I want to live in America* eyes.

"Benny, stop." But Ben is in a frenzy, and a silent one at that. It's anger, and it's not as simplistic as anger at my work once again taking me away from him. It's anger, it's confusion, it's fear. How can I explain that immersing myself in my work at this frenetic pace is what keeps me calm, sane? How can I explain any of it? "Stop," I say, pleading—begging. "Please stop." But it only intensifies his agitation. I put my hands to my face, sob. As quickly as he bolted in, he disappears, silent still. I crouch on the floor, stoop over each paper, each file. I start over with my sandcastle. I rebuild as I cry.

Raysa comes into the bedroom. I keep my face turned from hers. In silence, she helps me sort through the chaos. "I can go to the office to help you," she says after a while.

I sit on the bed, shake my head. She walks to me, puts an arm around me. I'm angry at Raysa and the Southern Bell reps. At Eddie and Xiomara and Mr. Ramlall and Jeff and David and the Key West fellow offering his properties for a one-week getaway and the copier technician offering his car for our mob getaway. My clients, even, anger me. All of them anger me. Because it shouldn't be casual acquaintances or utter strangers or paying clients who are supporting me. It should be Isabel. Mily. Cary. Janet. Barbara. More than staff, friends. Especially Lazara. When I last talked to her, I pleaded, "If not for me, then my kids." Maggie always beamed when Lazara introduced herself as Maggie's second mother. Lazara took Katy on trips with her to Iowa or to Cambridge so Katy could visit boyfriend Eric at college when I couldn't take time off work. Lazara organized slumber parties for Paula and friends filled with wild crazy tales that Paula believed. And when I got pregnant with Sadie and Ira was initially—seemingly?—ecstatic, then began pulling back, "Fuck him," Lazara said, "We'll raise the baby together."

Who would have thought? Unwavering, unconditional Lazara. The staff; my *support* staff, my friends. And Isabel. Who would have thought she'd fold so quickly or fold at all, and that shy, demure Miriam would have stayed firm. *Firme.* "*Estoy firme*," she said to me on the phone. The media ran up to her outside the office the day before yesterday as Mily was in the throes of her nonexistent political-prisoner-father cries, as Barbara was cheered on by the crowd, as Janet basked in her new Queen for a Day status, as Cary too reveled in her fifteen minutes of fame, and as Isabel stood by silently and let it happen. And when the media sought out Miriam, she stood firm. "Leave me alone!" Irma told me Miriam screamed and slapped at them and at their cameras. Irma drove quietly home; never once were Miriam or Irma contaminated with the contagious hysteria. Firm in their position, unwavering in their support.

———

My sister married her high school sweetheart a year after graduation. She put him through college. Only after incessant prodding by our parents did she grudgingly get her degree. But she is smart as a whip. When her three kids were little, she sold clothes from her garage. When she realized that bypassing the middleman meant better profit, she flew to New York, stayed at the homes of New Jersey Cubans and drove a rental to New York's garment district. She met Raysa while haggling with Orthodox Jews for designer (or faux-designer) clothes at cut-rate prices. She and Raysa go to Publix. They bring me back Oreos.

Raysa begins. "When I saw your sister at the airport—"

"—Miami, mind you, not even Fort Lauderdale—"

"—and with her hair blown straight, I screamed, *¡Muchacha!*" Raysa gesticulates in *cubanasa* plentitude. "'Go to the bathroom right now *y alborotate tu pelo*! With your hair straight like that, you look just like your sister.'"

"And all those warehouses we went to in New Jersey," says Maty, "full of Cubans—never mind we were in enough danger there already, all that stolen merchandise—"

"—and I kept saying, 'We're gonna get thrown out,' all these old *viejas* whispering *chiquichiqui* the minute they saw us." Raysa nods in deep pleasure.

"And then I call home," says my sister, "and Joe tells me, 'Your sister's coming' and I say, 'Coming? Coming where? To our house?' And he says, 'Yeah, I'm not afraid to die.'" A deep sigh. "I looked at Raysa and said, 'My *kids* are in that house.'" Her hands in the air. "This is like Hurricane Andrew II invading my house. I'm *still* recovering from that."

Andrew. It hit us less than two years ago, August '92. After evacuating Key Biscayne, we came to my sister's—the kids (minus Paula), Mami, Ira and I, Goblin and Chaucer, plus Mami's Catholic saints and Afro-Cuban deities. Armed with my boxes of journals (going back to '81, when I left Paul and took up with Ira, and took to journaling like a fiend), my campaign files (the hurricane hit smack in the middle of my race), and my office work, I worked by candlelight.

At Maty's home of chrome and glass, we weathered the storm. Category 5 winds, flying fences, and tree trunks. The next day, the news: The damage throughout some parts of the county was far worse than forecast. Key Biscayne and every district favorable to my congressional campaign—the Anglo districts, particularly those with a high concentration of women, even Republican women, likely to vote for me because of my pro-choice platform—were wiped out. And Ileana Ros-Lethinen's Little Havana districts? Virtually untouched.

"Listen," says my sister. "First, it was Jeannie." Jeannie, her sister-in-law, who was flown to LA to appear on *The Jenny Jones Show* for a special segment, "Women Who Fall in Love with Gay Men." Folding one foot under her, "Here I am sitting in front of the TV thinking, Thank *God* the show's over. Maybe my mother-in-law didn't see it. And all of a sudden, it's"—she circles the air big—"Breaking News. Something about a woman lawyer in Havana. And I thought, nah, it can't be. And then sure enough, I see your purple Tahari coatdress and Fidel leaning over you and the crazy Cubans screaming and shaking their fists and Rick Sanchez saying, 'Remember you saw it here first, on Channel 7.' No, and the worst was Mami calling, '¿Que esta pasando?' I'm telling you, I thought Hurricane Andrew was a circus, but this takes the cake." She leans back on her wicker loveseat, combs her long manicured fingers through her highlighted do. "And then JoJo looks at me and says, 'Mom, I have *just* one question for you. Which aunt is crazier? Aunt Number One? Or Aunt Number Two?'"

———

"Get in the car," I tell Ben and Sadie. So what if it's 11 PM and they're in their PJs? There is no logic to our lives anymore. "We're going to Eckerd's to pick out a toy." It's a holdover impulse from childhood. The best part of being sick was Mami's call to the *farmacia*: a twenty-nine-cent trinket, maybe even a truck delivered to our Nuevo Vedado doorstep in no time.

It feels good to step out into the night, to walk the parking lot, the aisles. But heading back to the car, reality hits. I take Ben and Sadie's hands, stand back, twenty feet. Pressing the red button on the bomb detector, I wait for the headlights to flash; the sensor is now checking for explosives. Starting at the back of the car, works its way up. When clear, the horn beeps five times. From afar, I aim, I click, I turn on the ignition. It is now safe for us to get into the car.

23

FUCK TRUCK

DAY 5 OF 3 (MAYBE 5)

———

Saturday morning, and this is my wake-up call: "Oh, Jesus." My sister stands over me, her arms folded. "Now the press is after me. They've been hounding me, calling all morning."

"How did they get this number?" I roll a half turn on JoJo's waterbed.

"And how do they even know we're sisters? We don't even have the same last names." We don't yet know that a *Miami Herald* reporter drove to my inner-city high school (doors locked, I'm sure) and examined my yearbook. Tomorrow, I will wake to front-page feature articles in the Sunday *Herald* and statewide edition. "The Odyssey of Magda Montiel Davis"; "Montiel Davis: She's No Longer Miss Popularity." Photos from my yearbook. "PEPPY: As captain of cheerleading squad" and "POPULAR: As Miss Miami Central High." From *Herald* archives. "POLITICAL: As a congressional candidate" and "ON THE RUN: Montiel Davis makes a dash for her car last Wednesday outside her office with policemen covering." The crux of the piece: How it is that a "bright young professional, U.S.-educated Cuban woman" could *think* this way, *do* such a thing?

———

Katy calls from Wellesley. She doesn't ask what we're doing at her aunt's house, and I wonder if she knows. She was to spend the weekend in Boston with boyfriend Eric, she says in quivering voice, but he flew home to Miami; his grandmother's health took a turn for the worse.

It's that quality in her voice, not just the trembling but its undertones, the currents of lingering hurt. The voice of Katy, five years old. The muffled sounds of confusion when Paul and I told her we were separating. We sat on the bed. Katy looked up at me, as if waiting for me to say it wasn't true. Paul cried. I was a cold, hard bitch.

As I'd dress for a night out with Cathy and Lazara, and later with Ira, "But where are you going?" she'd ask. And I'd shrug at her compulsive questioning. "You'll be all right." But always I wondered if Katy *was* all right. And listening to her voice now over the phone, I wonder if Katy knows. Has it hit Boston?

Once, she asked: "How come you never had us watch *The Wizard of Oz*? Marah's mom was surprised I didn't know what the Yellow Brick Road was." And I wanted to scream: "Three little kids to support, no help from your father, a home in Key Biscayne I can't afford, your grandmother and *my* grandmother to support, and all you care about is that fucking Yellow Brick Road?"

At times, Katy will be painfully blunt, using my lapses of memory to her advantage. I missed her high school graduation, she recently said. This time I stopped her, stone cold, only because I remembered. "I *asked* you ahead of time. 'Katy, I have to speak at the immigration lawyers' conference this year. Should I ask to speak another day?' And you said, 'No'"—I simulated her shrug—"'it's *only* high school. Not as if I was graduating from college.'" And she smiled. Smiled! A slight involuntary smile, but a smile nonetheless. "Yeah," she retorted, "but once I was there, I was sorry you weren't there. Sashi's mom said, 'Oh, you poor dear'"—now Katy simulated patting the seat next to her—"'Come sit with us.'" Of course I should have known to be there. All Good Mothers know to be at their daughter's high school graduation, *insist* on it.

And now my daughter calls with that familiar quiver in her voice, and I don't know whether she knows that the mother who stripped her of her father's companionship, who shattered her Dick-and-Jane existence, who didn't lead her down the Yellow Brick Road and who spoke to a packed audience of lawyers instead of attending her high school graduation is on TV and almost every newspaper throughout the country, outside the country even; in the Boston area, where she and her Wellesley roommates may see it, and in Cambridge where boyfriend Eric will see it. And in Miami where Eric's parents have seen it—and seen it. And I don't know whether to address it with her. She, the parent, me the *I didn't mean to screw up again* kid.

I dial 411; relief, Debbie Anker—Ira's and my friend, an immigration law professor at Harvard—is listed. Debbie knows. I don't ask her how she knows. Sure, she'll take in Katy for the weekend. "Have her take the bus to Cambridge from Wellesley." The *Fuck Truck*, Katy told me the Wellesley sisters call it, that takes them to the MIT or Harvard campus. And I thought then, Isn't it cool Katy feels comfortable enough to tell me about the *Fuck Truck*?

———

Sadie is perched on my sister's bathroom sink, melon-orange lips puckered at the lighted mirror, half-shut eyelids like rainbows of color. "Be-ehn!" she hollers, disgusted. She hands me a flashlight. "Give this to him, Mom. He's in charge of the lights for our play," and when I look at her inquisitively, "I'm Queen Esther." Turning back to the mirror, "Where *is* that boy?" she holds the eyeshadow wand like a Crayola, smearing yet another coat of Maty's lipstick on her cheeks. "Mom, how come you don't have all this stuff?"

"Has Daddy called?"

"How come you don't paint your face pretty, like me and Aunt Maty?" No sooner had Ira and I begun dating than he rubbed his thumb on my cheeks as if wiping dirt. "Why do you wear all that war paint?" The first time I stepped out without makeup, I felt as if in the midst of one of those dreams in which suddenly you're out in the street naked.

"Sades, has Daddy called?"

"Uh-huh." She nods.

"He did? What did he say?"

"Mom! I'm busy." She tosses her curls. "B-s-e. Busy!"

"Yeah, Mom. She's busy."

I whip around. Ira. We smile reflexively at each other, then catch ourselves and stop. Radio Rebelde. Sadie and Ben shriek, do little circles about him. Ira tosses Ben in the air, swings Sadie full circles around him. "Whee!" "Me next!" "No, me!" He picks up Sadie with one arm, Ben with the other, pecks one kiss, "Mua!" then another. Sadie pulls his face toward her, smacks wet kisses on his cheek. I stand back, wait for Ira. When he looks up, I'll know.

He talks only to them. "So what have you been doing? Tell Daddy what you've been doing." Without looking at me, he hands me an envelope.

On gold-embossed, fine linen stationery, engraved *La Oficina del Ministro de Relaciónes Exteriores*, an impeccably typed, perfectly spaced letter.

It ends: "I always admired you and now do so much more than ever. Affectionately, Roberto Robaina, Cuban Foreign Minister."

"How did you get this?" I look at Ira.

"Never mind how I got it. You think I'm gunna tell you?" He walks to me—"You'll tell Radio Rebelde"—and pinches my waist.

I turn my face, don't let him see me smile.

"Aruca," he says after a while. Ira's client and friend. And owner of travel-to-Cuba Marazul Charters.

"Daddy's commie friend," Sadie says.

Ira and I turn our heads at her.

"Uh-huh," Ben comes to Sadie's defense. "That's what Paula says."

"Well, Daddy's gunna have a talk with your sister Paula. Now can I please talk to your mother? Amscram."

Enter my sister. "Hi, Ira," she says in that amused tone of hers. Now next to me, she skims Robaina's letter. "Oh, Jesus! This is all we need. More fuel for the press." Then, as if in afterthought, "Damn, Fidel sure works fast, getting that letter over to you." She looks at Ira. "Yesterday, I received a nifty little call from some stranger with a communist voice saying he had a letter he needed to get over to this one." She juts her chin at me.

"It's not Fidel." I say. "It's a *government*."

"Yeah. Uh-huh." A twist of the mouth. "A government."

———

On the long ride home, I break the silence. "You think I could go back to work?" Ira looks away, doesn't say anything. "Tomorrow's Sunday," I say. "It'll be quiet." He says for a few hours, maybe. He says he'll drive me. "Did they . . . have the parade?" I ask finally. "Yes," he says. "It was wonderful, sweetie. Two thousand Cubans dressed in black parading two blocks from our house, on a pilgrimage to Requiem Mass at St. Agnes Church." Two thousand? I ask. "Well, I didn't go, sweetie. I was busy bazooka-training with our SWAT team. But yes, two thousand. That's what the news said this morning. And Lieutenant Angulo confirmed it."

"*¿Qué dice, Beba?*" Mami wants to know. *Nada*, I tell her. "*Too Sou-Sen*," she says. "*¿Vinieron dos mil 'pa comer mierda?*" Two thousand came to eat shit? *Fuck around*, in Cubanspeak. Ira flexes a nonexistent muscle at her. "*No importa, Abuela. Nosotros mas fuerte.*" "*Si*, Daddy," she says, "*Venceremos*," and blows out her *heh heh heh* laugh. *We will prevail. Venceremos* on signs and billboards and at mass gatherings at Revolution Square and everywhere else. *Volveremos* on the wormy *gusano* decal my father affixed to his 1961 Corvair.

Butt first, what the security experts told us, park butt first. Harder to get your license plate number that way. Harder, but not impossible.

"Sweetie." Ira turns off the ignition. "Forget what I said about all the nuts coming out of the woodwork or your terrorist countrymen." He looks down the block. "It's the *Mafia* we have to worry about."

"Mafia?"

"Yes, sweetie. Don't you remember? Right after the hurricane?" When the county finally lifted its keep-out order, we navigated our way back past overturned yachts blocking the causeway, giant fish sprawled dead atop the bridge. Massive wooden beams crisscrossed our front yard. "You recognize it?" Ira said. "It's the fence at the Silver Sands." The oceanfront motel a few blocks down. A mix of muck and salt water gushed at us when we forced open our front door. But for our next-door neighbor, whom we'd never seen, it was a totally different ballgame. Workers nailed and hammered, morning to night. Ira tapped the ankle of one high on a ladder. "Excuse me. Sir? How did . . . whose house is this?"

"Whose house is this?" The worker laughed. "The Gambinos'."

"Oh." Ira pointed to the next house, also in tip-top shape. "And *that* house?"

"The Luchesses'."

"I'm telling ya sweetie," Ira says. "It's the Mafia that's gunna get us first. If there's one thing the Mafia doesn't like, it's anyone around them attracting publicity."

Mami holds my arm as we walk through the courtyard. "*¿Que dice, Beba?*"

"That the Mafia's gonna get us."

"*Ni pinto, ni doy color,*" she says. Cuban lexicon: Nothing fazes me anymore.

But as I near our front door, "What's that?" A big fat envelope leans against a potted plant.

"Don't pick it up!" Ira says. "Everybody back in the car. Magda, get everybody back in the car." So off we go, back in the car. Then, "It's safe." Ira waves from across the road. "Come on back." And as we approach him, "It's a Priority Mail package."

From Barnett Bank of Broward County. "Welcome to the neighborhood!" reads the letter. "Our newcomers package contains relocation information about your new community." I look at Ira. "What is this? Somebody telling us they know I was at my sister's?"

"Or sending us a message to get out of the neighborhood."

24

YELLOW JOURNALISM

DAY 6 OF 3 (MAYBE 5)

———

I sit on the living room sofa, waiting for the sun to rise. It is still dark and probably safe for me to venture outside. I open the front door, look up at the high-rise condominiums overlooking our block. "From up there," Lieutenant Angulo had warned, pointing to the patio roof of the Key Colony complex, "anyone could have a clear shot at you." I look right, left, right again, then laugh, as if that could make a difference! I sprint barefoot, the pebbled rocks on our driveway murder on the soles of my feet, pick up the heavy yellow plastic bundle, run back inside the house. Once safe—*más o menos* safe—I look down. "Start your day off right with the *Miami Herald*," the yellow plastic reads, amid musical notes, flying butterflies, and smiling suns.

I walk in the bedroom, lay the unwrapped newspaper on my night table. I need to rest, I tell myself. I can't go on like this, getting just two, three hours of sleep each night. I lie spread-eagled on my side of the bed, one arm flopped across my forehead, the other across my stomach.

It will not win. It's going to stay there, the *Miami Herald*, unwrapped, unopened, ignored. *El mejor desprecio es no hacer aprecio.* At precisely timed intervals, little noises come from Ira. That snoring again. I turn on my side, then on my stomach; I put a pillow between my legs; try dangling my feet off the bed.

"What is it, sweetie?" Ira asks hazily.

I want to cut you up in little pieces. "Nothing." And then, "Every morning I hate picking up the *Miami Herald*."

But those noises again. I look over; he's back asleep. "So? Don't," he says as if he'd stayed awake the entire time.

"Don't *what*?"

"Don't pick up the *Miami Herald*." He leans over his night table, turns off the alarm before its usual 6 AM blast of NPR. More noises. *Click, click, beep, beep.*

"Yeah, right." I twist my lips. "Not *one* has written about free speech."

"Sweetie, it's the *Miami Herald*. What do you expect?"

"Even Carl Hiaasen sold out. He writes of me as if I'm some sort of star-struck groupie, clamoring after Fidel. Jesus! Now I'm *really* fucked—"

"I *wish* you were fucked. And I wish I was fucked too—"

"—he's not just some *Herald* reporter. I mean, he's *with* the *Herald* but . . . he caved in. Just like the rest of them. And he never even *spoke* to me!"

"I thought we agreed you weren't going to talk to the press."

"But Carl Hiaasen I would have talked to."

"Well, Liz Balmaseda you talked to." *The* progressive Cuban American reporter at the *Herald* who seemed utterly dumbfounded when she said on the telephone, *I know you. You're not some sort of Machiavellian character.* "A lot of good *that* did," Ira says.

"Yeah. Now I know what happened. Liz Balmaseda walked her big self into Carl Hiaasen's office, her mouth full of *pastelitos* and babbled *her* version to him, and *that's* what he based his story on."

"Sweetie, will you get off the fat thing? Here, except *this* fat thing." He pulls me to him.

I pull back. "Stop. This is serious."

"This is serious too. Very serious."

"Did you see what Liz Balmaseda wrote? That I was a nauseating sight. You know why she's nauseated? Too much Mexican food. Every time I'd see her at the gym, she'd rub her stomach and moan, 'Ohhh! I'm so sick! Too much Mexican food last night.' Or French or Italian. I'm telling you, she was like a hungover drunk."

"Well, some don't have the balls to speak out. It's more important for them to keep their job at the *Herald* than to do the right thing. And others are just—fat! Fat and nauseated."

Michael Putney isn't fat. *He's a friend*, Michael Putney. On his talk show, my exasperated "You have to hand it to the guy. He [Fidel] stuck to his guns" of last Tuesday inspired Michael Putney to intersperse my words with an old grainy black-and-white film of a burly man shaking a fist at a firing squad moments before he's gunned down.

He stuck to his guns / man shakes fist, gunfire explodes.

He stuck to his guns / bursts of gunpowder cloud TV screen.

He stuck to his guns / man sprawls dead to the ground.

When next year, Meg Laughlin, a *Herald* reporter with *cojones* (an oxymoron, I know), quotes Michael Putney ("The First Amendment should not take precedence over what Magda did") in *Tropic*, the newspaper's Sunday magazine, Ira will send Michael Putney a "Dear Michael" letter:

> On the day that the article about Magda came out, exile radio said that Magda would be killed by an agent of Fidel Castro—in effect, that it is perfectly acceptable to execute Magda because "it was done by Fidel." My wife and children are now prime targets of Miami's open season.
>
> The shameful part of what you said was not only its profound ignorance of the First Amendment but that as a journalist it signals that intolerance, bigotry, and violence are to be condoned. During the McCarthy era, it was not the ranting of the right wing, it was good people like yourself who refused to defend "those communists" that propelled this country into one of its darkest periods.
>
> Unless responsible journalists vigorously defend unpopular speech, the violent, extremist elements of the exile community will find it perfectly acceptable to execute people like Magda because no one will really protest.

Michael Putney will respond. He was misquoted.

———

Ira and I lie on one side, the *Miami Herald* in plastic yellow wrapper of musical notes, flying butterflies, and smiling suns on the other. "Let me tell you something." I snap to sitting position. "If the media asks Clinton about me, I'm gonna say, 'At least my finances aren't being questioned, and I'm faithful to *my* spouse.'"

"Sweetie." A little chuckle. "I really don't think you're that important, that they'll ask the president of the United States about you kissing Fidel."

Thank God. Thank God I'm not important.

25

TOSSED COINS

————

rma's small figure stands patient and solitary in the Sunday afternoon heat. She smiles, walks to the car, her sandals slapping the pavement of the office lot. *"Hola, Magda. Hola, Ira."*

The three of us step into the dark, closet-like elevator. No one makes a move, utters a word, a tacit understanding of what the others are thinking. After a few seconds, Ira pushes the elevator button. Ira, unusually quiet, unusually humorless, steps out on his floor. When the door shudders open on our floor, Irma and I breathe out in unison.

I fish in my backpack for my keys. I try this key, that key. None fits. I take the elevator back down to the second floor. Does Ira have spare keys? I remember giving him an extra set, but to this *new* space? Or the smaller space we had had before we graduated to a higher, better space on the third—the top—floor? The day we moved, Cary swaggered a pretend George Jefferson swagger, breaking out with *Well, we're movin' on up / To the east side / To a dee-lux apartment / In the sky*, and the rest of us joined in: *We finally got a piece of the pie!*

But that was my other life. In this life, we'll soon be movin' on down into a much smaller space than our original office. And in my other life, I would have known which keys for which office and the precise instance I handed them to Ira.

In this life, as in his other life, Ira doesn't remember, but now he doesn't gloss over his absentminded professor lapses, doesn't deny I gave him spare keys. In this life, he searches and he doesn't know, he says, he may have lost them; he's sorry.

I call Ira's paralegal, Monika—German—and "the ice princess," the staff would call her. Sure, she has an extra set of keys, she says. Sure, she'll drop them off. It doesn't matter that it's Sunday. It doesn't matter to Irma. She waits by my side in the airless space outside my office.

Monika arrives, hands me the keys, her blue eyes alight in a smile. I look at her keys, my keys, compare them. I try my key; it turns. "It's the same key I had all along."

Irma flips her head in a *so what?* motion. Monika rubs the top of my back in quick strokes. A familiar feel. I turn to her. "Were you here with me the day of the office mob scene?"

"Sure. Don't you remember? I rubbed your back when you were cold," says the woman I too called an ice princess.

————

Inside the vast, gloomy space, I am at a loss. Where to begin? I walk to my work station, into the kitchen. I tell Irma, "Pull out all the files, line them up in the hallway," but don't know why.

"All of them? On the floor?"

"Yes," and when all the files are lined up along the wall, "Not such a good idea," I say. "Put them back."

I circle the office. Swivel chairs empty and unmoving; letters cold with unfinished thoughts; *Magda Montiel Davis, PA* stationery curled limply over typewriter rolls. *Presence without name surrounds me*, Octavio Paz's poetry at my ears.

"Deadlines," I tell Irma. "Look for deadlines." I begin with Janet's desk. Her cowboy boots—I'd brought back a pair for each after my last visa trip to Mexico—still under her desk. Memos taped to walls, reminders pinned on bulletin boards. Next to her typewriter is a gold-trimmed, glossy black Mont Blanc fountain pen like the one I own. A matching pen stand like the one I own.

On Cary's shelf, one of the porcelain dolls I brought for each from the Dominican Republic. Long, white flowing skirt, floppy straw hat, cut flowers in hand, but no face. No eyes, no mouth, no face. I sort through each file, each paper, carefully. Slowly, a system seems to develop. I scribble a to-do list: cases to be prepared here, cases to be filed there.

Irma tells me a woman named "Cati" is on the line. Isabel's mother, I think. Isabel is hurting, she'll say; Isabel wants to come back. But when I pick up the line, "Who is this?" I say. "*¡El pueblo Cubano!*" she says in martyrdom. "*Ay, señora,*" I say, "*no coma tanta mierda.*" Don't eat so much shit, but in Eddie Murphy down 'n' dirty: *You're a fucking idiot.*

I leave Isabel's desk for last. Personnel files, time records. And the credit call bill, due tomorrow. A charge to Trias Florist. I didn't order flowers. I call Trias. Flowers ordered by Janet Thessen. I take a hard look at every single charge. Bovee's Office Supply. I call. Ordered was the Mont Blanc fountain pen and matching pen stand on Janet's desk. I call American Express. Do I want to press charges? Yes. Janet Thessen, I say, T-H-E-S-S-E-N. I give Janet's address, phone number, repeat it.

––––––––

The sound of the door buzzer that Ira had installed as a condition of my returning to work. On the other side of our white French doors stands Mara. "I knew you'd come!" I shriek.

She smiles cautiously. Mara's mom and dad were one of my first clients seventeen years ago, when I was fresh out of law school. Yesterday, her mom called—from Argentina. She heard about *it* from Mara, yes, but it was in the Buenos Aires newspaper. "Marita is a lawyer now." "Marita" was in grade school when last I saw her. "Marita can help you."

I unbolt the door, stand to the side in *step this way* motion.

"Do you have the case ready?" Mara says in a crisp Argentinean accent.

"Yes. All ready for you." I try hard not to grunt, lifting a boxful of files. When I hand the box to Mara, her arms drop with the weight. I ignore her look of alarm. "Here." I pat Elisa's old chair. "Sit here and warm up with Omar Nuñez's I-797."

"What's an I-797?"

I shrug. "It's just an RFE."

"What's an RFE?" She flips the pages of the request for evidence sent recently by Immigration. "What is this? Seventeen pages—"

"It's not seventeen." I look at the RFE. "It's thirteen. *Qué exagerada.* Stop being so Jewish, so Argentinean. Jesus!"

"Thirteen pages of *small* print. *What* is a specialty occupation? How do you *prove* industry standard? How—"

I toss *Kurzban's Immigration Law Sourcebook* at her. "Here, all the answers you need are in Ira's book."

"*Jefa*, I just passed the bar exam. I am going to lose my license before I even start practicing law. *Oy vey!* Jewish mothers! How did I let her get me into this?" She shakes the pages at me. "Look at this! How do I answer this?"

"It's easy," I assure her. And neither one of us believes me.

Good work, I tell myself, as I slide into Ira's front seat, sit behind tinted windows. Building blocks, layer upon layer, baby steps, that's all it will take.

Ira drives, small talks, falls silent.

I pep talk myself: Good work. Small steps. Till I open the front door to our home.

My mother stands silent before me. "Beba," she slurs. She tries hard to sound casual, but she slurs my childhood name. "Are you selling *la casa*?" Her small eyes search my face.

"No," I say. A child's no. A *no fair!* kind of no.

"Then why would—"

Ira walks to her, "*¿Qué pasó, Abuela?*" his voice tender.

"A woman came to the door, all dressed up. '*¿Está Magda?*' She said she was a realtor. I said, '*No, Magda está en la oficina.*'"

My first thought: My mother is not to open the front door to anyone except family. Lieutenant Angulo's orders. And she is not to tell anyone our whereabouts.

"The woman looked around our porch, then all of a sudden, walked away. Then she stopped, turned and said, 'Hah! You'll be lucky to get fifty cents for *la casa ¡de la comunista!*' She opened her purse and threw coins at me."

"Abuela," says Ira. "That woman came to get us to leave Key Biscayne and sign papers so she can sell the house. Make money." He rubs his thumb and forefinger. "*Mucho dinero.*"

Mami nods. "*Sí*, Daddy."

"And when she saw *casa bonita* and that we are still *aquí*, here—"

This makes her smile.

"—she *furiosa*."

Mami extends her arms for balance. She looks behind her as if reassuring herself that a place for her is still here, then lowers herself onto the chair.

I stare at her. How long did Mami wait for us to come home? *Moving*, she thought. *Selling the house.* And do what with her? Leave her? "Place" her? Where? At my sister's? Mami could never live with my sister, nor could my sister live with her.

I leave, look out the French doors of Ira's and my bedroom. The patio, the pool, the little spot where she sits. The over-the-bed rolling table, the kind they keep in hospitals, where she keeps her cigarettes, her radio. And this woman, hurling coins at my mother. I see it, my mother's eyes, filled with that unfocused void of yellow-brown. For years now—thirty-three years—since the shock of losing Cuba, the same unfocused void.

Right before leaving—I was just a child, had no idea what awaited us—I'd ask her, "How old are you, Mami?" We'd ride in the back seat of my grandfather's Buick, my head on her lap, her long red fingernails running through my hair. "Thirty-three," she'd say, and look out the car window, suddenly sad. "The same age as Jesus Christ when he was crucified." And now, thirty-three years of her own private exile in this "cold country," as she would call it. "*Qué país tan frío*," she'd say, and look out the icy window those dark wintry days in Pennsylvania, where we first stayed.

Already my mom had a hard life. The stabbing death of her sister Migdalia on the outskirts of Havana where they grew up. Mami was sixteen, Migdalia seventeen, Tía Tíita eighteen. Migdalia seventeen and stabbed seventeen times. It was an ex-boyfriend. He threatened her with death, time and again. He told the townspeople. They warned her, but she went about her life, focused on her future, her studies. He asked her to dance at a town-square event. He slapped her when she said no. He tried to smash a bottle over her head when he saw her dancing with someone else. The townspeople intervened. My mother and Tía Tíita were there. I don't know if my *abuelos* were there, if they too witnessed the slap and bottle assault. The fifty-year-old newspaper page that I hold in my hand is silent. And so am I, silent. The specifics, I dare not ask family. The conclusions and questions that follow—Did you not know? Did you not see to it that measures were taken against the ex-boyfriend, that Migdalia's life would not be endangered?—I dare not ask. Because to ask means to validate, reinforce, the culpability and regret I know that for a lifetime has weighed every one of them down. And to dismiss the defense mechanisms—Such things don't happen to me or my children or anyone I love—that we employ when confronting grave danger.

A month later, Migdalia lay sprawled on the sidewalk amid barking dogs and down the block from the site of the town-square dance. It was April 5, 1942 late at night. Migdalia was coming home after sitting for finals at Teachers College in Havana. She got off the bus, crossed the town's major thoroughfare. Across the rail station was my *abuelo*'s kiosk, where he and my future uncles grilled *fritas* and made mango shakes and where she stopped to tell my *abuelo* about her finals. She left, books in hand. My grandfather told the town newspaper it was 9:45 PM when last he saw her. Mami was in the bedroom that she shared with Migdalia and Tía Tíita.

She was trying to go to sleep, she told me years later, but *¡Ay!* she told herself, *those* perros, *they're barking so much tonight, so loud.* "But it was my sister Migdalia's wails."

Often Mami will say that when Fidel rose to power, he freed the man who murdered her sister. "That son-of-a-bitch Fidel set him free. The man who murdered *mi hermana* Migdalia." Always, she prefaces Migdalia's name with "my sister," as if to bring back those times, stay connected to the loss; as if assuaging the finality, enigma, pain that comes with death.

Shortly after the rise of the revolution, the new government granted amnesty to most prisoners, as many were political prisoners under Batista and it was nearly impossible to tell who was who, what was what. So I knew that Migdalia's killer, though there was nothing political about his crime, had been set free pursuant to amnesty and that he was *descaradamente*— audaciously, Mami would say—walking the streets of Punta Brava, where the poor family of seven children, then six, grew up. I knew because on my first trip back to the island, I made it a point to visit Punta Brava, and was told just that. But the fact is, the man had already served at least fifteen years. So I asked Tíita, and she confirmed the man had been sentenced to precisely that, fifteen years' imprisonment, which he served fully.

In 1980, the continued US embargo and a spike in oil prices made the Cuban economy suffer as never before. President Carter's loosening of US travel restrictions three years before prompted many exiles to return to the island with ample displays of material wealth—many say false displays. Tensions ran unusually high. In Havana, a man crashed his vehicle into the gates of the Peruvian Embassy, demanding asylum. Within forty-eight hours, ten thousand Cubans crowded the embassy gates. Fidel then announced that any Cuban wishing to leave the island for Florida could do so over the next six months via the Mariel port, no paperwork needed, and Cubans in the US could even bring their own vessels. Jimmy Carter welcomed Cubans to the US "with open arms and open hearts." Upon arrival at the Mariel port, Cuban Americans were told that in addition to their relatives, they had to make room for others wishing to leave. In the end, as many as 125,000 disembarked at Key West—some with histories of serious crimes and/or mental illness, while a bewildered Immigration was left to process their admission. Day after day, as exile radio read off the names of those arriving, Mami listened morning to night for the name of the man who murdered her sister, Migdalia. But the man never landed on US shores.

When I converted to Judaism, in honor of my aunt, who never had a chance at life, and in reverence for my mother, I chose "Migdalia" as my Hebrew name.

Right after my bid for Congress, I flew to New York to hear Foreign Minister Robaina speak at Riverside Church, and the air was freezing, the sidewalks packed with layer upon layer of ice. When he thanked us for traveling on such short notice to *"ésta ciudad, este país tan frío"*—this city, this country so cold—my thoughts weren't on the US's then latest draconian legislation to try to destabilize the Cuban government. Nor was my mind on Fidel's for-sure imminent and masterminded payback to even—to raise—the score. Through Robaina's eloquent, spirited talk, my thoughts were with my mother. Her hard adolescence losing her sister Migdalia. Her hard marriage. The hard, scrutinizing stares once in this "cold country." The looks of *rechazo* thrust at her—her voice, her gestures, too animated, too foreign. Too *too*.

While still in Cuba, when my father said she couldn't hire a housekeeper, she said fine, I'll pay for it with my own money. And she did, took two buses to get to the public school on the outskirts of Havana where she taught, then two buses back in time to make his four-course meals; only she could cook for him, not the housekeeper. Always I felt adored, protected by her.

The strength it must have taken for a woman in 1960 to have left her homeland; her husband, father, five very close siblings; to have left by herself with her two little girls. When I pack, often I wonder, How did my mother know what to take, how did she choose? One suitcase each was all we could take. The strength it must have taken to have come to a country where she didn't speak the language, had no notion of the ways.

Shortly after we left, a tumor grew in her pituitary gland, so disfiguring her that the features of her face, her feet, hands, her once-beautiful hands, grew to monstrous proportions. She lost sight in one eye. Her mind was dumbed, stayed dumbed; often I'm sure of it. Her wit stayed, but always, that unfocused glaze of the eyes. I thought it was because she never quite learned English. But no. Once, she asked me to call Caballero Funeral Home, order a *corona* for an old acquaintance that had passed away. "Mami," I protested, "they speak Spanish there. That's *all* they speak. They don't even speak English." But no. She was *atolondrada*, overwhelmed. I saw it in her eyes. And so I made the call for her, probably with some disapproving word or gesture.

Was it the effect of the tumor that finally broke her? Are *we* selling the house? Not *she*. Not *she* for a long time, who knows if ever *she*. When it was clear that my marriage to Paul was falling apart and he said, "I can't take it anymore, living with your mother," I agreed, my mother's daughter, and I agreed. "*Yo sé que yo apesto*," she said, when I broke the news to her that we were moving out. I know I smell, she said. A metaphorical smell; my mother never smelled, not even when she smoked. She only smelled of Shalimar perfume and pink Chiclets in those days of long ago, when she would lean over and kiss me then run out the door down three flights of stairs to hop into my father's new Impala and go with him to Havana Sugar Kings ball games—every night during baseball season she would do this.

Without telling Paul, I canceled all moving plans; I would not live without my mother. As soon as I left Paul, I bought this home for my mother, Mami, who's always lived with me. A bright, expansive home with entire walls of French doors thrown open, the ocean air billowing throughout the house. My mother always wanted a house by the beach. In Cuba, she and my father were at the point of buying one, and then came the revolution—and then we were gone from the island.

And then so was he.

It will take me years, decades, to realize fully the impact on my mother of the murder of her sister Migdalia in relation to the likelihood of that of her daughter. Mami, silent in the background, her daughter fathoming that she's slaying dragons, thinking, like Migdalia, that she's invincible, that it won't happen to her, to her children.

And years, decades, to realize that it wasn't my mother's uprootedness of leaving the homeland that finally broke her. It wasn't my father's unfaithfulness. It wasn't the pituitary tumor or the ensuing disfigurement of my mother, her once-beautiful self.

It was her strength.

26

EVENTUALITY

DAY 7 OF 3 [MAYBE 5]

————

I sit in the back seat of Ira's Chevy, wedged between Sadie and Ben strapped tightly in their car seats. We play rock-paper-scissors, twenty questions, or connect the dots from the time we leave home until we pull up at the curb of their preschool at Beth David Synagogue.

Last night, as I read *Sylvester and the Magic Pebble* to Ben and we reached the part where his voice always bubbles and he tries hard not to cry—Mr. and Mrs. Duncan's grief at their son Sylvester the donkey's mysterious disappearance—I was on the brink of telling him, "If somebody takes you and hurts you and tells you I don't love you, it's not true." How can I tell him this? But how can I not? And not prepare him for the eventuality.

————

My office is a ghost town, my first day back. It is the Monday after the Wednesday that I was besieged by mobs here at the office, Ira driving the getaway car.

The mirrors in my reception area, an entire wall of them, once reflecting movement, sound, color—clients in and out, glass panels of French doors tinkling against white wooden panes, the lively chatter of staff—all is unmoving, a deadened grey.

My first day back, open for business. I arrive early, feeling like the new kid in school, her first day.

And it is so cold in here.

————

Miriam, my receptionist, calls. She talked it over with her family and made her decision. "And?" It can go either way. I never know. "And this is the right thing to do," she says. "I'm coming back, Ms. Davis." Not right away, but she will come back. "My husband wants me to wait until . . . you know, until things calm down a bit." Eventually, she says.

"Soon," I say, in childlike attempt at self-encouragement.

Is "eventually" soon? "Calm down" could be never.

———————

The office fills up slowly, a balloon half filled. Irma is the first to arrive. Of course, Irma. Then Tío Marino, my mom's "baby" brother. Then my sister, her friend Raysa in tow. I jump springlike from my seat. "You look like you did at your *cumpleaños*," your birthday parties, Maty shouts through the glass. "Blocking the front door, asking everyone who came in, 'Where's my present?'" She mimics what I fathom she heard in my voice then, extending an open *gimme-gimme* palm. Grinning, I unbolt our new security locks.

My sister left her day-spa business in Broward County—closed? unattended?—and drove in Monday-morning rush hour traffic to Miami, where its narrow, congested streets and skewed highways have yet to recover after Hurricane Andrew.

"An hour and a half." She snaps her fingers. "That's all it took me."

"*Mi sobrina*," says Tío Marino, "*¿Y como lograstes eso?*"

She stretches both arms before her, turns a pretend steering wheel. Drove in my sleep, she says. "*Amanecí manejando.*"

Each scuttles to a desk. Irma quietly, meekly; Tío Marino carefully, orderly; my Maty . . . my sister throws up her arms, pulls at her hair. "*¿Donde empiezo?*"

"*Mira, chico,*" Raysa says into the phone. Leaning across the desk, her butt U-shaped into the air. "If you're so *valiente*, why don't you go to Cuba and plant that same bomb on Fidel?"

"The calls," my sister says, breathless. She lifts her head from her desk, a last-place swimmer coming up for air. "Look at this. Every line is lit up."

"Remember to keep a record of every threat, every call," I say.

My sister puts a hand on her hip. "How many times are you gonna tell us that?" Raysa waves a time-out at us. She's straining to listen, dark eyes squinted, handset cradled at shoulder.

"We need to call them every couple of hours with a complete—and accurate—list," I say.

We = Raysa and Maty on the phones. The three of us had a conference call last night and decided not to put Tío Marino on the phones. And Irma speaks no English. But I choose my words carefully, use *we* to pass on a spirit of sisterhood, solidarity.

Them = FBI agents. Oscar Montoto or his partner, Luis Rodriguez, and now a new addition, Dick Something, with his deep FBI voice. But they all have deep FBI voices. You'd think their voices were prerecorded discs rotating furiously inside their robotic bodies.

"The FBI has been great," my sister says.

But in her words, I hear Ira's words to me earlier, "Yeah, but are they watching you for you? Or watching you for them?"

———

Joe Beeler calls. Before I thank him again for the use of his law office, "Say, Magda, did, dah, anything come of Lincoln Díaz-Balart's letter to Janet Reno that you should register as foreign agents?"

"No. Should it?" I shrug. "I saw it as a dog-and-pony show."

"Well, you know, Magda, it could, dah, very well start as that and then turn into something more."

"As in?"

"As in indictments for failure to register as foreign agents."

"Aw, come on! You mean the US Attorney would indict all two hundred of us who attended the conference?"

"No."

A silence. "Joe, how could they indict me? How am I a foreign agent?"

———

Ira and I walk the Village Green, the new park that the new Village of Key Biscayne built. Key Biscayners voted to secede from the City of Miami so property taxes of Key Biscayners go for perks to Key Biscayne, like immediate dispatch police, and not anywhere else. Like the inner city. The Key Biscayne Council cut down a farm of coconut palms and built this fabulous park with ergonomic baby swings and state-of-the-art toilets. Ira said I could take the dogs on a short walk as long as I was careful. As long as he came with me.

I walk Chaucer. "If the authorities—"

He walks Goblin. "Who would the authorities be?"

"Say, the FBI."

"Okay. The FBI."

"Wait, what other authority could it be?"

"Could be the Office of Foreign Assets Control."

"Okay. OFAC, FBI. They barge into my office, and . . . can they *do* that?"

"Yes. They can do that."

"Without notice?"

"Yes."

"With no right to a hearing?"

"Yes. They're not arresting you. They'd have a subpoena."

"A subpoena? For what?"

"All your records."

"All my files? Ledgers? Client cards?"

"Yes."

"Then the office shuts down."

"That's the idea."

FBI, on the line. "I have a report on the phone numbers we traced," says Oscar Montoto. "Ready? Write this down. Herzog, Nall—" He spells it. "Obviously, you don't recognize it." He waits. "It's a CPA firm. In Coral Gables."

"CPAs? Why would serious professionals . . ." I know CPAs lead boring lives, *pero coño, le zumba el mango*. And in upscale Coral Gables?

"Probably some lower-level employees working there."

"O-ooh." An *I get it* intonation.

"Next, Manuel Castañedo. And the machine gun sounds—those came from E. Garcia de Bustos." He reads both addresses. "Know them?"

"Negative," I say, wondering if I might build some FBI camaraderie using what I fathom is FBI lingo.

"Remember." Another pause. Jesus, do they train these guys to pause at just the right time, for the precise length of time? Or is it to give their surveillance apparatus time to kick in? "Call me or my partner, anything funny, anything suspicious. You have my numbers. And my partner, you have my partner? Luis Rodriguez. 787-6519. That's his pager. Our pagers are on at all times."

"And Dick too?"

"Who's Dick?"

Who's Dick? And Where's Waldo? "Dick . . . Granati."

"O-ooh." An *FBI gets it* intonation. "You mean Gianati. Dick Gianati. Yes. Dick too."

27

RAISE THE ANTENNA

The Telemundo van is across the street, Irma says. She saw it a while ago, didn't think much of it. Now she went back and it's there still. I go to the window. White van. It's always a white van. Big antenna protruding from the roof of the van, erected high in the air. Bright lights.

I call Ira. "You gotta leave, sweetie." A hiss. "You know why they're doing this, right?" He doesn't wait. "It's been relatively quiet the last couple of days"—*relatively*, yes—"so they have to stir it up again, park their van in front of the building so a crowd comes." *Relatively* because the city manager just plead guilty to federal obstruction for trying to derail an FBI investigation into corruption at city hall and was sentenced to a year in jail. "You're a lucky woman," Ira said upon opening up the newspaper. "You're secondary in the news today."

Now he says leave. "Evacuate."

"Again? I can't practice law like this."

"Well, you ain't gunna practice law if you're dead."

"Make you a deal. Irma stands watch by the window. Crowd builds, we leave."

Two hours later, no crowd in sight, the Telemundo van pulls away, its enormous antenna shrinking back to size. "I bet Fefita and Pepito said, 'Oh, it's just Magda Montiel again,'" my sister says, "and went back to their *chismes* and *churros*."

A back pain that is off the charts—I can't sit, can't stand, can only walk backward. Or sideways. A *cangrejo*, my sister says, a crab. Maybe I can check cases standing on my head. Or on a new office chair.

Irma drives me to a quiet furniture store on a quiet side street in quiet Coral Gables. We are inside the store twenty minutes, tops. When we return to the car, a poem is taped to the window of the front passenger seat where I sat. Were we followed? If so, since when? Since we left the office? How? Someone sat outside our office building and waited for me? Someone inside the building—Ira's office, another office—alerted him/her/them? *Okay, here she comes.* Or someone just happened to spot us as we drove, on US-1, maybe? We even made a quick stop at Coral Bagels for a cinnamon raisin. Did someone watch me lumber out the passenger side, walk my crab-walk into the bagel shop, search for the perfect bagel?

Or was someone already there? Maybe someone who works on the same block, or next door to the small office furniture store on quiet Aurora Street? But the poem was *taped* to my window, not wedged between glass and windshield wiper like a parking citation. And the poem was typed. It was margined and centered. Someone just *happened* to have a typed, margined, and centered poem handy? And Scotch tape too?

Both Irma's and my mouths drop open. Then we laugh. Like children, we laugh. We don't know what else to do.

Back at the office, I call Oscar Montoto. It is then that my hands shake, my heart thumps.

"Send it to us," says Oscar Montoto in that curt FBI voice of his.

"What? The poem?"

"No. The incident."

"Oh. Because the poem is bad, really bad. Some nonsensical stuff about some guy named Mendive, whoever he is. The only Mendive I know is Armando Mendive, my CPA, ex-CPA, and he just fired me. I read the poem one, twice, couldn't make heads or tails of it. The poet is no José Martí, I can tell you that—"

"Ms. Davis," his voice firm, "Write it up."

Write it up, write it up. Okay, Oscar. Right-o, Oscar. Write it up.

———

"Okay." I lie on the couch, my feet on Ira.

He watches TV.

"Say the FBI burst into my office, news cameras—your *friend* Michael Putney—right behind them. . . . Okay." I poke him with my toe. "Are you listening?"

"Roger."

"What do I do? Keep calm?"

"Yes." He nods once, an appeasing, go-away nod. "Keep calm."

"Smile?"

"Yes. You have a great smile."

"And call you." I jab him with my big toe. "Keep your phone with you. On. Charged."

But Ira turns off his phone when he meets with clients and *buena suerte, Magda*, trying to get past his new secretary to get him to pick up the line. "Did you hear me?"

Yes, he says. No, he did not. "How can you watch such stupid shows?"

He turns to me. "And what would you like me to watch? 'Magda Montiel on Telemundo'?"

Come to where no man has gone before. "Here comes Starfish."

"Starship." *Whoosh!* Huge, small, tiny, Starship Enterprise disappears into the screen.

After a minute or two, "I can't believe you won't wear the beeper I got you," I say.

"You wanna keep tabs on me—"

"I *asked* you: 'If I get you a beeper, will you wear one?' And you said yes. You said yes."

Newsbreak: "Current temperature ninety-two degrees, humidity eighty-nine percent."

"Keep tabs on you?" If I could recount all to Lazara, she'd say, *"Ay, Magda, ¡por favor!* You're delusional. *¿Ese enano?"*—that . . . let's just say it's a person of extremely short stature.

"Who's got the time, energy to worry about those mundane things? Like your husband fooling around on you."

Mr. Spock looks like my first boyfriend, eighteen-year-old linebacker at Miami Springs High who I lost my virginity to. I was fourteen. Back to Ira: "At first, I thought it was a given all my clients would ask for their files back."

"And that all your staff—and your friend Lazara—would stay."

"I'm so lucky. So lucky my clients stayed."

"And you know why else you're so lucky?" He stands to face me, bowlegs akimbo, pink open palms at his side. "You won the lotto when you met me, Davis." A *what you see is what you get* pose. "The goose who laid the golden egg."

Actually, Mr. Spock's not looking bad these days.

28

NOTHING COMES BETWEEN
ME AND MY CALVINS

———

Like having the scale soar to 138 pounds and trying to fit into the size 2 Calvin Klein stretch jeans Ira gave me for my last birthday. That's what it's like moving our office across the hall. But the rent is one-third of what we paid, and Ira said: Keep the overhead low. Business will surely go down. And yes, Magda, clients will walk.

I exhale hard, belt out an internal Tarzan call. I take the U-shaped modular sofa bordering three entire walls of mirrors in our old reception area and disassemble the sofa myself. Take a screwdriver and figure out how to do it. Me, who couldn't change the paper in the copy machine or send a fax. I drag the two corner pieces across the hall and angle them in opposite corners in our new tiny reception area. Two pieces of how many? But at least I still have the prints with purples and fuchsias and aqua pastels. The oil painting of breezy royal palms I picked up in the sidewalks of Old Havana fits just so, and so does the framed poster of Monet's waterlilies, bringing out the colors, of course bringing out the purples, what other colors are in your color spectrum, Ira had said in our other life.

Back across the hall, I say one last good-bye to the things I can't bring with me, press the intercom button, swoosh open the front door at the sound of the security buzzer. Not a set of double French doors like before, but a French door still and white-lacquered still. Already two clients wait for me. No back door anymore for me to sail in and out of to avoid running into antsy clients. One client, then another stands, their little children swarming about, climbing up, sliding down the tiny remade sofa, a wife with long sad eyes looking up at me, too tired to stand.

"*Doctora.*" They're fraught with worry, one says; sleepless, the other says.

I smile, reassure them. A genuine smile, a genuine reassurance. Not like before. Not like when I'd distractedly skirt past them or tell Miriam to say I wasn't in. Not when I'd reassure them by rote, smile frostily, go hurriedly on to the next complication.

Miriam sits behind a security-wired wall separating her from the public but still behind the sea-green receptionist workstation. It fits. Miriam fits.

"Miriam, what's the balance on the operating account?"

"I'll have the numbers for you right now, Ms. Davis." She has taken on a Jane Austenish persona and pronounces "I'll" *AY-eel*. I tell her: Please call me Magda. "Oh no, Ms. Davis." She smiles, pleased. "I couldn't do that."

Behind Miriam, a lineup of two, three, four sea-green Formica desks. No empty space, every inch of our small office used to maximum potential. Smaller space, in anticipation of business going down.

Different space, sorrowing the memories.

My sister is the forewoman in the assembly line of desks. She stops me. Of course, she stops me.

"Yes?" I drag out the yes in a *you rang?* tone.

"What about"—she rakes wisps of copper-cellophaned bangs off her forehead—"this fucking E-1 or L-1 or H-1 visa case—whatever the hell it is." No one can say "fucking" the way Maty says it. A whispery "fucking," emphasis on the *f.* "I've never prepared one of these type cases before." She's never prepared *any* cases before, but okay.

Mara, whose *oh vey!* Jewish mother, one of my first clients, volunteered her for the job, stands up. "Oh, that's never stopped *la jefa* before. She'll tell you"—here Mara waves my sister away, mimicking me, "'Oh, just *look* at Mr. Such 'n' Such's case': Mr. Such 'n' Such of twenty years ago whose file you can't find anywhere, not even in cyberspace. *Oy vey!* You know how I got that renowned painter I got thrown at me approved? That Brazilian kid with *tres carajos* of notoriety that she told me to prepare as an 'alien of extraordinary ability'?" Throwing up an arm, "I asked him to bring me a painting," she says. "And he brought me this . . . this painting of these two huge *tetas*." She cups her breasts. "He called the painting *Landscape*. So I packed it up, sent it to Immigration, and got an approval back, instantly. Never got the painting back, but I got the approval. *Jefa*, I hope you won't ask me to get an approval for a furniture maker, because I don't want to have to pack up a sofa and send it to Immigration."

"Well you can send this one." I point to a corner piece in our tiny reception cubicle. "It'll fit in a FedEx box."

Maty is on the phone with the day spa that she owns. "What do you *mean* she went home with pink hair? Oh my God, of all customers for that to happen to. Don't you ladies *know* you can't go from blonde to red? Let me speak to Leslie. . . . Yeah, Leslie, what's going on? She looked like . . . Oh, great! She left looking like the Pink Panther. You know what? Call her back . . . the customer, who do you think? Offer her a free pedicure. Never mind, raise the ante. Offer her a two-hundred-dollar gift certificate." She hangs up, looks across at Mara. "How do you say it, Mara? *Oy vey?* And this one"—she lifts her chin at me—"is in La-La Land. Hello-oh? You need to *hire* people. I can't stay here forever. And Mara—"

"*Jefa*, what was it you said? 'Oh, just a few hours each day?' My husband's ready to change the lock on our door. You forget, I have *babies* at home."

Tío Marino, wearing well the banner of my mom's baby brother, looks up from his desk of neatly lined-up No. 2 pencils and stacks of ledgers, half smiles.

My sister waves more messages at me. "This woman named Lazara called. No, not *your* Lazara." She looks at me, wide-eyed. "She has immigration experience, sounded pretty good—"

"I'm not hiring anyone by the name Lazara."

I plunge ahead, dig into my pile of work. Irma knows to stay close, an operating room nurse handing surgeon all necessary instruments. She knows what I mean often without my saying it, sometimes a hand gesture, sometimes a misspoken word. Once, I said, *Traeme la copiadora*"—the copy machine; bring me the copy machine—and within seconds I had the Xerox copy I needed in hand. Stitches and scalpel, nurse to surgeon.

But now Miriam walks to the workstation, stands before me, shaken. "Ms. Davis."

"What?"

"I'm really sorry, Ms. Davis." She bites her top, her bottom lip. "Isabel is on the line."

Isabel has been calling for days; I have refused to take her calls. "This time she says she won't get off the line till I put you on the phone." She always did intimidate Miriam. Once, Miriam resigned because Isabel was short with her. I'd just given birth to Sadie, was dealing with the chaos of three teen/preteen girls at home, my recent marriage to Ira, the usual client stress and fragility of office finances, and didn't need a whiny, *majadera* Miriam on top of all else. So I let it be, made no effort to call her. When her replacement was offered a position at the state attorney's office, Miriam returned the instant I called her.

"Okay," I tell Miriam, "I'll take the call."

"Ooh, thank you, Ms. Davis."

"But you owe me, big time."

"Yes, yes. Thank you, Ms. Davis."

I need to tell her, I owe *her*, big time.

I pick up the telephone, my hand heavy. Did I receive her fax? Isabel asks. Yes. Hers and those of the other dogs, I tell her. "So many mixed feelings," Isabel had written. "Regardless of the telephonic insults and/or threats we underwent, we never left the office because we waited for your call. You know where to reach me. Call me. Despite what you think, I am not your enemy. None of us are." She did have to add: "It's only fair the girls be paid for their accrued vacation time and/or the last two days they came in."

And from Cary: "What the media didn't mention is that we all spoke very highly of you. The reason for the radio interviews was to find employment, not to bad mouth you. Believe it or not, the girls and I wish you the very best. You are a strong woman and will not let this episode destroy you. Remember, during the campaign everyone was saying, 'She's got bigger balls than any man.'"

Janet and Barbara wrote the same thing. They didn't know what to say but felt they should be paid their vacation time. Barbara added, "I care for you very much." The letters were sent together. From Mily came nothing.

I'd started to throw them out, then laid them gently in my desk drawer, feeling a certain peace, sadness—resignation—as I closed the drawer.

"I want to talk to you," Isabel says. Her voice steady, restrained.

"No."

"About the office account."

"No."

"Payroll taxes."

"No."

"The visa lottery, deadlines—"

"I will figure it out." I speak through clenched teeth.

"Let me come in." She cries.

"No."

And cries harder. "I heard you referred to Elisa as *una dama*—" The attorney who quietly resigned immediately following my return from Havana.

"Elisa *did* behave like a lady. Unlike the five of you."

"*¿Una dama, Magda?* And you were at the point of *firing* her?"

"I had touched base with you about the *possibility* of letting her go only because the money situation was so bad. I figured I could take over her attorney position much more easily than trying to do the paralegal work myself, trying to type . . . those *godawful* forms."

In between sobs, little whimpers, Isa belts out a laugh, that spontaneous laugh I so loved. In high school, I steered clear of Typing I and II, afraid I'd end up being someone's secretary and not go to law school. So I never learned to type. And now that I'm a lawyer, I have to handwrite every single damned motion for staff to type. But I'm softening, so "That's right," I say, "*una dama*. Elisa stood much more to gain by parading herself before the press, radio—"

"You don't know—"

"—TV. She would have become the hero of Cuban exiles, built up a name, stolen my clients, my entire practice. But she did not."

"You don't know what it was like for us. The threats, the panic, the fear. But we didn't leave. We waited for you—"

"You *did* leave."

"We left when—"

"Miriam didn't leave. Irma didn't leave—"

Sounds, deep and guttural. Shallow intakes of breath.

"Elisa didn't prostitute herself."

"And now you have Miriam there," she says, as if suddenly she regained control, "like the Queen of Sheba, not even putting my call through—"

"That's right. Miriam."

"And Ira's paralegal, pretending she cares about you, when all she cares about is the almighty dollar."

"Monika? You mean Monika? She *stayed* with me, Isabel. She's not even *my* paralegal and stayed with me that day I had to leave the office under police protection. Risked her life as the five of you were downstairs selling yourselves to the highest bidder."

"What about your father? Telling the press, 'This is the worst thing that could happen to me.'" Yesterday's *Miami Herald* front page "Odyssey of Magda Montiel Davis / No Longer Miss Popularity / De la Más Popular a la Más Criticada / De Reina a Objeto de Repudio," with yearbook photos in its Sunday statewide edition. "How come *that's* okay?"

"He's an old man, Isabel. And besides," I lie for my father, "the article's okay." My heart will burst from my chest, beating so hard, so fast.

"They used us," Isabel screams. "All those job offers, they were bogus."

Isabel is sobbing and I am eroding, breaking down. All those years together, the trust, the spoiling, indulging. The taking care of each other.

The time I tantrumed, "I want my soy burger," pounded on our kitchen table even. I was pregnant with Sadie and Granny Feelgood was late in delivering. I craved a hamburger, some protein, but no meat, never meat. So soy it was and soy pronto. For years thereafter, Isa would mock me, smilingly, lovingly, "I want my soy burger," any time I insisted a case be prepared a certain way—however impractical. Or the time Benoit, our sexy French-Canadian executive, gifted us with a baker's dozen of Montreal bagels on Isa's and my trip to Canada to see the human circus perform its award-winning production—the circus had just retained us, they were on their way up—they'd just won an Emmy—and so were we, we thought, on our way up, our first corporate client. Benoit was aghast when the bag of fat, very fat bagels that he gave us was almost empty. "Magda," Isa whispered, "You ate *eight* bagels?"

"No," I said. "Not eight, maybe nine. Or ten." And for once I didn't feel that postbinge remorse. Montreal bagels, they were that good.

Memories. Affection. A feeling I am beginning to forgive her. But Ira. He'll never forgive *me*. If I take Isabel back, even if she doesn't work for me again, even if all I do is maintain contact, any contact with Isabel, Ira—God no, it's not in the cards. I force myself to hark back to that day in the kitchen, my talk with them—"I can do this, but I can't do it without you"—their cold, hard eyes, telling me *gone*, your practice is gone, wishing that on me, as if all I had built had been gifted to me. All those wretched years of hard work, sacrifice, wading my way through law school—feeling so far behind all the other students—despite my unexpected pregnancy with Katy, despite an incessantly crying colicky infant, then thrown into the practice of law. Giving birth to Paula right after that, then Maggie right after that too, building the law practice, nurturing the clientele—but not the kids—into what it is today.

"What you did," I say to Isabel. "Is *imperdonable*. I hope God can forgive you. Because I can't." And with that, I hang up. And she doesn't call back.

29

SCOUNDREL

———

My father. He's not exempt. At the bank, he receives a post-card: "*Hijo de gato, caza raton*." Son of cat hunts mouse. In American-speak: The apple doesn't fall far from the tree. "That's why your daughter Magda *es tan mala*. She learned it from you. . . . The bank is laying down the banana peel to fire you. Bye, *viejo zorro, ladrón, sinverguenza*." Conniving old geezer, thief, scoundrel.

When my father shows it to me—he makes a special trip to my office this Monday morning—I feel the air taken out of me. I say to him—I don't know what I say to him.

The instant he leaves, I go downstairs to Ira's office. "Maybe he didn't do right by someone," I say to Ira, "a customer or coworker at the bank or something. Why am I to be blamed for that?"

"Why do you think he's blaming you?"

"Why did he show it to me then?" I wince. "I hate how he makes me feel around him, still like a little kid. I hate that he calls me Magda."

"Well, that *is* your name."

"When he says Magda, it sounds so artificial, so contrived. Why doesn't he call me Beba? Like my mom?"

"Sweetie. Get a grip. All this baggage about your dad. Jesus, you have the memory of an elephant. You don't forget." Then, "And don't forgive."

"You'll think he'll get fired, though? 'Cause he's old? 'Cause of me?"

———

"Ira."

"*Si, mi amor.*" Mee ah-mohr.

"Okay. So FBI, CIA, you name it, they raid my office. Then what? Hire Joe Beeler?"

"Uh-huh."

"And I'd get my files back when?"

"Probably the next day. Not bad—"

"Yes, it is bad. The government raids my office, my practice would not survive that. Not—"

But he's mumbling. Something about *a pretty good system*—that it *works*? This? From the drummer who shaved his head when Martin Luther King Jr. was shot? Who was arrested for disobeying the bobby's order during a Vietnam demonstration while at the London School of Economics? Who wore clogs and jeans to court (though later he did add a tie) when I first met him?

"How can you say that?"

"You think Janet Reno would allow a witch hunt?" Clinton's third pick for attorney general. First pick, corporate lawyer Zoë Baird—no cigar. She and her husband had hired an undocumented foreign national as nanny for their three-year-old and had failed to pay Social Security taxes. Second almost pick, federal judge Kimba Wood—no cigar. She and husband had hired an undocumented foreign national as nanny for their six-year-old. It was legal at the time of hire. And they had paid Social Security taxes. But still, no cigar. Two of Clinton's male cabinet members, the secretaries of commerce and transportation, had failed to pay taxes for a housekeeper and babysitter, respectively. And were confirmed and remained cabinet members.

Janet Reno, unmarried with no children, posed no risk of this so-called Nannygate scandal. Elected time and time again as top prosecutor for Miami-Dade County, Janet Reno had always lived in Miami. And Bill Clinton is Bill Clinton.

The New York Times
Oops! Snapped with Castro

Washington—For decades American officials have done everything but backflips to avoid even making eye contact with Fidel Castro on the rare occasions when diplomatic duty lands them in the same room.

But who was that bearded man next to Mike Espy, the Agriculture Secretary, in South Africa this week? It was Mr. Castro himself and it is said aides to Mr. Clinton aren't too pleased about Mr. Espy's Kodak moment.

Hillary Rodham Clinton, who like Mr. Espy was part of the official

United States delegation to Nelson Mandela's inauguration, knew enough to stay on the other side of the room from the Cuban leader. So too did Vice President Gore, who led the contingent honoring South Africa's new President.

But Mr. Espy, who has spoken sympathetically in the past of Mr. Mandela's affection for Mr. Castro, had no such qualms. And his choice of company at a reception in the Presidency building has left Clinton Administration officials agog at the apparent cozying up to the Cuban leader. So far, the photograph has not turned up in the press, but the picture taking was witnessed by reporters at the reception.

"Boy," says Ira, "Hillary Clinton sure managed to make that picture disappear awfully fast." The *awfully fast* he singsongs. "That's what you needed, sweetie, to have Hillary Clinton with you in Havana."

————

Assistant US Attorney Willy Fernandez will be interviewed next year by Meg Laughlin of *Tropic*, the *Miami Herald*'s Sunday magazine, regarding the ongoing threats against me. There was some talk of prosecuting those making threatening calls, Willy will say, but after consultation with the FBI, the US Attorney decided that "stern warnings" would suffice. Willy will say most (careful not to say *all*) of the threats came from exiles in their seventies and eighties who were told on Little Havana radio that it was their patriotic duty to tell me what they thought about me and promptly scribbled my home, office, fax, and beeper numbers, given out by the radio station. These "septuagenarian and octogenarian" callers couldn't leave their houses, Willy will say (*not* careful to say *most*), because they were "invalids" or without transportation. But none of the voices of those making threatening calls are those of seventy- and eighty-year-olds. Not one.

Years later, Ira and I will file multiple applications under the Freedom of Information Act for release of information held by the FBI, CIA, DIA (Defense Intelligence Agency), and NSA (National Security Agency). Among tasks entrusted to the NSA is listening to international calls, but unlike Cuba, it's not Fidel's one-man band listening to every single call but an army of NSA agents. The government will claim exemption from release of information "in the interest of national security." We will appeal. The government will then send a trickle of news articles and photocopies of threats that I myself had given to the FBI. Again it will claim exemption as to any other documents. We will file suit in federal court. And receive another useless trickle of documents, though in all fairness this one will contain FBI records of visits paid to a dozen or so of those who made threats; a trickle, you could say, of the vast number of threats.

Notwithstanding representations made by Assistant US Attorney Willy, not one document will record visits by the FBI to "invalids." Rather, they will contain descriptions such as "white male, black hair, 5'10", 180 lbs." Visits were to workplaces such as Office Max, where "employees are, for the most part, young people who do not care about politics." One employee was on vacation and agents never went back to interview him. Some admitted calling but denied making threats; they said nothing, they said, then hung up. When asked why the duration of calls were far longer than the time it takes to call and hang up, some stayed on the line "just to listen." One said his calls were nothing more than "an attempt to have fun agitating [her]."

A woman interviewed at home denied making any calls but, she said, her husband may have. A man said his wife was the only one at home at the time of the calls; always, he came home late. And a father said it was one of his two sons.

Every week my office gave the FBI a number of cassettes of recorded messages. One of those cassettes was returned to us pursuant to the FOIA application. The transcript: "Whoever made this recording has to be the lesbian bitch of Magda Montiel. You think you're gonna become a judge? Ha! Ha! Ha! Hahh! Let me laugh. I'm still waiting for you. I'm just giving you time. I am gonna get you, baby. I am *just* giving you time." The woman, with little accent and distinct voice, is no seventy- or eighty-year-old. A seventy- or eighty-year-old is, in addition, highly unlikely to speak fluent, barely accented English. A second call immediately follows, now in Spanish. Translation: "Illiterate, dyke [*tortillera*] whore, whoever made this recording. When you least expect it, whore lesbian Montiel, when you least expect it, I am going to get you, when you leave your house or at a restaurant, any place, when you least expect it. And if I can get Ira—get Ira! Ira! Ira!" she goes on. "Bunch of communists, disgusting, I am going to get the two of you. When you least expect it."

Voice recognition could easily have been used in these other cases to provide evidence of probable cause, necessary for the issuance of an arrest warrant. As for fingerprint evidence, because "numerous written communications addressed to MS. MAGDA MONTIEL DAVIS . . . all of a threatening nature, were all handled by MS. DAVIS' office staff as well as numerous postal employees and/or delivery service personnel, it was not feasible to process [them] for latent fingerprints." And yet, every threat, in its original, was turned over to the FBI. Writing analyses could easily have been made as most were handwritten. Every envelope, also original, was turned over to the FBI. Its gummy flaps were hardly, if at all, "handled by MS. DAVIS' office·staff." They were not handled at all by "numerous postal employees and/or delivery service personnel." Fingerprints could easily have been lifted and DNA evidence gathered even by the likes of Cousin Vinny.

And yet, on January 17, 1995, the US Attorney will decline prosecution on every single case, hundreds of them. Because "most authors of threatening communications denied having made such a call . . . stated that they do not have control of their telephone on a 24-hour basis . . . were admonished and advised of Federal statues [sic] prohibiting such behavior . . . it was clear to investigators that most were elderly Cuban exiles that had little or very restricted mobility and were limited to their home environment, incapable of carrying out the threats"; therefore, "based on lack of physical evidence linking subscribers to the actual threats, subjects denied writing letters," and because "no statements contradicted their stories," prosecution will be declined after "consultation" with an unnamed FBI special agent (SA).

Six weeks later, March 1995, I will be attacked by a large crowd at Miami International Airport. Widely disseminated by media, details of the attack will be contained in FBI records. My choices midattack were: Board the plane that many attackers were preparing to board, be in a confined space alongside them? Board a plane that could already be, or soon be loaded with, explosives? Or go back to the terminal and face the rest of the mob?

The following month, marking my first anniversary of threats, a sticker bearing *Abajo Fidel / Frente Liberación Cubana* will be affixed to the window of Ira's study (no easy feat, given that to reach the windows one must climb a ladder or measure the height of Goliath). Soon after, a second such sticker will be affixed to my mother's car window. And soon after that, a man will drive up to the house and hand Maggie an envelope as she exits the courtyard. Thankfully, the envelope will contain no pipes, wires, or shrapnel. Just another threat. Details of those two incidents will also be contained in FBI files.

A second attack will occur at Miami International Airport, this time on arrival. FISTS FLY, the *Miami Herald* headlines will read.

Special Agent in Charge (SAC, MIAMI) will, on June 1, 1995, send the following memo to FBI Director, Headquarters, Domestic Terrorism Unit. "All logical investigation has been completed by Miami. Should the Dept. of Justice concur with US Attorney Miami, Headquarters is to advise Miami so that this matter may be placed in a closed status." And it will.

FBI Miami will, on April 30, 1996, wire FBI Director Louis Freeh the following details of a plot underway, provided by a confidential informant.

CONSPIRACY TO BOMB PERCEIVED SUPPORTERS
OF CUBAN GOVERNMENT.

SOURCE ▮▮▮▮▮ (RELIABLE) REPORTED ▮▮▮ ▮▮▮▮ EXPLOSIVES WOULD BE UTILIZED IN THE ASSASSINATION ATTEMPT OF SEV-ERAL CUBAN EXILES THAT ARE BELIEVED TO BE COLLABORATORS OR SYMPATHETIC OF THE CASTRO GOVERNMENT.

▮▮▮▮▮ STATED THAT HE AND HIS COLLABORATORS ARE VERY MUCH AGAINST THE ACTIVITIES OF SUCH INDIVIDUALS SUCH AS ▮▮▮▮▮▮▮, ▮▮▮▮▮▮▮, MAGDA MONTIEL DAVIS, AND OTHERS.

AT PRESENT TIME, IT APPEARS A GROUP OF INDIVIDUALS ACTU-ALLY INTENDS TO MANUFACTURE EXPLOSIVE DEVICES IN ORDER TO CARRY OUT THE ASSASSINATION OF MAGDA MONTIEL DAVIS, AND OTHERS.

30

MOTHER'S DAY

DAY 13 OF 3 (MAYBE 5)

———

Sades!" This morning I brighten. Sadie sits on the living room sofa, reminiscent of Katy, the same age, waiting for me to get home from a night out with Ira. I'd tiptoe through the front door before sunrise, when Katy would say, "Is this any time to get home?" and look at a pretend watch. "What are you doing up so early?" I ask Sadie.

She holds up a paper. "Mommy, why do you draw those things?" One of the drawings sent to me, sent to Ira, of me kneeling before Fidel, puckering thick-lipped kisses on his dick. I don't know how I could have left it out.

"I didn't draw it," is all I can say. I wake fully when in both the English and Spanish version of the *Herald*, I see MAGDA AND FIDEL—FIDEL'S OBJECTIVE, THAT THEY SHOULD KILL HER. By Roberto Luque Escalona, *escritor cubano*.

Ira calls. He was at the gym, at the drugstore, at the cleaners, what am I doing? Reading. And I give him a synopsis: If Fidel has me killed, it will give him more ammunition to attack *la mafia de Miami*. If *el exilio* kills me first, it will save Fidel the trouble. This I translate: "I can well imagine what they would do with Magda Montiel's cadaver. What Fidel would do, because it was he who ordered the sale of the videotape of the *cumbancha* ..."

"I hate him!" says Sadie. "The guy who wrote that." She stomps outside, and it's raining. I chase after her. "No!" She slaps at my arm: "Leave me alone!" and disappears into her Playskool dollhouse. It's thundering and the dollhouse is next to the pool. And there's lightning. But Sadie crouches further into the dollhouse to a place I cannot reach her. "No!" she says, each time with a slap at my extended arm.

How can I explain to her who this self-proclaimed *escritor cubano* is? Why the *Miami Herald* publishes what he writes? That I didn't know that she knew the words "cadaver," "assassination"? This is not the *Father Knows Best* episode I grew up watching, Robert Young talking a puffy-cheeked, pigtailed Cathy out of her dollhouse, making it all right.

This mother knows nothing.

————

I won't open the tiny gift envelope paper-clipped to the Mother's Day roses Ira sent me. I won't open the cellophane wrap squeezing life out of the roses. Poor roses. Set us free, they cry out. We promise to open big and red and beautiful.

From the corner of my eye, I see Ira looking at me looking at the roses. We cross paths in our living room and say nothing.

I am angry at Ira, again. I have to get to the office—Saturdays and Sundays are my best days to work. During the week, it's not so much the taking care of business, putting out fires, stopping deportations that jar my concentration. *That* I'm used to. It's taking care of death threats that permeate my everyday life—and now Ira has decided that this is the day to put his college LPs in order, their covers soggy and smelly after Hurricane Andrew.

"Wow, sweetie!" he calls out from his study. "Kids! Come look at this! Mississippi John Hurt, Joni Mitchell." We know. He got her to come to Berkeley right before she made it big, when he was president of the student union. And because he also got Bobby Seale to come to campus and the faculty was pissed that to attend, they too had to pass through metal detectors (the Black Panthers demanded it), he was not allowed to deliver the graduation speech as had all past presidents.

Phil Ochs, Mississippi John Hurt. Who cares? Not my world. And I can't just take off to the office, can't take off anywhere. He has to drive me.

————

Mother's Day and "Why is it Mother's?" I grump. "In Spanish, it's *El Día de las Madres. Madres.* In the plural." *Huh*, is all Ira says.

My Mother's Day presents: a homemade card authored by Sadie that she had everyone sign; my own Reebok step, and a step-class video to go with it. "Maggie's idea," Ira announces proudly. He took them Mother's Day shopping yesterday. "Mommy's staying home," he said when they asked, "so she can get her work done."

So she won't get shot—or blown up.

"I picked out the Reebok step," Maggie says quietly, "since I figured you won't . . . probably won't wanna go to Streetdance, for a while."

"Good job, Mags," I say, and turn back to my files.

"Just what Mom needs," says Paula. "Another video."

I work until the last minute, past the very last minute, prepping files, checking and rechecking: Passports? Birth, marriage, divorce certificates?—now called "dissolutions of marriage." And death, death certificates too? Yes, death too, and all must be originals. I-20s from the schools? Ditto—for the F-1 and M-1 students. I-797 Notices of Approval?—for the H-1B, L-1A visas. Alphabet soup. Slurped, digested, regurgitated. I look at my watch: 11:45 is my absolute cut-off time. My deadline. Must be off to Irene's—Ira's mother—by noon, the latest. Mustn't fall behind schedule. Or else. Or else Ira. He's hot, he's cold. And be late to his mother's house, he'll be a long time defrosting.

My mother shuffles into the kitchen eleven or so, debunking medical studies that old people sleep less with age. I walk to her, kiss her cheek, hand over a card with cash inside so she can give it to my kids and my sister's kids, play the Florida lottery, and buy cartons of cigarettes. No store-bought gift for her. (Not that I could have gone to the store, but I could have sent Ira). I've learned. For my mother, cash, only cash. Clothes? She'll hold them up, give them the scrutinizing eye and frown. Puckered hems— she will point—and stripes that don't match at the seams. "Americans don't know how to sew," she'll say. "Don't take *pride*." Not like when she used to sew. Used to before the tumor in her pituitary gland that left her fingers devoid of dexterity and one eye blind. Not like when she used to sew, she'll repeat, and then say, "I hated sewing." She'll say this every time.

No store-bought gifts for her anyway because my sister *si sabe, ella si sabe*, really knows how to buy for her. But this year, this *Día de las Madres*, my mother eased up on me and didn't go on about my sister and all my sister knows and all my sister can do.

Barely do we make it inside mother-in-law Irene's one-bedroom Miami Beach condo than she pipes up, "Is he giving you enough, honey?"

"Grandma!" Paula's golden-brown eyes alight, her cheeks flushed pink.

"No, Mommy needs to tell me, because if he's not, I'll whop him one." Thin, fuchsia-painted lips, teased-and-teased-again orange-red hair. "Sadie, Benny, Grandma bought you some rugelach and some babka. But first, a little nosh." Stacks, mounds, bowlfuls. Matzo ball soup, gefilte fish, brisket, kugel, candied carrots, everything on mirror-shiny platters.

"Irene," I say. "You use your best china?"

"What am I saving it for, honey? Here"—she points to a chicken's up-turned butt—"I made this just for you."

"I don't eat meat," I say. A déjà vu all over again.

"Oh." A look of surprise. "You don't eat meat?"

"Ma, you know she doesn't eat meat."

"But this is chicken, darling." She looks at Paula and Maggie, "Your mom needs some meat on her bones," wiggles her tush in the chair. "Now tell me. You girls have a fellah yet?"

"Irene!" I say.

"What?" A look of innocence. "I'm not a supposed to say that?"

"Girls don't need a fellow."

"A nice fellah," she continues, looking up at the girls. "So he can carry your pocketbook while you shop at Loehmann's."

Ira reaches for her plate. "Ma, that's enough, Ma."

"Just a slivah, Ikey. Just a slivah." She pulls back the plate.

We clear the dishes, everything back in neatly divided drawers, perfectly stacked cabinets. "*Look* at this house," Ira says. "Everything in its place. Now that's what I call—"

"I don't want to hear it, Ikey," Irene says. "Didn't you always say you wanted to marry a career woman? A career woman can't keep a perfect house too."

"Ma, we're nowhere near perfect. We need to get to zero before we can start the climb to perfect."

Irene hands me a silver-etched tea server. "Take this home with you, honey. It belonged to my mother Sadie." Last time, she gave me an antique opal bracelet, and the time before that, a string of pearls Ira's dad Benny had given her. "No, Irene, you keep it." She flaps down her hand. "What am I saving it for, sweetheart? The years," she says, squinting out the sliding glass doors, "Where did they go?" She walks us to the front door, long necklace of oversized aqua beads swishing between big, cone-shaped breasts. "Ma," Ira says. "You okay, Ma? You need anything?"

"Yeah. Vitamin F."

Paula says, "Grandma!" Maggie puts a hand to her mouth.

Irene leans down to Ben and Sadie. But she doesn't have to lean far. The proverbial high heels add height to her 4'10" frame, but not much.

Out the door now. Almost. Irene turns my face to her. "Why are you wearing your glasses, honey? And not your contact lenses? You're so much prettier without your glasses."

"Oh, I ah, am about to get on a plane. The flying—dries out my eyes."

She stands in the doorway, watches us walk down the long stretch of corridor. Then, "You tell those messhugeneh Cubans," she yells, "to go fuck themselves."

31

F = FBI

DAY 14 OF 3 (MAYBE 5)

———

Monday, May 9, which happens to be Ira's birthday, and yesterday, Mother's Day, and I spent it on a plane to Mexico with my clients in search of their visas. Ciudad Juarez, the hot place to come for visas, hot as in the US consular officers aren't terribly abusive, as in most other US consular posts. Not hot as in illegal, oh god no never illegal. Especially now. I sit outside the consulate, my butt hard on a concrete planter with no plants, only desert sand and dry soil gone dead under the hot Mexican sun.

The little Chiclets girl hovers as she usually does, distended belly and dirty, brown bare feet, this time selling not just Chiclets, the pink and the yellow kind, but balancing a rusty, peeling white tray of *café con leches*.

It's strange sitting here. Things are normal.

Sometimes I plunge on normally and forget the big changes. Like the two foreign students at Miami-Dade College behind me in line early this morning. Instantly, they knew who I was. "Oh, you're the lawyer who—"

Yes, the lawyer who, what? Who takes care of her clients. Who thinks—or doesn't think, depending—she takes care of her children. Who has at least one kid belly flop onto her bed most mornings and lift the Tempur-Pedic pillows she stacks over her head. And who thinks about getting up but can't. For a long time, she can't. Yesterday, it took her an hour and twenty minutes to get up. Mostly, she lies in bed and marvels about the new lying position she just conjured up that makes her feel cushioned and loved and childlike. Then she does, finally lifts herself up—one two three, she says but not aloud—rolls to one side, thrusts her torso to sitting position, belts out an internal Tarzan call, all the while thinking, *No, keep going, up up forward, do not go back down.* And she shuffles across the living room, the dining room, the family room into the French country kitchen. And has a hearty breakfast of two aspirin.

And then she looks at the refrigerator door no longer taped with her Streetdance schedule but with all the phone numbers in black, Magic-Markered letters of Key Biscayne, city, and county police. And before her husband drives her to work, she'll peek in the Filofax organizer a client gave her years ago—Carlos Something-or-other, she used to remember but now she forgets—the Filofax organizer with her name gold-plated and engraved with a comma and Esquire after her name, the organizer where now B = Bomb Squad and F = FBI.

———

It's hot and cold sitting here. The place brings back memories of coming with Elisa—the one overnight trip for which she agreed to leave her husband and child, then mentioned casually that her husband thought she should be paid extra for her day and a half away from home and family, but how many times am I going to remind myself of that?

And memories too of calling the office to report success. All the clients, every single one of them, got their visas, and the women in the office, every one of them, Mily, Cary, Isabel, Barbara, all of them, ecstatic. And I felt cushioned and loved and protected and safe.

———

Ira was good about my leaving despite Mother's Day, despite his birthday. But he's hot. And he's cold. Sometimes he gets off on a show of support here and there: from Aruca his client-friend, from fellow attorneys (all non-Cuban, most non-Miami); from big names, good names: the writer/feminist Kate Millett and TransAfrica's Randall Robinson; from worldwide media coverage (though when Ira heard The Kiss was on *NBC Nightly News*, he did say, "Congratulations, dear, now you're famous," in a nondescript—questionable?—tone). When he says I "acted like a jerk" though, I wonder whether he means I was sexual toward Fidel. I didn't mean to be. Or is it that he's irreversibly angry and unforgiving? Or that the sexist epithets are leaving a mark on him? Sometimes he's quick to point out it was dumb. That's the word he uses, "dumb." "You couldn't have picked a worse choice of words. One sentence alone wouldn't have been as bad, but together . . ."

Friday night, after I met with clients past 9 PM—no Shabbat dinner again—finally I shot back. "I don't *feel* dumb." He said he didn't fault me for *feeling* that way. About Fidel, the revolution. But that I didn't have to *say* it. "Didn't you know? That the cameras were there?"

Yes, I knew. "Didn't you know? That your words would be *spread*?" When he said that, I had a sudden urge to laugh, visualizing the spreading of ashes from an urn, a bronze one with my name engraved in gold swirly script, ashes spreading like desert sand off a cliff into the mountain wind, huge rocks and crashing ocean waves beneath an enigmatic and hooded Meryl Streep in *The French Lieutenant's Woman*, Ira's and my first movie date in '81.

Still, I can't say I wish it had been different. Were this my other life, I'd still be bogged down with staff, overstaffing, really; my vulnerability, weakness, not letting anyone go despite the too heavy payroll. With the pseudoacademics, wannabee intellectuals of the CCD. Perfunctory commitments, obligations that did nothing but weigh me down, *glub glub*, a ship's anchor around my neck. Now, it's as if something, someone—call it God, the universe, my guardian angel—cleansed me of the negative forces around me. Now, I focus on clients and family as never before. I'll never humiliate Mami again and have buried, I think, the pain of Dad's emotional neglect. Now I can pass on *real* values to my kids.

Maybe I'll have a delayed reaction. Maybe I'm okay right now, this minute, because my weight has dropped so much. Or maybe it's the overdose of *café con leches* from the little Chiclets girl that brightens my spirits so, then plummets me to the depths of I don't know what. Meryl Steep's cliff, maybe.

———

Inside the cold visa room, I tell my client, Esperanza ("Hope," she reminds me), "Do not stand in that line." I point. "Actually," I add, "stand right here, *don't* move." I draw an imaginary line. A guard then flips through Mohammad's Iranian passport, signals to him to stand in the line of Mega-Bitch Officer. I pull him into another line. Mega-Bitch Officer raises her head, motions at me sergeant-like. Obediently, I walk to her window. She flaps her *bembas* up down, up down. "Excuse me?" I say daintily, leaning my ear to the small, grilled circle on the thick glass dividing us. "I said, 'You are *not* to control which lines your clients stand on.'" In a tone of disbelief, "Oh," I say. "I wouldn't do that." She sneers. I wait, I watch. She walks to the back. I walk to Mohammad, barely moving my lips. "Go to the bathroom—" I say. His thick, hairy eyebrows curl in all directions. "Go," I say. "Take off your jacket, wait a while, come back, stand in this *other* line." A slight bend of my head. From him, a look of terror. "Just do what I say." And he does. But when I scan the room for my clients, Esperanza/ Hope, is back in Mega-Bitch Officer's line. I take long, determined steps her way. "*What* is the matter with you?" I shake her arm. "Did I not tell you not to stand in this line? Not to move?" She squeaks, "But *ah-tohr-nee*, the guard, he push me here." "Well, I'm pushing you *there*." And I do, push her, to Mohammad's line. Mega-Bitch Officer is still in the back—probably out to lunch—so I'm safe. I find an empty seat in one of the endless rows of chairs, plop onto its creaking plastic. Mohammad now back, I stand before him. "You take good care of your clients, Miss Magda."

And I forgive even Hope.

It's cold and hot here. Inside the grey visa room, the air blasts full speed. Outside, the sun exhausts me, but strangely, I shiver with cold. Strange that cold is hot and hot is cold.

The little Chiclets girl comes by again. I don't tell her I gave already this morning. I give to her again. She is silent and inexpressive, like the beggar woman in those years of long ago.

It's 2 PM and still no visas. And Joe Gonzalez, chubby and sweet-smiling Joe Gonzalez, the nonimmigrant visa section supervisor, is not even here today. I asked first thing this morning, just in case. "On detail," the guard said. So, if a problem emerges, who can I turn to? Still, I'm not scared like I was on earlier trips. I wouldn't loosen up until all of my clients' passports were safe and visa-stamped in my hands.

This is nothing compared to what I've been through.

Awful turbulence on the flight back to Miami. And all my Hail Marys and Our Fathers didn't work today. Maybe they won't work now?

I couldn't get the visa for Mohammad.

Are you testing me, God?

I won't give up and I won't give in. Is this what you want of me?
Or do you want me to break down, apologize, full of remorse?
What are you telling me, God?
Give me a sign.

God, the turbulence, it lets up, then starts up again.
Okay, the pilot sounds calm and casual. It should be smooth in a bit,
he says.
I wonder if I needed this to *humble* me.
It's now been two weeks.
What is it that I'm afraid of? The pain? The gagging, choking? The panic
at not being able to get out?

THANK YOU, GOD.
It stopped. The turbulence.

32

EXIT VISA

DAY 23 OF 3 (MAYBE 5)

———

Oh God, should I even be talking to them? Miriam just came to me, whispered, "The Cuban consul called from DC."

"Why are you whispering?" I looked about me exaggeratedly to make my point. "It's only you and me here." But I got her point. I walk into my tiny office, shut the door, reach for a quarter. No. If you use a payphone or your sister's car phone or the fax line, it will look even worse. Oh Brother, Big Brother. Our regular phone line, I decide—and line 1 at that—punch-dial the Cuban Interests Section in DC. But why am I leaning into the phone, crouching, squeezed as if I were *Get Smart*'s Agent 99? (short hair, cute straight-banged cut, long legs, thin frame. One and two, I could pull off; three and four, no.)

"*Sí,*" I breathe into the mouthpiece, "*es Magda Montiel devolviendo la llamada de . . .*" Hugo Yedra. Yes indeed, the Cuban consul. He picks up right away. "Magda."

I press the phone to my ear and mouth, swivel my chair to face the back corner. As if that could make a difference!

Yedra rattles off a list of my clients' names. All my exit-visa requests, granted.

"Oh," is all I manage to say. Then I thank him awkwardly, my tone pitched high and low, replete with childlike cracks. Cuba prohibits those who fall into certain categories from leaving for a certain amount of time: medical doctors for five years, because Cuba can't pay for their education and then be left with no one to take care of her people; those who defect while on a mission representing Cuba—"defectors" to the US, *desertores* to Cuba; those privy to sensitive information, such as those high in the

Communist Party, and others. The cases I presented to an official while in Havana fit into every one of the prohibited categories, but I thought, worth a try.

The Cuban consul explains the procedure. I take robotic notes. Wait a few days for the news of the approvals to reach the immigration offices of the municipalities where each client resides, then a *tarjeta blanca*—the exit visa—will be issued to every one of them. Green card here, white card there, must keep all these colors and ins and outs in order. Then I realize it's my turn to speak. "They should be out . . . when?"

"Before the month is out. In a matter of days. Two, three weeks at most."

"Oh, wow."

He laughs. At what? At my Americaness.

"Okay, Magda." Not okay, the Yankee pronunciation. *O-kah.*

"O-kah," I say. "Please thank—" thank who? *Ay Dios mío*—"whoever is responsible."

"*Tus gracias serán comunicadas.*"

I'm sure they *will* be communicated, thank you. I picture Fidel's Pope-like singular nod.

"*Oye, Magda,*" the consul says, "I have a funny story to tell you."

Yeah. I have one too.

"I was just in Cuba and Fraga"—Alfonso Fraga, the chief of the Cuban Interests Section, who was on the flight back with me from Havana. But who is *us?*—"was telling us that while he was here at the Interests Section, *la compañera* told him Magda Montiel was on the line and he picked up the phone: '*Hola, mi vida,*' and some woman screamed '*¡Viejo, maricón, hijo de puta! ¡Ah, sí! A Magda si le recibes la llamada . . .*' And still Fraga thought it was you. He said he thought, 'Why is Magda calling me *viejo maricón?*'" Old faggot.

I chuckle. It is not until I hang up that I register the significance of the news. A keen awareness that I'm about to deliver life-changing news. I think of the medical doctor who while on a medical mission overseas, had . . . lest I take sides, let's just say "flew the coop." He'd been in to see me about his wife, also a medical doctor, and two daughters back in Cuba. Had no money to pay me, *ni un centavo,* but I'd taken on the case anyway.

But dessert comes last. First, the Big Feast. The Feast of Revenge: The young Cuban mother who'd come to me to get her toddler son out of the island. *Dos añitos,* she'd said. Just two years old, "and they took him from me."

They didn't take him from you, I said from inside my head. You opted to leave the island and your son as well. But along with the medical doctor and six others, I presented her case to a Cuban official while at the conference. Then, right after The Kiss, the young mother left a message on our answering machine. She didn't want a *comunista* for a lawyer. Not even a free one.

So now I call. An elderly sounding woman answers. I identify myself, remind her of my mission to get the woman's son out of Cuba. "Every case, every single client on that list, got approved. It's too bad she chose to fire me as her lawyer. Her little boy would be here with her. Within the month."

"*Ay 'mija*," the woman cries that endemic *vieja cubana* whine. "*Es que ella esta enferma de los nervios con el trauma de la separación.*" *Enferma de los nervios*, my ass. A nervous breakdown, she says, a "sickness of the nerves." The trauma of separation.

"Is there anything you can do?" the woman says. "To put her *niñito* back on the list?"

"Nope." I say this with great satisfaction. "When she fired me as her lawyer, I asked Cuba that her son be taken off the list." True. But I could easily put him back.

"*Ay 'mija—*"

Ay 'mija, nada. I hang up midsentence, leave her hanging, but in Spanish, it sounds better: *Su palabra en el aire.* Leave her word in the air. And don't think about the awfulness of what I have done.

———

Now I call the medical doctor. "Granted," I squeal, a second after his *Oigo* greeting. "The exit visas, granted."

There is silence.

"For all three."

"Are you sure." His voice is devoid of tone, emotion. It smacks of annoyance.

"Yes! I just spoke to the Cuban consul himself, not ten minutes ago."

"Well, I don't know. With these people, you don't know what to believe." A long pause, as if measure for measure, he weighs his words when speaking to me. "If it's a trick, a set-up."

"It's no trick." There's childlike hurt, defensiveness in my voice.

Finally, "I would like to ask you not to divulge, discuss my case with anyone."

"Divulge?"

"Yes. I read in the newspaper something about your helping the family of a medical doctor get their visas, and I don't want . . . *no quiero prob-lemas, aquí, con esta comunidad y con la revalidación de mi licencia*." Wants no problems with the community here. And no problems revalidating his medical license.

"It was an article. That I wrote for the *Sun-Sentinel*. The Fort Lauderdale newspaper. Before I left for Cuba. Before any of this happened." I note apology in my voice. But that's it; I only note and still I plunge on. "I didn't even use your name. Nobody will know."

I hang up. Understanding I should be outraged, but calm, the strange placid acceptance of a servile sellout.

33

ORDER

It's all about order, I decided, life in place amid all I can't control.

As soon as Ira leaves on Saturdays—every weekend he takes the kids so that I can get work done—I dig in, the vortex of a tornado, eye of a hurricane, sifting through files, checking every sentence, word, signing off on stacks of cases. Quickly. Not like before. Not like before, when it took me two, three weeks to check a case, return it to staff for corrections, additions. Always corrections, additions; cases were never perfectly (many times not even adequately) prepared.

Not like before. So now clients can't complain. At least not about getting their cases filed. After the cases, I go crazy with the house, cleaning out clutter. I heard Mami on the telephone the other day with my sister. *"Tu hermana esta más loca que un chivo. Le ha dado por limpiar."* Crazier than a goat, your sister. She's taken up housecleaning.

It began with my closet, tossing out tightly packed rows of Madonna-style lace-over-denim jeans and palazzo pants I didn't even remember I owned; don't think I even wore. Then I cleared out entire shelves of Jane Fonda leotards and old Reebok baby pink and baby blue sneakers that had no support and made my fallen arches fall further. But they were cute and everyone at Streetdance wore them. The same shoes I wore—that I do remember—agonizing over Ira, all he'd done those early years, all the times he'd hurt me. Three- to four-hour daily bouts at Streetdance, trying hard to exorcise my heart, Ira-free.

Last Saturday, I organized my jewelry drawer, paired earring with earring, dragged the English planter by the bay window, clipped the yellow leaves off the *malanguitas* in dire need of water and sun. I wanted an extra day of cleaning, even just a few hours of cleanup, a wild frenzied cleanup, like a pregnant woman who "nests" right before she gives birth, like I did with Katy.

It's all about order, I decided, life in place amid all I can't control. I read that once, the thoughts of a woman with terminal cancer, at peace with herself.

————

D-Day. Just as Tuesday is trash pickup day, so is this Tuesday, the day the ex-staff will pick up their things. Where? Where can they pick up their things? Isabel asked Miriam. On the sidewalk, I told Miriam to tell her. I throw their *mierditas* into old cardboard boxes, seal, then reopen one to throw in a note to Janet: "Your unauthorized use of my American Express to buy yourself a Mont Blanc fountain pen and a bouquet of flowers for your mother is a *criminal* offense." I don't sign the note, end it instead with a forward slash.

I warn Otto, who I summoned for the event, "Do *not* be nice. Just stand there"—I stand, a Buckingham Palace guard—"cross your arms, make sure they take everything, and leave."

He goes, he comes back.

Was he nice?

Yes, he was nice.

Why was he nice?

"*Porque son damas.*" How could he *not* be nice? he says. That's the way he is, and again he says, "*Son damas.*"

Ladies. They are ladies. And he, what? Sir Lancelot?

Two police officers were there, he mentions.

"Police officers?"

"Amador Diaz."

"Oh. That's nice. Isabel's boyfriend. In police uniform?"

Yes, in police uniform.

"Nice," I say again. "In uniform. On City of Miami time." I should report him, the boyfriend. "And the other?"

"Detective Diaz." Then he says, "The two looked exactly alike."

"Detective Diaz?" I look in my address book. Detective Diaz, all right. He's supposed to be working on *my* case. Protecting me. And he's Isabel's boyfriend's brother. I remember now, Isabel's boyfriend's brother was a detective. "Wonderful," I say. "Small world," I say.

34

FLYING CARPET

DAY 33 OF 3 (MAYBE 5)

———

Down the jet bridge, into the plane, trying to balance myself and my baggage through the skinny aisle. First class, business class, I do a sideways crab walk into coach, the aisle skinnier still, all the while grumbling, *Cubana de Aviación* doesn't have first class, poor class, beggar man, thief, when suddenly, Ira. "Sweetie, come back."

I do an about-face.

"We're in first class." A sheepish look. "I got us upgraded."

"What kind of socialist is that?"

"A tired one, sweetie, what can I tell you?"

Roll call: Paula, Maggie, Sadie, Ben; Katy too, home from Wellesley for summer break, the seven of us filling an entire aisle and then some. No-nonsense black canvas duffle, that's Paula's; Katy's KMD-embroidered J.Crew backpack in still perfect condition since middle school; Maggie's last-minute, thrown-together nest of a mess; Sadie's pink Little Mermaid carry-on; Ben's pocketful of T-Rexes. The seven of us en route to the annual immigration lawyers' conference, this year in San Francisco.

"What's the matter?"

I pretend not to hear him. Ira.

"So, what've you got to say for yourself?" Trick question. Used to trip me up some very long years ago, but no more.

I take my seat. "Why'd you say hello to Luis Cordero?" The best defense, an offense, especially with Ira Kurzban.

"I *didn't* say hello. He said hello to me."

"Well, why'd you answer *his* hello—so nicety-nice?" Luis Cordero and his law partner, Eugenio "Gene" Hernandez, fellow immigration lawyers.

"They stopped talking to me. I've known them for years, and they stopped talking to me." *Click click*, my seat belt. "And right before we got on the plane, Marisol told me they chastised her for talking to me." Marisol used to work for me. On my return from Cuba, she volunteered to help pump out my cases.

"Luis? And Gene? They're not even political." A flip of the head. "But they're Cuban."

"Yeah, well, neither was some of my staff—*ex*-staff—Cuban. Janet, Cary—"

Luis and Gene enter the plane. Luis smiles at Ira. I look at Ira. If he smiles back—

He does. A tiny curve of the lips, but a smile nonetheless.

I lean in to the children. "That," I point to Luis, "is what a fascist looks like."

"Shh, *Mo-ohm*!" Maggie looks behind her. Paula reaches under her seat. Sadie looks up at me with silent eyes. I avert mine from Katy's; she is watching me intently as if processing, what? My stability, reliability. My motherliness.

"Sweetie," Ira says, "you're losing it." Then, "You're becoming just like them."

———

Our thirteenth conference together. As I lay in bed this morning, I harked back to those early years, how I'd seethe in silent fury because Ira wasn't *with* me. After each session, colleagues would stop him, relishing his scholarly slickness, his "take" on precedents, legislative updates, due process issues. And he would light up with the complexities of law, but also the adulation, and I was left to go back to the room by myself (not that I let on about my childlike feelings of abandonment).

"One, two—" Ira and Ben hammer their fists—"three! Paper, scissors, rock!"

"How're things, sweetie?" Ira faces Ben, his back faces me. "At the office, I mean."

I shrug. "I like doing the math. Payroll. Receivables. Gives me a sense of—" What? I forget. Just like that, I forget.

"Scissors, Dad!" Ben cackles, throwing back a bubbled head of curls.

"Sometimes I work so hard, so long, I lose perspective. I have to check every single case, every single letter. Why?"

But he doesn't ask.

"Are you even listening?"

"Dad, *play* with me."

"Hold on, Ben," and "Yes, listening."

"Because," I say, "who else is going to do it? It's not like before. When I had Elisa. Plus, now there's even more pressure to pull through for the clients, get them results. If I get a case denied, first thing they'll think—say—is: 'It's because she's *controversial*.'"

"Sweetie, every lawyer gets a case denied here and there. Even me."

"I love how Elisa and *husband* aren't coming to the conference this year. Now that it comes out of *their* pocket. Imagine if I would've said, 'Elisa, sorry, but this year—'"

"Forget this year. When *could* you afford it?"

"Never. And still I paid for her. Imagine, though, saying no trip. She would've come down on me, hard—bad financial planning, bad . . ." I miss her. "I'll be right back." I go to the bathroom, pat—more like slap—my face, the same way Mirtha de Perales would slap her aging self on Havana television; my aunt Tíita slapping as well; Mami behind Tíita telling us, *Tu tía esta loca*. It didn't matter that Tíita was well within earshot.

"Anyway." Back in my seat now. "Maybe it's—"

"No, Dad," says Ben. "Say it after me. *Ar-kee-op-terics*. Archaeopteryx."

"Maybe it's better I don't—" I look at Ira. "Ikey?"

He's asleep.

Maggie said I looked better this morning; what did I do? Sleep, I said, forced myself to sleep. And washed my hair. I lean over. "Mags, you like my hair?"

She shrugs. "It's all right."

"I'm glad I like it again."

Silence.

"Would've been a mistake to cut it."

Sadie sings "A Whole New World."

"You know why she's singing that?" Maggie says to Paula. "'Cause of Aladdin. He and Jasmine sang that as they flew off on their magic carpet."

"A flying magic carpet," I say. "That's what I need."

"Oh, Mom, you're so dramatic."

———

"Mmm," Sadie says, "This OJ is good, Mom." *Oh Jayee*. "You should've had some OJ." She extends the cup my way. Oh god. Two bagels (and a third inside my carry on). Two skim-milk cappuccinos. And it's only 10:30. This morning, 136 lbs. Two mornings ago, I was 130 and a half. Right after Havana, I was 121. And happy. Bomb scares, death threats, but skinny. And happy. Now my skirts are too short because my stomach is so big. It's when I get home late at night that I eat, even though I started the day not with 1 or 2 but 3 jumbo-size bagels. That Ira gets while I sit in the car behind tinted glass.

"Here." Sadie puts her plastic cup to my lips. "Taste it," the foamy yellow of the OJ marking a smiley-face smile clear up to her cheeks. I do the motherly thing, I taste it.

After a while, "I'm so mad at myself," I tell Ira. "I sent Alfredo Duran a note, telling him he can start sending me cases again." The lawyer once opposite Ira in the case of the fourteen-year-old Cuban girl who'd sailed to Miami on a raft with her eighteen-year-old boyfriend, who the court said could stay in Miami with him and not return to her parents in Cuba. Duran, also ex-Bay of Pigs invader; ex-son-in-law to former Cuban President Carlos Prío Socarrás; ex-chair of the Florida Democratic Party. For years, Duran has been a steady source of referrals of very wealthy Latin American clients.

"Why can't Duran send you cases?"

"He *can* send me cases. But I wrote him that he *could*."

"So, what's wrong with that?"

"Because. The CCD, remember? I got kicked out. And because he wimped out with the press. Last thing I said to him that day at my sister's—when he *insisted* I fax him my *written* resignation—never mind I told him I had no staff, no typewriter, no fax machine, nada. Anyway, last thing I said was 'All I ask is when you speak to the press, speak about my freedom to speak.' And you know what he said when I called him on it later? 'I *have*, but you know how the press is. They just print what they want.' Cuban Committee for Democracy; democracy my ass."

"What do you want, sweetie? He's Cuban. None of these guys have any balls."

Except your husband.

"Except your husband. And listen, speaking of sending you cases. When you get to the conference, don't start talking to everyone about what's happened. They're all gunna wanna know, but that's only 'cause they're curious."

"No. They should all know—"

"No one wants to send business to someone with *problems*."

"The world should know."

"So, who are you now? Jackie Kennedy?"

"I *love* Jackie Kennedy. Love that she married Onassis. Did whatever the fuck she wanted. Not what the Kennedys and you Americans wanted. Can't believe she's terminal." Thirty-three thousand feet, little trembles, big jerks. "Can't believe I lowered myself like that with Duran." We fly through walls of clouds. "Anyway. I asked Mara to go to the next immigration luncheon with me. So I can show 'em. Introduce her." I extend my arm. "'My associate.'"

"That's right, sweetie, you show 'em. Show 'em all, all those bastards." We bounce in unpredictable rhythm. "I can't wait for my wife to show 'em when she *shows* up at the luncheon with her new bodyguard."

"Otto?"

"No, sweetie. Bond. James Bond."

"Sure hope Otto at least knows to leave Ringo at home."

"Why, sweetie? Why would you want Otto to leave Ringo at home? What's so unusual about a lawyer of my stature having his lawyer-wife walk in the immigration lawyers' luncheon with her bodyguard and a Rottweiler?"

———

Flick, flick, my cuticles. Scrape, pick, rip off little threads of skin.

"Magda." Ira takes my hand, not in an *I Wanna Hold Your Hand* way. He slides his glasses to the tip of his nose, brings my hand to his eyes. "What's the matter with your fingers?"

"Stop." I pull away. "It's from all the cleaning I do."

"Yeah, right. Come up with a better one."

"Nothing's the matter. I'm overdue for a manicure. The girl who does my nails, she told me not to dare show up at the salon, not even to call her. Said she'd call me about coming over, and when she didn't call, I figured, well, she's Cuban, her husband and in-laws are Cuban, they probably wouldn't let her come."

"Why does it have to be her?"

"Because." I thrust my face at him. "Because the last one used to dig the dirt out from under my toenails and then put it to her nose and smell it."

"Sweetie!"

"I don't want someone smelling my dirt."

"Yeah, well, it's a little late for that."

"And this one digs deep. She goes under my toenails, pulls out all the dead skin—"

"I can dig deep."

"This is serious."

"This is serious too." Then, as if speaking to himself: "Speaking of *dead* skin—"

"Anyway, it's not like I can just go anywhere else, to another salon, *now*." I raise my leg, lift my long, peasant skirt above the knee. "And my legs are getting hairier and hairier."

"So? Shave 'em."

"She doesn't shave, Daddy," Sadie says. "Mommy *waxes* at Toni & Guy."

"Ah aah," Ira singsongs. "What kind of socialist is that?"

"A Frida Kahlo one." I pull back my hair—"Look at my eyebrows"—daub my upper lip—"my mustache. Frida Kahlo."

"So?" He pats his belly. "I look like Diego Rivera. We'll be a pair, sweetie. We're a pair anyway. Right, Sadie?" He licks my nose. "You're beautiful, *Doctora* Davis." What clients from Ibero-American countries call lawyers. "Extra pounds and all. I like you like this. You feel better. More"—he pinches my side—"cushiony." A pause. "And hairier."

CNN flashes on the overhead screen. "Oh my god, Ikey. Can you imagine if they play The Kiss?" But it's Jackie instead. Jackie, dead. Who used the Camelot fairy tale to reinvent her husband's legacy—not the womanizing Roman Catholic husband with mob ties who lied about US orchestration of the Bay of Pigs. Maybe she did it for her children. Or maybe for herself. Good for her. Jackie, dead, days after taking a walk in Central Park with longtime Jewish companion, he steadying her, tenderly adjusting her scarf.

"If Kennedy's assassination was today, you know what the media would focus on?" I say. "Her trying to crawl out the back of that convertible as soon as the first shot was fired."

"Just like you, dear. You'd be like, 'Nice knowin' ya and throw my brains back at me." A hurling motion. "'*You* figure out how to put 'em back in yourself, buddy. I'm outta here.' I just know, somebody's gunna take a shot at you and hit me instead."

———

On the descent. Ben connects constellations of stars on his travel game pad. Big Dipper, Little Dipper. "Sweetie," says Ira, "set your clock back."

"Three hours?"

"No. Six weeks."

Splat. We land. San Francisco. "Mommy." Benny's eyes, a halo of wonder. "How come when we land here, nobody claps?"

"That's because we're landing in the US, Benny. Not Cuba."

"Sweetie."

"Hmm?"

"Have you been back to the gym?"

"To Streetdance?"

"Yes. Streetdance. What else is there besides Streetdance?"

"Not yet. I will, though."

"You'll feel better, when you do."

"Why? I'm fine." And as our entourage of children and J.Crews and pocketful of T-Rexes exit the plane, I call out to Ira, some long steps ahead, "I'm fine." I catch up to him. "Perfectly fine."

Made it back to the room by 9:30 after my breakfast meeting with other panel members. In five hours, I am to speak to hundreds of immigration lawyers. I spread out my notes, rewrite everything neatly and in outline form:

    I. Exclusion and Deportation
       A. Relief:
          1. Political Asylum
             a. Well-founded Fear of Persecution on account of:
                i. race
                ii. religion
                iii. national origin
                iv. membership in a particular social group

And what else? Mustn't forget:

                v. political opinion.

I don't want Ira to see me put so much into it, so on his way out to his next *something*, I ask casually, Will he take a quick look at my notes?

He can't, he says, and the phone rings and I pick it up and it's "Hold for President Aristide, *s'il vous plaît*," so, of course, for this Ira does stay, and now the phone doesn't stop ringing and now I'm *Madame This* and *Madame That* and would I kindly ask *Monsieur Kurzban.* . . . What monsieur? He's no monsieur, he's a fat little Jewish guy from Brooklyn and fuck all these *Madames* and *mercis* and it's "Hold for President Aristide" again and I can't concentrate.

So. The breakfast meeting. The immigration officer on our panel, Skerrett, was nice enough looking and affable (even if he does work for the government). I'd worried: Might he refuse to be on the same panel with me? What then? Bow out quietly? Vociferously protest, let loose the Cuban *chusmeria* in me? But then the media would catch wind of it, the news would reach my clients, confirming what I suspect they suspect: *She's no good as an immigration lawyer any more, a high-ranking immigration official refused to sit with her on a panel*, and there goes my life's work. But, no. I worried for no good reason.

So now Ira hangs up with his third call with President Aristide and tells me *now* he can help me with my talk. I tell him to just leave the room, take Ben with him, and let me be.

Every speaker was to have submitted an article for publication, and given the death threats and all else, Ira volunteered to write it for me. "Will take me just an hour or two," he said. Would have taken me an entire day. More than an entire day. But he missed the deadline. Overlooked it, he said. "Sorry, sweetie. Overwhelmed." I was ticked off but powerless to say anything.

When he comes back, I am in bed. I get under the covers when I hear the door.

He asks, am I okay?

Yes, just tired.

Am I *sure* I'm okay?

Yes. And no, I don't want to go downstairs to the lawyers' reception.

He shows me a draft from our colleague-friend Denyse Sabagh, soliciting contributions from association members for a one-page ad in the *Miami Herald* supporting my freedom to speak.

"No!" I spring up. "The letter shouldn't say 'Magda and Ira *want*' or 'It's Magda and Ira's wish.'"

He shrugs. "I think it's okay, sweetie," but pencils it out. He leaves. After a while, he calls. He spoke to Denyse; she'll make the changes. *Now* will I come downstairs?

I tell him it's nice to be in the room, alone.

I rehearse my talk once, twice before the mirror. Delete, add, draw arrows across the page: *Deportation, political persecution, asylum.*

Ira is worried it's getting to me. "Psychological terrorism," he said.

"That's always been their MO. If they can't break you economically, they do it psychologically."

Still, I imagine Ira filing for divorce, fighting for custody of the children. I could never get a fair shake in Miami, that's for sure.

———

I go downstairs well before my talk. But who walks ahead of me but the Three Amigos: Luis Cordero, Gene Hernandez, and now, Raul Javier Sanchez de Varona—RJSdeV. A letter from RJSdeV awaited me when I arrived from Havana. It was postmarked April 25, 1994, the same day that the seconds-long video clip of me and Fidel was first played on every South Florida TV station. The day that I ran along the Malecón seawall and sang *Nosotros* and danced with Ive, unaware. Dictaphone to his mouth, "I denounce . . . condemn you," he wrote. "Your hands are now dirty with the blood of proud martyrs whose only crime was to stand up for what they believed. . . . You are totally unqualified to become an immigration judge, as you so desperately are seeking to become." I foul shot the letter into the trash.

RJSdeV wrote Ira. Ira wrote back. "My wife's statements stand, and she will either explain it or not in the future. As a lawyer, you should be more concerned about the protection of constitutional rights than the condemnation of any statement. Instead, you simply followed the media. Why have you remained silent while persons engaged in physical violence against me and my wife, simply for something Magda said? You are more concerned about freedom in Cuba than in Miami, and that, for a lawyer or anyone, is not acceptable."

I marveled at Ira's use of the possessive—*my* wife, which I interpreted as *mi mujer*, my woman. It rang more sexual to me than sexist. And at his affirmation too of not just my actions but my autonomy. But "Why'd you write back?" is all I said. "He's a lightweight, a nobody."

"Because. He's a fellow lawyer."

"You know who he is? That *comemierda* with the short neck and barrel chest who hasn't been out of law school long enough to realize he's as unimportant as the rest of us."

"Oh? That guy?"

"Yeah, that guy. Such a long, fancy name for such a piece of shit."

That same day, several messages from *Exito* magazine lay untouched on my desk—about my application for immigration judge, Miriam's hurried scroll read. But the call from EOIR, the board that decides our clients' appeals, that one I did take. On the line was its director, Chris Grant. Their offices, he said, were inundated with letters, faxes, phone calls—"a campaign," he called it, "vehemently opposing your imminent appointment to immigration judge." Was I still interested in the position? He sounded demoralized and embarrassed. I told him he could take my name off the list. "It's okay, Chris, truly it is." He was relieved but profusely apologetic.

At Ira's suggestion, I'd applied for the position while pregnant with Ben. True, five kids *was* a lot, especially with the coming of Ben so soon after Sadie. No pressures of running a practice. And with an 8–4 schedule, time for the kids, even a higher, a steady, salary. EOIR invited me to interview. I was pleased, though surprised. I'd envisioned a roomful of government yes-men scrutinizing my application. Kurzban's wife, an immigration judge? Kurzban who's always suing the government? The missus holding a not-too-kosher political opinion on Cuba? Who had the audacity to lead an aggressive, offensive (albeit destined to fail) campaign against congresswoman Ileana Ros-Lehtinen? But then came the call from Chris Grant, and I realized I did have a shot at becoming an immigration judge, maybe becoming the *mommy* I'm expected to be.

In a few years, after a series of mishaps with the law that finds RJSdeV disbarred and selling real estate instead, he will have a change of heart about Cuba—that is to say, investment opportunities in Cuba—and will go on record about all there is to gain in the no-longer-forbidden land that is Cuba. And Luis Cordero too will have a change of heart about shunning me (presumably a change of heart as well about chastising those who don't) after a good-paying client is in need of a lawyer with connections to Cuba. Luis Cordero will call my office time and again in fruitless effort to talk to me. Gene Hernandez will tell Ira that he "feels very bad about Magda." Talk to her, Ira will say, "but I have to warn you, my wife doesn't forget—or forgive." Which will leave me thinking.

―――――――

I walk the long conference aisle head on, no stopping. Don't look right, don't look left. Will they or won't they? The Three Amigos—Luis, Gene, and RJSdeV—who, like my ex-staff, conveniently sprouted an exile mentality. Then again, maybe they won't. No Cuban *chusmeria*, not in a packed room of Anglo colleagues.

I step up to the dais, the handrail loose, pull out the metal folding chair, *scrape* and *scrape* again—too loud my scrapes. I sit, ankles crossed, hands folded on my lap, as do First Ladies. I lift my head to the audience. What if I forget and smile reflexively at someone? And get rebuffed, again.

Can I really do this? Talk about well-founded fears of persecution based on political opinion, *como si nada*, while my life hangs by a thread?

Something is behind me, at my neck. A presence. (A specter?) "Sweetie," Ira's voice is gentle, "you're gunna do great."

I lean into him. He smells boyishly handsome; his breath, his hands, everything.

"You're good at this. You've done it a million times." And then a notch above a Rosie the Riveter can-do: "You will do it."

My hand cupped to his ear, "If someone begins shooting, where's the best place to hide?"

"Behind me."

A big shot with an up-and-coming Chicago law firm is introducing me in the past tense. It sounds like my obituary.

I cross my legs at the knee, shake the top leg, shake the bottom. *Stop it.*

Big shot is wrapping up my obituary.

I hope hard no one will boo.

My obit comes to an end. I hear only light applause.

Ira sits front row.

I stand, find my voice, and speak.

————

Oh God. St. Theresa, Little Flower; Jackie Camelot Princess, thank you! As I stood facing the packed audience in that vast convention hall, I wondered if Jackie's spirit, just a bit, was in me. Instinctively, I put down my notes and talked. Not intellectual, convoluted; simple and practical and me. I smile, a Cheshire cat. Applause.

Ira eye-smiles. His whole face eye-smiles. A thumbs-up, the same thumbs-up halfway through one of my televised debates against Ileana Ros-Lehtinen. He walks to me. "I'm taking you back to the room, Davis, so you can *relax*." He raises a finger. "As soon as I go to the reception." He pinches my tush and is gone.

No one booed. I didn't get shot. All is well—better.

My colleague Josie Gagliardi comes from behind, gives me a back-wrapping hug. "I was so nervous when you stood up to speak," she whispers. "So afraid someone would boo."

A grand San Francisco day, and Ira and the kids and I walk up hills and more hills on the Berkeley campus, and Ira is sure the rooming house he shared with his friends—he was the only straight guy in a houseful of gays—is just around this corner. But it's not, nor around the next, and we walk up hills and more hills and have scones and hot chocolate at Caffè Strada, and Katy says, "Ira, is Berkeley where you became a communist?" and he says, "No, I was one long before that," and she laughs and I take a nap on a grassy slope under a fat tree.

We go to a National Lawyers Guild reception at our friend Marc Van der Hout's house. Guild members ask if I'll say a few words; they're concerned, they're friends, they're liberal, and I talk and talk, I talk about everything and my mouth hurts but I cannot finish, cannot finish, I am going to drop, drop to the floor and Marc knows, he knows, because he received my letter and would know anyway because he's my friend and he huddles close and holds me up.

We go to dinner. We break bread, Ira and I and our children and liberal friends, toast a chilled red Napa Valley wine at the Cliff House overlooking the gargantuan Pacific waves, and Ira says, "Unbelievable. I've busted my ass all these years to build a name, and I run into a federal judge that I argued the first Haitian case before, when I still had hair. And you know what he says? 'How's Magda.'" He chomps on a piece of bread and then another. "I'm now known as Magda Montiel Davis's husband."

And Marc says, "Well, there are worse things."

"Not in Miami," Ira says, and we laugh, we all laugh, Ira and I and the children and our liberal friends. I don't tell him that our other liberal friends Eddie and Xiomara told me that the media now refers to Ira as "Magdo."

And so we ride back to the hotel and the children go upstairs, and Ira and I stroll the sidewalk, just the two of us, and it feels good to walk the streets and do it freely. We're laughing and I stop, I try to pull my jacket over my ears but cannot. I pull, I tug but the lapel is not long enough. Ira keeps walking, realizes I'm not with him, turns around, says, "What's the matter?" alarm in his voice.

"My ears are cold."

"Sweetie, it's not even cold out."

"I know. But my ears are cold."

"Wanna put 'em between my legs?"

I laugh, he giggles, then I blurt, "Ikey, I don't want to go back."

"Back where?" But he knows. And he takes my hand and pulls me and we take to walking again, and he is trying hard, "Oh, sure, dear. How about a kibbutz? We can go live in a kibbutz. I would love to see my wife working the fields and doing house chores."

And I say, "No, Ikey, I'm serious."

And he says, "I know you're serious." And then he stops and looks at me, for a long time he looks at me. "But you have to." He *looks* at me. "They can't win."

And we go upstairs to our room. Ira starts to take off his clothes, his white belly jutting over the belt of his pants, and Maggie knocks on the door, quick, hard knocks, and says, "Mom? Mom, I think that guy with the long name—"

"Raul Javier Sanchez de Varona?"

"Yeah, that one. The one you said wrote you and Ira a letter, Mom. I think he's the one who left that message on our answering machine, 'You lesbian bitch, you think you're gonna be an immigration judge,' because I was standing right behind him after your talk and I swear, Mom, it was the exact same voice."

And then I sit on the bed, turn on the TV, my eyes skimming an aerial of a white Bronco on the LA freeway. "O. J. Simpson is riding in that white Bronco," says the newscaster, "his good friend A. C. Cowlings driving." One good friend risking his life for another good friend, guilty or not, and I flick and pull at the dead skin around my fingernails, one two three four fingers, flick and pull and rip off dead skin, and all I can think of is Lazara. Lazara and the sweatshirt I'd mail-ordered, an early birthday present, two Kewpie-doll friends pointing up a hill, *To the Ends of the Earth* on the front of it, the sweatshirt that now sits folded and dusty in my closet, that twice I have started to throw out and cannot.

And Ira grabs my hand and says, "Sweetie, your fingers are bleeding."

And I say, "Oh," I say it blithely, "it's okay. It's just the cuticle. Just a manicure I need." I pull away. "That's all. Just a manicure."

35

STREETDANCE

DAY 38 OF 3 (MAYBE 5)

———

I roll out of bed, s l o w l y, half a turn, a quarter turn, tiptoe away from a snoring Ira into the kitchen, grab Mami's car keys, and drive—drive!—to Streetdance. To this old warehouse converted into a no-nonsense, hard-rockin' dance studio on a woodsy, winding side street of upscale Coral Gables.

I enter in attempted *Hiya, toots* normalcy, stare straight ahead, a horse with blinders, sideswiping a look here and there. Nothing has changed. No one. The aspiring actress who understudies for Cameron Diaz. The gargantuan lawyer who never combs her hair. The leggy fashion model with a full mane of curly black hair, who after class will romp about the locker room with a thin line of neatly trimmed pubic hair.

The Heavy Metal class—our leader Paulette's version of free weights—just ended and now she whistles and we burst into the studio, a pack of hungry dogs.

We wait for Paulette to start; she will when she's ready. Paulette, dressed in all black, always black, even the hair, black. Eagle wings tattooed on shoulders as if they could lift her in flight, not in a delicate swoop but with an Orville-Wrightish *I'm gonna fucking make this thing fly* determination. Tattoos on her feet, as if wearing shoes, but she does not. Paulette never wears shoes, not when on the dance floor. A tattoo of a teardrop of bright aqua falling from her right lid, bringing out the wet blue of her eyes. Forearms tattooed with burgundy roses, thorny vines cascading onto her wrists, yet hands that are graceful; fingers, delicate and long.

Fish is here today. She's here every day, zippered money pouch under her arm, collecting $21 from each of us for an hour and a half of Streetdance.

Judy Fish is her name but we call her Fish. She too dresses all in black; on her right ankle is a tattoo that spells P-A-U-L-E-T-T-E. Paulette calls Fish's twenty-two-year-old daughter Nikee—who never wears black—"my daughter," and they are family, a close and loving family of many years.

Paulette lifts a muscled, tattooed arm, says not a word, and the music begins. At rapid-fire pace, she digs in, the vibrations of the sound system making the bare raw wood of the floor, warped from years of our sweat, tremble under our feet. The cautious wear earplugs; the rest of us do not.

The warm-up always slow, erotic. Today, it's *Boléro*, rising to electrifying heights. An array of numbers, hundreds of them, that we could do in our sleep; often I do, I dream I am at Streetdance and do the numbers in my sleep. Step with the left, step with the right, the choreography a mishmash of Paulette's concoctions, the traditional eight-count an anomaly; the steps bearing no names, the dancing based only on beat and rhythm.

Arms above the head, I twist the length of my body to Elton John: *For each man in his time is Cain | Until he walks along the beach | And sees his future in the water.* And I process: Eddie and Xiomara called. Seems a *repudio musical* was staged against me last Saturday night at the annual dinner of the Institute of Cuban Studies, directed by Maria Cristina Herrera. Emilio Cueto, who I last saw at the Havana conference, flitted past the crowd, plopped before the piano, and belted out a Magda-Fidel parody. Wrote it himself, he did, and along with the flans and *cafécitos*, it seems I was the dessert of choice.

Kick, jump, slice left. Watch the media pick it up now.

It's not funny, the terror.

Then there's song no. 2, "La Boda" (The Wedding). Recorded in someone's garage, sold at a Little Havana pharmacy, and played by WQBA "La Cubanísima." That one the media did pick up. "People love it," Agustin Acosta of WQBA told the *Sun-Sentinel*. "The song really expresses the sentiments of the people."

"Haven't heard it and don't care to," I told the *Sun-Sentinel*.

"And what do you think of Pilar Casa-Gatto?"

"Pilar what what?"

"The composer. Her picture's in the paper."

"*¡Bien conocida en su casa!* She's no Carole Bayer Sager, I can tell you that."

"Song's going nowhere," Mami said when I got home. She did a number on it. A number on the number. An upside-down glass of water and ammonia on the top shelf of her Afro-Cuban etagere, flickering candles making la Virgen de la Caridad look like she's moving her lips, though I hope not singing "La Boda."

The cooldown. Ambrosia: *make a wish, . . . / So we could wash away the past / So that we may start anew.* I sway, glide, circle. And I think of Lazara.

I sent her Cristina Garcia's *Dreaming in Cuban.* "Read this," I scribbled inside, "and go to Cuba. *Then* you can talk to me with some intelligence. *Y te jodistes.* You missed out on all the cute FBI guys." I sent it quickly before I changed my mind. I didn't hear back from her.

Miriam said that Lazara (now I see, Miriam stays in touch with her) told her that she was going to call me. I hope she does. So I can get a message out to the five dogs (*ex*-staff) that I'm fine. More than fine.

It's my revenge.

"Thank you. I love ya." Paulette lifts an arm in a *get the fuck outta here* wave. She's gone, the music gone, but not the feeling.

No, Paulette is not gone. "Magder." The addition of *er* to my name, her way of showing affection. "Any shit around here, you tell me. I'm not gonna have it."

"Shit? What shit?"

"I don't care what happens outside. Let 'em kill themselves outside my dance studio. But in here, I'm not gonna have it. Not in my dance studio." It's not her dance studio, but okay. As long as I've been a Streetdance regular, eleven years now, Paulette has had to rely on this diamond-glittering follower or that one for financial backing. This time, it's Mirtha Garcia, sister-in-law of actor Andy Garcia.

"Okay." I shrug. "But there's no shit."

————

My legs sticking to the driver's seat like *chicharrones* to frying pan, I roll down the windows, flip the air on full blast. The radio too, full blast. Music, I want more of it. Streetdance. So glad I mustered the courage, not to sneak out of bed this morning—that was the least of it—but to go back. Just like that, *como perro por su casa.* Go back.

I zoom up the big bridge, feeling the power of driving, feeling I could do anything. At the stoplight, WELCOME TO KEY BISCAYNE, PARADISE FOUND. The old gas station. And something behind me. A big motorcycle. I drive along Crandon and still it follows. *Que jodienda,* this. What to do? Use a payphone? I can't just stop anywhere. I can't stop anywhere at all. I can't go home, that's for sure: Communist Mother ambushed by gun-wielding

Easy Rider right at our courtyard with its tiger orchids and yellow shrimp plants. Right here at my children's feet.

I circle our neighborhood: Atlantic, then Gulf, then Caribbean. And still, the motorcycle, now flashing headlights, now approaching me. Unthinking of the consequences, as in shot-between-the-eyes consequences, I turn to face him. Jesus. A police officer. He dismounts as if dismounting a horse. "Your license."

I make no eye contact, say not a word, flip my driver's license his way.

"You were going around in circles."

"That's 'cause you were following me. We've been having"—now I look at him—"some security problems."

"Ah." A sudden awareness. "You're Ms. Davis."

"Yes. Live and in person. So far."

"I'm one of the officers assigned to patrol your street." He leans into my window. "Look, you're just trying to *educate* these people."

"There's no educating them."

A faint notion he feels sorry for me. "Let me escort you home."

"No." A too quick no. "No need. Really." That's all I need, pull up at our driveway in a most unquiet way. Madame Bovary here, conjuring alibis, without the carnal benefits of good, old-fashioned adultery. Cheating on Ira—with Streetdance. I squeal a U-turn, catch sight of the officer in a cloud of dusty pebbles.

I knot my hair into a bun, throw a T-shirt over my wet clothes, stroll in the house, *como si nada*. If I cheated on Ira, I'd be damned good at it.

Ira is on the telephone. President Aristide again? No, not President Aristide. Covering the mouthpiece, "Human Rights Watch is coming to Miami," he whispers. "And they want to talk to *you*."

I shrug. "They'll wimp out. Just like the ACLU." Then, "When are they coming?"

———

Three, four hours later, still feeling that endorphin high, I pick up the phone. Silly. Silly for me to have assumed that my call to schedule Ben's haircut hadn't been returned because of all this *alboroto*. An affable "D'Angelo's" from the receptionist, and *"Si, yo llame unos dias atras—"* from me.

"Un momento, por favor," she says, as if expecting that I would call back. As if strict instructions had been handed down from the highest levels of D'Angelo Salon: D'Angelo himself with his satin-tied ponytail and tight

black flare jeans and too skinny hips. D'Angelo whose name is probably José Luis, who now makes weekly appearances on Univision or Telemundo, I forget which. Or maybe not. The receptionist's footsteps wane, then, "*D'Angelo*," I hear her call out, "*es Magda*." That's when I know. I toy with the idea of hanging up, but no. D'Angelo styled my hair the day I married Ira. I took my bouquet to the salon, and he put tiny pearls and matching orchids in my hair.

"*Mira, Magda*," says D'Angelo. "*No quiero problemas.*"

"*El* appointment *no era para mi*" is all I manage. "It was for Benny. My son. I wasn't going to take him myself, his nanny Gladys"—I am in disbelief. And still, I go on. "*Yo iba a usar discreción.*" Discretion. I was going to use discretion.

"*Sí, pero tus empleadas—*"

Ex-employees.

"*—vienen aquí a arreglarse.*"

Yeah, but I was first. They go there because I recommended him. I was there first.

"*No quiero conflicto.*"

"*No hay problema.*" I hang up. A servile sellout, that's what I have become.

The phone rings almost instantly. It must be Asela. Asela who has been cutting my hair for years, even before she joined D'Angelo's. I followed her there.

But no. It's not Asela. It's Xiomara, Eddie on the other line. "*¿Como estas, querida?*"

I talk fast, spill all.

"Well, look at it this way, baby," Eddie says. "At least Benny can now go down in history as being the youngest recipient of *un acto de repudio*."

36

ARISTIDE

DAY 62 OF 3 (MAYBE 5)

———

ra's Chevy Caprice, what all the Haitian cabbies drive now, except Ira's is space-age blue, not yellow-taxi yellow, pulls up to valet parking at the newly built Colonnade Hotel in souped-up, swanked-up Coral Gables. A princely parking attendant extends his hand to me. I float past flowing fountains, colorful Moorish tiles, and casings of exquisitely carved mahogany on beveled glass doors. Up the escalator, my heels sinking into the carpet, through a narrow hallway, two US Secret Service agents walk, silent and earphoned, at Ira's and my side.

A gold-plated doorbell announces our arrival. The double doors glide open. And there, wide-eyed and toothy smiled, much like the skinny, bookworm kid in third grade, is President Aristide. Jean-Bertrand Aristide—*Titid* to those close to him—who, through Ira, extended an invitation for me to visit with him.

In fine business suit of navy blue and a red tie, he lays his palms on my shoulders as if still a Roman Catholic priest bestowing blessings upon me. But *au revoir, arrivederci, adiós*. No longer is he a Roman Catholic priest. The Roman Catholic Church ousted him. Roman Catholic priests are not to get embroiled in politics, said the Roman Catholic Church.

"What about Peter Pan?" I asked Ira. Operation Peter Pan was at the onset of the revolution, when Roman Catholic priests on the island worked closely with the US government on a secret mission to save thousands of children from communism. When unaccompanied Cuban children, some as young as two, were put on planes by their parents for destinations unknown. When once in the US, many were physically and sexually abused.

When for years some did not see their parents. When some never saw their parents again.

And Ira had laughed. "Sweetie, it's the Catholic Church. And the US government. *That's* how Aristide was stripped of his priesthood."

President Aristide stands at eye level—he is of small svelte stature—pecks a kiss on each of my cheeks in the tradition of the French, ever-present in the Haitian people. He dabs his mouth delicately with a white linen napkin—he has just finished lunch—and I wonder whether Ira at least knows to temper his Brooklynite table finesse when eating alongside the president. I expect to see spiritual foods of sorts: a panoply of fruits, fresh vegetables, whole grains but no, I learn, the president is a big meat eater.

In a small but elegant parlor, we sit. He speaks to me slowly and in Spanish—Ira told me he speaks eight languages, including Hebrew, which he learned while a divinity student in Israel. In a very short time, he has now learned English. His thin legs are crossed, his hands folded at the knee; impeccable etiquette, but with a warmth that quickly puts one at ease. On the coffee table is the latest issue of *South Florida Magazine* with its one-page layout of the photo of me and Fidel; "Kiss of Infamy," it's titled, with a caption from Reinaldo Arenas's *Before Night Falls*: "They should envision the rope from which they will swing in Havana's Central Park." It's the same one that I received immediately upon my return to Miami, which I now see was a draft of what would be converted into a full-page magazine article. I sent its editor Glen Albin a note. Albin is young, cool, affable—and a liberal. He was supportive of my campaign. Albin wrote back; something about the use of juxtaposition in artful expression. What juxtaposition? The excerpt, in its entirety, reads: "All the pretentious people who dream of appearing on TV shaking Fidel Castro's hand and of becoming politically relevant should have more realistic dreams: they should envision the rope from which they will swing in Havana's Central Park, because the Cuban people, being generous, will hang them when the moment of truth comes."

Initially, I assumed that Arenas directed the anvil, or *mejor dicho*, the noose, at me. But Arenas had died of AIDS in New York four years ago. So it wasn't directed at me specifically but me generally; our enclave of Cuba activists. And juxtaposition, *nada*. Arenas's words could not have been clearer.

It was Maggie who first saw the magazine at a Coconut Grove news-stand when out *mataperreando* with a friend. She paid for it, brought it home, and asked me to pay her back. Paula wrote to the *Miami Herald*: "*South Florida Magazine* is provoking more than the murder of an idea. It is provoking the murder of a mother of five. Instead of envisioning her being hanged, envision the aftermath, a motherless family." She signed it "Paula L. Davis, 15-year-old daughter of Magda Montiel Davis." I cried for her but said nothing. What could I possibly say? I didn't understand it myself, especially given Glen Albin's role in it.

President Aristide now asks me about the children. Fine, I say. My mother? His eyes carry an odd tinge of sadness. We talk of the time we visited his home in Tabarre on the outskirts of Port-au-Prince. We sat in the round, all-white living room, white beams forming a cross on the ceiling, the entire house emanating the same simple elegance and spirituality as the man himself. The minute we'd taken our places at his white-laced breakfast table, Ben had asked, "When are we leaving?" An oh-oh silence and Holy Crap! said my brain, but President Aristide threw back his head and laughed. Then Ben gagged. And gagged some more. The cherry-flavored Robitussin I'd just given him for his spray-all cough. I prayed hard: Please God, if you're up there, Baby Jesus, Santa Barbara (Changó in Afro-Cuban), St. Jacques (Ògún in voodoo), Moses and Abraham too, don't let Ben spurt red all over the president's white lace tablecloth and white linen napkins and white carpeted floors and white upholstered chairs and white cross on the ceiling.

On the chauffeured ride back up the mountain to our room at Villa Creole, Ben was happy. "Now I know *two* presidents. President Aristide— and the white guy." Clinton.

Democratically elected—he beat the US-choice candidate with sixty-seven percent of the vote—President Aristide has been living in exile nearly three years; first in Venezuela, now the US. Yet he was ousted from his presidency and from his land, where one percent of the population holds forty percent of the wealth.

From looking at him, his unassuming style, you'd never know he's the president. From talking to him, you'd never know he'd been done in by the Catholic Church, by the US government, by some of his people, in a deftly orchestrated coup d'état. He rises suddenly and with a swift sweep of the hand, catches a fly.

"A fly," I say, "here at the Colonnade?"

"They're everywhere. There's always one or two you think you can't catch, but eventually you do. You just have to persevere"—he opens, closes his hand—"until you do."

I find it strange that Ira sits with us but stays silent and mention as much on the walk back downstairs, Secret Service agents in front, in back, at every turn. "I know the president," Ira says. "And it's you he wanted to speak to."

"But he never even *mentioned* anything. When I saw the *South Florida Magazine* laid out on his coffee table, I kept waiting for him to bring it up."

"That's the Haitian way of telling you he saw it and is in solidarity with you."

———

Beyond the prettily etched, beveled glass doors of the Colonnade lobby, Ira pats frantically at this and that pocket of his frayed navy-blue blazer—he always thinks someone has taken his wallet. Finally he finds it and tugs at the too fat wallet in his back pocket. He nods a quick good-bye at the Secret Service agents, as if it were up to him to dismiss them, as if natural he should be calling the shots. Catching my smile, he grins.

It's steamy and hot. I go back inside, stroll into the gift shop. Strange that such an upscale hotel would have such a tiny gift shop. Instantly, a feeling of being watched. More than watched, scrutinized. I ho-hum sort through greeting cards—a funny one about friends growing old together that in my other life I would have bought for Lazara. I reach for a bag of cookies, put it back, scan the shelves, try hard to be breezy, casual, feeling the encapsulated space getting smaller, Big Brother eyes on me. Ira waits outside for the car. I skirt past the Moorish tiled fountain and exotic tropical foliage. The ceiling fan whirls; a smell of heat. Clasping my hands behind me, I stand on the top entrance step, my back ballerina erect, my head high.

A woman buzzes about. Now she stands before me on the sidewalk, three steps below.

My arms crossed, my knuckles pressed against my ribs, I listen to her small talk, and for a minute, I think I'm wrong. For a minute, I think I ought to know her, remember her, and how awkward I do not. She speaks rapidly, her words garbled. The parking attendant swerves Ira's car into the driveway. It is then that I hear, "Cuba."

The attendant pulls open the car door for me, graciously he does this, but I stay standing.

"*¡Hipocríta!* If you like Cuba so much, why don't you go live there with your *maestro*?"

And like that, amid the breezy musical chimes and trickling fountain water, comes my first one-on-one, my first of many, and for many years to come.

37

BASEBALL BREAKFAST

DAY 71 OF 3 (MAYBE 5)

———

I can drive! Officially. No more sneaking around, taking Mami's car, timing my return home so that Ira doesn't catch wind of what I'm up to. This Saturday morning, Ira surprised me with a teal Chevy van (okay, not purple, but next best thing). He was careful to purchase it in West Palm Beach so the tag doesn't read Miami-Dade County. And in his name so no industrious bomber can single out my name. No Magda Montiel Davis anywhere.

———

The phone rings. "You get it."

"No, you get it."

"I got it the last time."

Gladys says, "*Yo estoy* busy." Ira likes to say "busy" is the only English word she knows.

Fourth ring now. "C'mon, sweetie. Be a good wife."

I shake my head, lumber to his study.

"Who is it?" This, from Ira, before I'm even there.

"I don't know. Probably one of your depressed, intellectual friends."

"At least I have friends. Real ones."

I pick up the handset. "*¡Flaquita!*" Eddie Levy.

"Eddie! Now I'm *flaquita*? I lost weight over the phone?"

"*Flaquita con las teticas chiquiticas.*"

"Xiomara!" I know she's on the other line; she dials the phone for him and stays on. "See? I told you your husband's been feeling me up. Pretend patting with that fakey blindness of his. Eddie, you're so politically incorrect."

"I don't have to be politically correct. That's for these New Age *americanos*. I'm a Jewban. Besides, that's how I like them. Small titties that fit in the palm of your hand like little mangoes, the kind you prick a little hole through and suck the juice out."

"*¡Ay, Eddie, por Dios!*" A pause, then a sober tone. "Magda."

"Xiomara—"

"No, Eddie, she needs to know."

"It's about your father," she says. My heart jumps, and then the rest of me.

————

It happened at the annual breakfast for retired Havana Sugar Kings baseball players. Dad must have gotten up early because my dad is always on time. He laid out his clothes carefully on the bed so he could dress in the way only my dad can. He picked out just the right suit, with just the right tie—a silk one with purple in it, because my dad loves purple, as do I—and a fine linen shirt, with J. R. M. embroidered on the cuffs and the also initialed cuff links. On his wrist, the 18-carat Rolex his boss Bobby Maduro gave him for all his years of service to the Havana Sugar Kings; the Rolex that my mom boasts to this day that she sneaked out of Cuba in her cosmetic case, the boxy one she brazenly laid on the olive-clad *miliciano*'s desk for inspection in those years of long ago.

And the morning of the breakfast, my father splashed whatever cologne it is he wears these days. I don't know what cologne my father wears these days, because my father has a new family. But for this scenario, this blur of imagination, I'll have him wear Old Spice, the sweet, minty smell of Old Spice that he wore when we lived on the hilly slopes of Nuevo Vedado. I'd collect the grey-blue plastic tops of his creamy white Old Spice bottles and make them into pacifiers that fit perfectly into my baby dolls' mouths, and when I'd show him, he'd beamed, "*¡Que inteligente, esta niña!*" The one advantage I had over my sister, duping my parents into believing this *niña* was so *inteligente* only because I did well in school. My mother would nod and smile, faint traces of Old Spice lingering on her and on his perfectly ironed white linen handkerchief, also embroidered with his initials, that he was careful not to leave the house without.

The morning of the breakfast, I bet he got into his Mercedes, an oomph in his step, purely happy about seeing the ballplayers he worked closely with at the Gran Estadio de La Habana for almost two decades. Players who were at his and my mom's wedding at Iglesia del Carmen down the hill from the University of Havana where they met and he wooed and courted her and won her over. Players who played dominoes with my mom late into the night on the front porch of our Nuevo Vedado home as he slept. Players who came to my sister's and my first Communions and costume parties and all other kinds of parties and gave us presents of baseball player figurines with Kewpie-doll faces whose heads *bop-bop-bopped* side to side and up and down.

And when my dad got to the ballplayers' breakfast that morning, his friends were waiting for him at the main entrance. Waiting for him, that's what he said. "You can't come in," they said, "not unless you renounce your daughter." I bet they crossed their arms over their chests when they said this. I bet they shifted their bodies right left right, blocking the entrance. I bet there were four or five of them, one the spokesman, the others the chorus. Those in attendance stopped what they were doing, what they were saying, and they watched and listened as a dead silence came over the room. And I bet my dad looked up and around, the scared bewildered look of a kid, waiting for one of them to speak up, sure that one of them would come to his defense.

And I know none of them spoke up for my father.

He walked away, head bowed, shuffling his feet with that tired gait now that he is in his seventies. And it was then that they called out to him, "Montiel! *Tu apellido apesta*." Stinks. His family name stinks.

———

I turn over in bed, press my face into the pillow. My eyes sting. They sting when they're open, they sting with each blink, they sting worse closed. I think about getting up. Putting one arm under me, lifting myself on my elbows. But I don't. *Move your toes, can you move your toes for me?* That's what the nurses in the recovery room told me after each cesarean section. I thought about moving my toes, in my head I was moving my toes, but I wasn't. I think about getting up, but I don't.

"Ikey." He stands over me on the side of the bed. I tell him. Then in palliative tone, "My father *did* say he would die before denouncing me. I called him."

Ira is silent.

"But did he tell them that?" I feel the heat behind my eyes. "If that was your mom, she would have told them all to go fuck themselves."

I think I see a slight nod, but instead he says, "That's not your dad's style, sweetie." And then he hugs me, a full give-all hug. "I'm sorry, sweetie." I think I hear him cry with me.

My father also said, *Que pena pase*. Embarrassed, he was embarrassed. I sob. I don't tell Ira, but I sob.

38

NAKED

DAY 77 OF 3 (MAYBE 5)

———

A dream I walk a narrow sidewalk, cracked, half lifted from the pavement, like the waterlogged sidewalks along el Malecón. But I do not walk the Malecón. I walk to a government building, massive and unimaginative and grey. It's a courthouse; my trial begins this morning.

To my right, a small wooden frame house lined with a white picket fence, like the dollhouses my mother used to make us from cardboard boxes. Behind the fence stands my father. He warns me not to stop; keep walking, lest I be late; I'm first on the judge's calendar. Relax, I say, it's 9:15 and the trial begins at 9:30.

A crowd builds with each step. From the crowd comes a pair of hands. It hands me a pair of shoes. I don't see a face, only a pair of hands. The shoes are a muted purple and low heeled. I climb long entrance stairs rising from the side of the building, and that's good, I think, because going through the front entrance would have taken longer, and Ira, my lawyer, will surely want to prepare me before trial.

But now I'm told that the trial will be held not inside but in the back on the slope of a hill. I sit; the table is long and white. The jury is comprised of those sitting next to me and those opposite me.

But it's time to start, and Ira is not here. A young woman is chosen to represent me; she's intellectual looking and court appointed. Cuban American, but Jewish and liberal. She has me stand and introduce myself. I try to articulate the "Magda," the "Montiel," the "Davis" but cannot get it right. The cry of a baby, the roar of student protest interrupt the young woman's opening statement. I look down; she has no legal pad. How will she able to proceed without writing it all down?

Now comes the part where I am expected to perform; not take the stand but dance, and I wonder if my low-heeled purple shoes will serve me well.

A door opens and Ira enters. Behind him a black priest walks in calm elegance. He wears a red tie, holds an etched gold box to his chest. An offering, of sorts. But his tie is too bright, he's told, too loud for these proceedings.

I wake, reach for my journal.

Yesterday I was ousted from Streetdance.

————

The lights were like nameless color. And something wasn't right. The same dancers, the same leggings, fishnets, see throughs. The same nicked, sodden floor. But something wasn't right.

It's when you know.

A *cubana* with big hair and big thighs entered, exited the dance floor, and then a battalion more, enter exit enter. Quarter past nine already, by now the throbbing heat should have bent my muscles into compliance. By now I should have reached that near-nirvana state.

It's when you know. Like the time some years before Ira and I married, and I went to the ashram for my what? my third, fourth visit, and even after two, three days of crystal-domed yoga and excruciatingly exhilarating hiking of the Calabasas trail, something wasn't right. And I dreamed BETRAYAL, the word BETRAYAL written across my forehead, saw it actually, woke, and whispered, There is betrayal but it's not from Ira. He's not with another woman; at least not one to permanently replace me. And even though ashram instructions were to disconnect, disassociate, not call the office, not home even, at 6 AM California time I called the office and discovered that the two women lawyers I trusted had joined forces and were out and about looking for office space, taking my then support staff with them, the then support staff I loved then. Not Mily or Cary or Barbara or Janet or Isabel. Some other support staff I loved then.

It's when you know. Like the time some years before Ira and I married and I stopped eating. Suddenly and inexplicably, I stopped eating, and I drove to Ira's apartment on our way to one of our Saturday-night movie dates and on his kitchen counter were two empty ice trays, *two*, when it was only Ira living in that small apartment, and I said, Hey! Why are two empty ice trays out? There were wine goblets too and he doesn't drink. Innocently, stupidly, I said this, and he looked at me then turned to me in fierce fury and said, Why shouldn't I go out with other women? I'm not married to you, and then he shrugged, and I felt the physical sensation of my heart cracking open.

It's when you know, that tiny mustard seed inside your gut. Call it intuition, call it Mami's *espiritismo*, your guardian angel, God—and you just know.

An egg-shaped man stood in the doorway of the dance studio. He stood as if someone had summoned him, *Oye, papi, ven 'pa 'ca.* Could anyone lock the doors, block the exits? Prevent me from leaving? A thumping static rose from the dance floor, slippery and wet, my purple Nikes not serving me well today, paining the soles of my feet. The egg-shaped silhouette of the man seemed to move as I moved, right left right. But maybe it was just the Sartre-like, *No Exit* eeriness of "Hotel California" that Paulette was now playing. This is what I told myself.

But I didn't know.

You can check out anytime / But you can never leave.

That's the hard part, not knowing.

Another *cubana* with stringy black hair and too long face and badly lip-sticked mouth walked up to me. A *cubana* I've been dancing alongside eleven years now, but I didn't know her name; I didn't know any of their names. I just danced there. She walked to me, a bitter pull to her face. "Did you go to Cuba?"

"Yes."

"Why?"

My first impulse: Because I fucking felt like it. Better yet, *Porque me salió de la papaya.*

"I want to talk to you."

And I want to dance, my second impulse. Dance, pivot, jump. But what if she thinks I'm regretful, shameful of all I've said, all I've thought, all I feel?

The music started again, and I held up a finger in *I'll get back to you* motion, then chastised myself as I danced. I should have given her nothing, nothing but a no; an irrefutable, categorical no; a no-means-no no. I should have set clear boundaries, rules—my rules.

You may be right / I may be crazy. A Billy Joel rasp filled the dance studio. Maybe I should give her my Jane Fonda quote. Before the next number,

I walk to her, say, This is not the right time or place. What else did Jane Fonda say? *It's a bad war.*

Donna Summer: *Give me*—JumpJump—*your unconditional love*—and a sexy sway of the hips, and no longer was it Jane Fonda in my head, but Ira. Ira and his words and that throaty, sexy voice of his even when he is saying something unsexual, like: "What you need to do is talk to these people." Talk to them, he said, and they'll understand, to which I'd "What?" I'd whatted him good. "What're you crazy? There's no talking to them." Still. Ira and the pink of his skin against the blue of his eyes. And his brain, no? His wisdom.

The end of "Unconditional Love," and I walked to the woman with the stringy black hair and too long face and badly lipsticked mouth. "Okay." I contracted my calf muscles. "We'll talk."

She headed outside as if on a war footing. I followed her out into the alley. The sun was bright and hot and cast a half shadow across her face. Before she could say anything, "I have children," I said, "and not a day goes by that they don't ask me for a glass of milk and I don't think of my two childhood friends who live in Cuba with children the same ages as mine who can't give their children a glass of milk." My heart beat loud and fast, and I couldn't tell whether my heart was constricting my breath or my breath my heart. "So, I'm three hundred percent opposed to the embargo because it hurts innocent people." The music inside came rapidly, hard, stilted drumbeats, meshed high and low sounds. "While I recognize there are problems in Cuba—"

"At least there was a life there before Fidel Castro."

"A life for whom?" Keeping my voice slow and steady, I talked to her about the beggar woman with a baby holding out her open hand to me, and my mother giving her nothing but a can of condensed milk. "That was Cuba, before the revolution."

"Look," she said. "I know you're smart. A lawyer."

And therefore inconceivable that I should think this way? But I knew: say it and lose the war. "Yes," I said, "a lawyer."

"Not an imbecile."

"No, not an imbecile."

"But things in Cuba are . . ." She made dusty circles with her sneakers.

"Scarce?" I volunteered in earnest attempt at cooperation. "Difficult?"

"No." She shook her head in frustration. And then, "That man robbed me of my childhood!" A vibration of bongo drums, bass sounds—dissonant, discordant sounds, the music no longer making sense. I heard her say,

"My father." I heard her say, "Political prisoner." And I tried to be—think—like her, and maybe I could have, had I seen my father in prisoner garb within the confines of El Morro, but a wall went up and all I could hear was Mily and her hyperbolic mourning of a never-before-mentioned father and Lazara's Telemundo-inflected *Fidel sends little kids this big—this big, Magda—into minefields!* And US hypocrisy with respect to, well, with respect to a multitude of matters, but for purposes of my situation, this moment, Cuba; a shining example of "the pot calling the kettle black" in its Human Rights Report on Cuba, in everything.

"Two wrongs don't make a right" was all I could conjure up. Then, "It's not good to be vindictive," and then, "to live with all that hate." The music clashing from inside the studio. Her breathing. The bitter pull to her face. *If you just talk to them. If you just talk to them*, running through my head, my entire being, and I'm about to lose the war and about to stop dancing. No pointe shoes for you today, baby pink and satin like Ive's and my sister's. No pointe shoes for you today or any day, your gnarled feet bowed and tied, not in pink satin ribbons but in too tight ankle-high orthopedic boots. And those boots hurt. They hurt.

"That's it," she said. "I can tell you've developed the socialist mentality." And with that, she was gone.

I walked back inside the dance studio. The egg-shaped man was missing—where was the egg-shaped man? And the women started again, enter, exit the dance floor, into the locker room. Donna Summer again, this time, *Last dance*, a soulful slowness, *Last chance for love*, then a quick pickup on tempo. I danced untamed, my arms over my head. An awareness that my raising arms would anger her, anger all of them, anger them further, but a pleasure almost at their anger. The woman with the too long face now back from the alley, she danced facing the big mirrors. She danced as if fragmented, the cut glass where two panels of mirror meet making her look as if she had three eyes here, half a head there. Or as if doubles, triples, quadruples of her danced across the dance floor in perfect unison.

"Thank you, I love ya." Paulette, black clad and barefoot, lifted a muscled, tattooed arm. Her partner, Fish, smiled widely, waved back. Their mutt, Goldie, lifted herself from the whine of the sound system.

I walked to Paulette. Strange I should always feel this way around her, diminutive, awkward. Unmoored, fidgety. Her sexuality, I've often thought, maybe her sexuality. The powerfulness of it. But strange, so unlike me. "The shit," I said.

"The shit?" Her voice was deep and throaty, her blue eyes wet and intent on mine.

"Yeah, the shit."

She thrust her head closer, opened her eyes wide.

"It's here." I rustled through my backpack and with damp fingers fished out a business card. "Remember when you said to let you know if there was any shit here?" I wrote with shaking hands my home, beeper, fax number, underlined my prettily engraved office number. "That you weren't going to have it, not in your dance studio?" Strobe lights sliced through the dance studio, circled about. "Call me." I pressed the card hard into the palm of her hand.

She nodded. "I will." Her voice was low, gravelly.

Inside the locker room, the too bright fluorescents marked a grid across the floor. I squirmed out of my wet leotard, stepped into the shower—boxy, airless plastic. Full blast, I turned the faucet hot to very hot, lifted my face to the weight of water. Danced, of sorts, made little circles inside the shower stall, my toes squeezing its slick surface.

And then it came. "Magda." It was Mirtha Garcia, *Garcia* as in Andy Garcia, Hollywood's own. Sister-in-law Mirtha, the now de facto owner of Streetdance, the latest in a string of investors hopeful that this time Paulette, founder, creator, will fathom that she's not the owner; hopeful that this time there's no fallout. "Magda." Mirtha Garcia again.

I turned my body side to side, like Irma's developmentally challenged son who needs to be constantly moving or else he loses the sense of the existence of his own body. I knew Mirtha waited, and some part of me thought, *I should be turning off the water.* And I will. But I didn't, I rocked, shoulder to shoulder, nipple to nipple. The pink vinyl of the shower curtain smelled of a brand-new doll, a pink-satined ballerina doll in those days of long ago. Finally, I did, I opened the curtain. Holding aside my towel, I stepped out fully naked.

"Jesus!" Mirtha muttered.

In silence, I lifted one leg onto the bench, exposing my innermost self to her.

"People have been criticizing me because I let you dance here." *Let you*, she let me. "I even got in a fight with my husband over it."

I sat on the bench, swished my towel across my back, much like Chubby Checker, twisting again like he did last summer. Except slowly, I swished slowly.

"Irmita," Mirtha said, "told me of your . . . your conversation with her."

Oh, so that's her name, I thought. The woman with the stringy hair and too long face and badly lipsticked mouth. Weird. Weird she should bear the same name as Irma, my Irma with the developmentally challenged son. Irma with her unconditional support.

"So," said Mirtha, "you admitted you're a communist."

I wanted to laugh. Laugh hard and laugh in her face and ask as I'd wanted to ask Mily, And what kind of communist would that be? A *tropical* communist? A socialist? How about socialist? In their eyes, all are *cortados con la misma tijera*, so let's throw in socialist too. "And you're basing all this on the report of—one person?"

"I know her," Mirtha whispered savagely. "Irmita wouldn't lie."

I put the Evian bottle to my mouth, took a big swallow. "And I would?"

"I'm sorry." She moved her hands in *just let it drop* motion. "Look. I worked really hard to open this dance studio, lure Paulette over from Wendy." Paulette's last investor. "I put a lot of money into the place." The smell of sweat and apple-cinnamon splash. "I'm not losing my business over one person."

Mirtha left. The women stayed, they stayed and watched me, corporate security ensuring fired employee leaves without ruckus.

Slowly, methodically, I clasped bra, hooked skirt, buttoned blouse. My hair wrapped in a towel, I picked up my *Jane Fonda Workout* bag, walked past the women and onto the dance floor. My last time. I heard Paulette grumble a complaint to Mirtha, but not grumbling enough. I made sure not to look down, not once to look down. Head straight, spine erect, ballerina erect.

Outside, I nearly wailed. The sun was in its 12 o'clock position; that's when it reaches its highest place in the sky, I read to Benny last night. Black shiny asphalt crunched the soles of my shoes. I counted twenty steps back, took aim, the automatic ignition-starter now scanning the fender, motor, seats, trunk. The beeps, five in all. Now I was okay. More or less okay, assuming no explosive and no left turn. I climbed into my new Chevy van. Locked the doors. Then I did. I wailed. Little whimpers. Big whoops of sorrow. A child's shuddering sounds of helplessness.

Finally, the release of tears.

39

BUT NOW I HAVE SUSHI CHEF

———

After my ouster from Streetdance, I drove straight to the office, alternating sobs and a business-as-usual resolve. In between a string of clients, I tracked down Ira in Haiti, but all I got was a recording at his usual room at the Villa Creole. "Sweetie," said Ira some time later when he called back, "you scared me. From the sound of your voice, I thought something happened to the kids." Still, I rambled on, blow by blow, feeling I was speaking only to the telephone receiver. Ira covered the mouthpiece, called out, "I'll be right there." Then back to me: "I'll be home Sunday." A distracted silence. "We'll talk then."

My head bent, I could see my belly, chest move with each breath. "It's just a dance class," he said after some silence. "No, it's not just a dance class," I said, "I can tell you're not the person to talk to about this," and hung up.

The staff tried comforting me. "Miriam even said she'll call you Magda," Mara said. They prodded me to go home. "Home?" I said. "To what?" then realizing the unmotherliness of my words: "At least here I'll keep busy." I tackled case upon case, stacks of them. As thoughts about Streetdance came to me, I stopped to jot a quick sentence or two, be it on trash paper, coffee napkin.

At 7 PM, my extension rang. "What are you still doing at the office?" Ira said. "Go home, your kids are waiting for you." That Ira pause. "And so is your husband."

I rushed home to a Shabbat dinner full of zaniness and merriment. Then all of us sat for one of Sadie's performances—she sings, dances, writes the script, makes Ben the lighting director with the help of the flashlight—and even Tía Tíita behaved.

I undressed for bed weirdly happy. All will be well, I told myself. Then,

Who said that? I was an English major. I should know, I should remember. *All shall be well, and all shall be well, and all manner of thing shall be well.* But I didn't—and fell asleep utterly frustrated. Angry.

––––––––

The morning after, I wake, instinctively raise my head at the clock. Eight thirty. The time I would have raced to Streetdance. I dig into my journal, a madwoman in hazed frenzy, write fast, write slow, write focused, write blank. Track every move, step, all that was said, all that was not, reworking the scene, rewriting the script to fit my needs, imagining quick, spiffy comebacks, but mostly filled with regret. If only this, if only that, if only I hadn't followed Ira's advice: *You just need to talk to them.* Them.

Now for my bomb-detecting dance, I click. Lights, beeps, I climb into the van, and drive to Coral Way, its tangled, age-old banyans, Sushi Chef. Miriam has been ordering sushi for me under an assumed name, but yesterday I told her to order a sushi boat, a big wooden one filled with eel and tekka rolls and California too, and though for staff, to deliver to Magda Montiel Davis, PA. And they delivered okay.

Time to take it up a notch, go inside Sushi Chef. And I do. And all of them, okay. The Venezuelan owner and the young woman behind the counter and even the ever-silent sushi chef, all of them, okay.

But when the young woman rings up my order and says, "How *are* you, Magda?" here we go, the tone, the *feel sorry* look. The sad puppy-dog eyes studying my face, waiting for me to have a breakdown any second. Step right this way, folks, an exclusive viewing of Hester Prynne, branded, scaffolded, crazed. When I have the meltdown, as my kids call it, I'll do it in the privacy of my own space, thank you, irrespective, in mockery of, the *feel sorrys.*

Like the time I spoke at the National Lawyers Guild with Arthur Kinoy, active in the Rosenberg defense, Montgomery bus boycott, Chicago Seven trial, Watergate prosecution, et cetera. Following our talk, an old hippie woman, uncombed grey hairs flying about, strode up to the podium, stroked my arm. "Oooh, your poor dear." The same puppy-dog eyes. "They've made you into a scapegoat," and I shrugged and walked off but wanted to push her away and scream, "Oh get real, lady!"

But now I have Sushi Chef. And another first, the movies. Last night, Ira, on his way to CocoWalk to pick up Maggie from a day of shopping, said on impulse—I think on impulse—"Get dressed and go with me to the movies." No B-grade sci-fi ("Ira, you're an intelligent guy. How can you stand to watch such idiocy?"), no smart, introspective character studies ("You owe me two movies, Magda," this, always from Ira, two fingers at my face, now four, now six as I ignore him and keep watching the film). So we compromised: *Forrest Gump*. But many of the songs played—*Break on through to the Other Side*, *On the Road Again*—were those to which I danced at Streetdance. Still, I sat in the audience, danced in the dark with my fingers, my hands. Did every step, every single goddamned step, circled my knuckles and wrists: turn, side step, jump. I felt sorry for Ira, trying to cheer me. Finally, "What's wrong, sweetie?"

"Most of the songs in the movie, I danced to them at Streetdance."

Back home, lights out. "Sweetie," Ira said, "if our marriage were to break up, you wouldn't be this upset."

40

REPENTANCE

———

I t is the season of repentance, when we are called upon to do teshu-vah, to return to God in truth and sincerity. Today, we do this at Alice Wainwright Park before the choppy bay waters that separate main-land Miami from Key Biscayne, the loop of the big bridge to our left, the tiny strip of island where our house rests melding across the bay into the thin horizon. A huge wall of sea rock rises behind us.

We are here to perform the tashlik ritual, when we cast our sins into the depths of the sea. As prayers are said in Hebrew, old bread brought from home is bit by bit, crumb by crumb, tossed to the waters. I don't much understand the Hebrew prayers, only the *Barukh atah Adonai,* so often repeated—Praised are You, Lord our God, King of the Universe—but the ritual is familiar to me, much like Mami's Afro-Cuban practices.

Each year, before my mother ventures into the water, she throws black pennies to the ocean floor as payment to Ochún for the right to use her seas. After a *despojo*, a cleansing with flowers, cologne, flying doves—sometimes blood—the wilted petals and other refuse are tossed to the waters as well. I have seen my mother do this, stop her car at the foot of the big bridge, look about her, raise her arm like a star major-league pitcher, and toss hard, toss far, the same way she tossed her diamond-encircled wedding ring into Biscayne Bay the day my father left us.

I tried today to get Mami to come to tashlik services, but she won't ven-ture out of the house. If she ventured little out of the house before—save perhaps to *la farmacia* or the grocery store—she ventures out much less, hardly at all now.

I stand before the water, its lull, its ripples and swirls, the sea wind at my face. Kicking off my Nikes, I sit on a slab of seawall, and suddenly I'm walking the legendary seawall of the Malecón, holding my mother's hand, my other hand stretched out to the sea for balance, enthralled at the power of the ten-foot waves, and hopeful. Hopeful el Malecón would one day be a beach, a beach with liquidy soft sand that would sift through my ringed fingers—always, I filled my fingers with twenty-nine-cent rings from *el ten cen*—Woolworths. A beach so close that I wouldn't have to count on anyone to drive me to the beach at Tarará or Santa Maria del Mar. And so, I asked my mother, would, could el Malecón one day be a beach? She said eventually the giant waves would pulverize the big sea rocks into sand. And yes, one day el Malecón would turn to beach. How much longer? I asked. One hundred years, she said. In about a hundred years.

I gaze at the bay and think of water, how it transforms: oceans to waterfalls to rivers to streams. Constantly moving, forever changing, relationships in flux.

Tashlik is about regret, Rabbi Riemer says to our small circle. Be regretful only of those things that you can change. And I cast my bread crumbs into the water.

41

PLOT TO KILL

———

In the middle of dance class at a small studio in the Anglo neighborhood of South Miami, I get tapped on the shoulder from behind. *Telephone.* I am going to tell Paula I will pick her up in fifteen minutes. Too bad, I will say, she has to wait. Because I said so. Because . . . because I'M THE MOTHER, THAT'S WHY (the words on the coffee mug Katy gave me).

But it's Miriam. "Sorry to bother you," she says slowly. "But the FBI just called. They said it's urgent and to call them immediately." Then, in afterthought: "And call us right back."

Is she worried about me? How sweet. Or worried about her? The other day while at the movies—Ira and I took off to the movies just like that, in the middle of the work day, though outside City of Miami limits—Miriam paged me, right as *Dead Man Walking* was the dead man walking, to tell me a client needed to talk to me. "Miriam," I chided her, "when you beep me, I picture the FBI bursting in our office."

I don't say thank you to her now. I realize I don't say thank you when, to my curt good-bye, I hear her say—not with a purpose, but as part of her good-bye—"Okay. You're welcome."

I call Oscar Montoto. He says they've been working with the US Attorney's office, says something about "an investigation." An investigation? My heart doesn't even jump. Let it be about me. A lot of good it will do them. There's nothing they can get on me. *Nada.* I report every bit of income received (they can't get me à la Al Capone), and I am most careful—vigilant—about keeping my clients in line.

"We've uncovered a plot to bomb you and eight others," Oscar says.

Lovely. "What should we do? What's your professional advice, I mean? The kids. Should we move out for now?"

"We think it will be only a few days before we make the arrest. But it's up to you and your husband whether you will move the kids out." A certain disquiet. "If not too great an inconvenience."

Suddenly, "Is this Oscar?"

"Yes, this is Oscar Montoto with the FBI." He reverts to his *Mission Impossible* voice.

"I had a dream they killed you." It's true, I did, but I don't know why I tell him this now.

"No. I'm still here."

"Okay. Just want to make sure I'm not talking to the underworld or am already in the other world myself."

Oscar tells me it's very important that I keep it confidential, lest the arrests—in the plural he says this—be thwarted. "Plus," he adds, "the informant's life could be in danger."

"Jesus. Then how much can I tell the office? They need to be advised, for their safety."

"Nothing. Miriam will tell her Cuban husband"—how does Oscar know that "Mr. Elias Rivero," as Miriam calls him, is Cuban?—"her husband will tell a friend—"

"No fair, Oscar, to keep it from them."

"Well, yes then, do tell them. This way, you can give them instructions to be on the lookout for packages received, the mail—"

I give the parking attendant my keys. He storms back inside. "It's alive!" My Chevy van. Then he recognizes me. "My mom's a *santera*," he says.

———

Miriam again. FBI again? No, not the FBI. Ira. Live and in person, upstairs in my office.

I cut short my phone call with a client. Heaven forbid he would stop what he was doing to attend to me. And heaven forbid I wouldn't stop what I was doing to attend to him. I tell him about Oscar's call. "Should I have a bomb detector installed in Gladys's car?"

"No. I just want you to take your mother and the kids and leave town."

"To *where*?"

"Disney World."

"Like the commercial? That's what Americans do."

"Well guess what? This is America, not a third world—"

"And what about you, Magdo?"

The *Magdo* he ignores. "I'll take out a larger insurance policy."

He calls Oscar. The bombers "don't even have the devices yet," Oscar says, so I'm relieved of my Disney duties. "But he said the men could get the devices on their own. Not wait for the informant, if they're on to him."

42

THE PERSON I AM BECOMING

———

Miriam is at another doctor's appointment; my sister is pulling out her hair—literally, physically. I saw her grab her copper-cellophaned streaks and pull hard at her scalp over an E-1 treaty trader visa case on short—very short—deadline. So Irma volunteers to work the phones. She juggles the rings and the buttons and the red flashing lights in her broken English.

"Magda Montiel Davis, PA." When she says my name, there is pride. "*Wa-ahn mee-not, plees.*" One minute, please. Her big dark eyes look up at me. She cups the mouthpiece. Will I write out for her—phonetically—commonly used phrases?

I make a list: Whom do you wish to speak to? I start to write, May I help you? Then decide, better not. Better not include the May I help you? Lauren Beckwith is bound to call with that heavily accented British-speak that even I have a hard time deciphering: "Hey there, luv. I'm ringing you again because I called on some bloke who was on the telly, but I'm quite unsure, luv, he seems dodgy, this geezer"—once I asked her, "Geezer? How old is this guy?" but no, geezer is any guy, not necessarily an old one—"just out to take a quid or two."

I hand Irma her script, smile. She grins, I walk to my office. A few minutes later, I ring her at the front desk.

"Magda Montiel Davis, PA." Poor Irma, she thinks it's an outside line.

"Irma—"

"*Hola*, Isa!"

I feel my eyes widen—"It is *not* Isabel"—hear myself speak though clenched teeth. "It's *Magda*."

"Oh." Dismay. "Sorry." *So-rree.*

I hang up, bolt to the front. "Irma, *I don't* want you talking to that woman."

There are little trembles in her eyes.

"Do you understand? You are *not* to talk to her." Okay, maybe I've gone too far, so I clarify: "While at my office. Not on *my* time." I turn, walk to my office at the back of our narrow and very tiny space. The caboose.

Sometime later, Irma is at my office door. The door is open, but she taps the glass of the single French door that used to be double French doors, *pero bueno*. "Can I come in, Magda?" Her voice is tentative, weak.

I nod silently.

She sits, elongates her arms down the center of her bony chest, squeezes her hands between her knees. "*Tengo que renunciar.*" Resign, she says, she has to resign. Her big dark eyes glisten, her voice shakes. "I've loved working here and working for you and learning, oh I've learned so much and am learning every day and I'm *muy agradecida* to you. But I can't work for someone who doesn't have faith in me. Doesn't know my loyalty."

"No, Irma, no." I grip my hand over hers. Her fingers are thin and cold. "I am so sorry, so very sorry."

"Magda, I would never—"

"I know. I know that. It's just—"

"I know." We talk a bit more, but she's careful not to make it long, to be considerate of my time, and I want to say: Irma, it's okay. My hurting you deserves in return at least some of my time, the same as any other staff member—current or ex—would demand of me.

She will stay, she says simply. But there is hurt and vulnerability in her eyes, in all of her. I turn back to my work, regretful, remorseful. Mostly, in fear of the person I am becoming.

43

SONESTA

DAY 79 OF 3 (MAYBE 5)

———

We lie together, Ben and I, on a chaise lounge by the seashore, the breaking waves sinking us deeper into the sand. "Whoa," Ben cackles. "Whoa, Mom." He says the clouds are like cotton candy, the pink kind, and you can lick them right off the sky, and, "Did you know, Mom? Did you know that seagulls are the descendants of pterodactyls?" I want to hold tight to this moment, the rubbery, milky smell of his breath; the speckles of sand on his white, round belly; the Scooby-Doo water shoes he refuses to take off. He gazes up at the purple blue of the sky. Then he says,

"She's a moron."

"Who, Ben?" I untangle myself from him, spring to seated position.

"That woman," he says, his eyes are paper-thin on the horizon, "that woman who was yelling at you."

It happened a good two, three weeks ago.

A three-year-old's memory is supposed to be short.

———

"Shotgun!" Benny yelled, and he jumped in the front seat of the double stroller. We headed to the beach closest to us, the Sonesta.

Sadie tapped him from behind. "You're supposed to wear your sunglasses, *Be-ehn*, not chew them."

"Shut up, *chocho de vaca*."

"Mom, are Sadie and Ben going to fight the entire time?" said Maggie. "Because like, I might as well, I'll just turn around and go back, okay?"

"You sound like a, what do you call them?" I said. "Valley Girl. That spoiled brat on *20140*."

"*Mo-ohm*," said Sadie. "*90210*."

"Brenda?" asked Maggie. "You mean Brenda?"

"They're *all* spoiled on that dumb show," Paula said.

"You're just jealous.

"C'mon, guys," I said, "chill out." And there was whirred laughter.

"Benny," Paula said, "when you're in high school, Mommy's gonna pick you up on a motorcycle wearing tight leather pants and silver chains."

"At least his mother will pick him up. That's more than we had," whereupon I came to my own defense.

Through the S-shaped sidewalks of our Holiday Colony neighborhood, we bickered, teased, grumbled. I pushed my weight onto the double stroller trying to make the steep incline to the hotel's entrance ramp as a stretch limo eased past us. A sudden slap of cold air as we entered the lobby, the geometric lines of its furnishings a bit too avant-garde for my liking, but a feel-good ambiance nonetheless, happy northerners in vacation mode.

We exited the lobby to the smell of salt and sea and childhood. My *abuelo* driving my grandmother, mom, Maty, and me to Tarará Beach, just a half hour or so from our Havana home. But for a three-foot Beba standing tall in the back seat of her grandfather's Buick, that ride seemed endless.

Struggling to hold on to the double stroller as we now descended the ramp to the beach, the weight pulling me down too quickly, I stopped, breathy. I noticed Paula. When did she start dressing like that? An extra-large grey athletic T-shirt; long, baggy pants. "Why aren't you wearing your bathing suit, honey?" She said nothing. Then Sadie jumped out of the stroller. "What are you doing?" I said. It was oppressively hot and already I was beat, all that push-pull, Maggie strolling along in *it's all about me* adolescent arrogance; Paula's silence.

"I'm four-and-a-half, Mom," Sadie said. "Too *big*, Mom, for peoples to see me in a baby stroller," her bebop sandals slapping noisily at the pavement.

I laughed despite it all, scanned the crowd. Below us was the bohemian-clad Filipino fellow singing "Kokomo" to the beat of his pedal steel guitar; one man, one instrument, creating the sound of a full-fledged band. There was a Brazilian-thonged woman sucking on a milky piña colada and a gold-chained, white-hair-chested man leaning into her watermelon-pumped breasts.

And there was a woman screaming, *Ahí esta la mujer que beso a Fidel.* Over and over, *la mujer que beso a Fidel.*

I stared straight ahead, said to Maggie through smiling teeth, "Let's go."

"No, Mom. We're staying."

I looked at her; fourteen, my little Maggie.

"If we leave, you're showing them they won."

We continued down the ramp, into the sand. Out of the corner of my eye, I saw people—locals?—leaving their palm-thatched huts, their macramé hammocks, the Seagrape Bar, balancing drinks and their drunken selves. Coming toward us.

"Maggie." I touched her arm. "These are Calle Ocho *chusmas*. They have forks—and knives." I looked at Paula for validation, support, but Paula was speechless, expressionless. "And they've been drinking."

Laughter, more roars. Shouts. I followed Maggie to the seaside playground—she, the lead engine; I, the caboose. She held Ben's hand, Paula held Sadie's. The shouting intensified, and I couldn't tell whether the crowd was getting louder or coming closer. Maggie lifted Ben onto a kiddie swing. "No, not the baby swing," he moaned. "The *big* swing."

"If anything happens," I said to Maggie, to Paula, "grab the kids and run. Don't worry about me. Once safe, *then* you can get help for me."

"No," said Paula, "now," and she spun on her heels. Maggie scurried to catch up with her. What to do? Grab Ben and Sadie and join them? But already they'd disappeared. I stood, motionless, save for the rise and fall of my chest. Rise fall rise fall. Heavier now, hotter. Rise fall rise fall.

Ben and Sadie spun the merry-go-round, tumbled from high-flying swings into the hot sand, wet curls sticking to laughing faces. They looked over at the seashore, children splashing, chasing white pelicans. I was sure they would run and join them, but as if in tacit understanding, they stayed—performing, it seemed, for me.

Ben climbed the gnarled trunk of a grapetree, began tossing berry pellets at us. "Benjamin Kurzban," Sadie said. "You stop right this minute. Do you want to hurt your mother?"

"Okay, Mags, *now* can we go? Paulie, tell Maggie we should go."

Paula said nothing. Maggie looked at me with narrowed eyes. She nodded.

I crouched eye level with Ben and Sadie. "We're going to leave now, and I want you to look straight ahead. Don't look down, don't look to the side." I held my head high. "Look straight ahead, like this."

"Like when you line up at school, Ben," Sadie said.

And the five of us walked, hands clasped, past the shouts, the mockery and laughter, and I marveled at the ability of little children to make themselves oblivious to the darkness and danger about them.

KEY BISCAYNE POLICE DEPARTMENT
Offense/Incident Report

Report Date: 07-11-94   Report ID: 94192008

DR# 94192008
IN# 94192008

Continued...

The Details are as follows:

I RESPONDED TO THE KEY BISCAYNE POLICE DEPARTMENT REFERENCE A WALK IN REPORT
OF AN ASSAULT. MS. P. DAVIS STATED THAT WHILE SHE AND HER FAMILY WERE AT
THE SONESTA BEACH HOTEL THEY WERE APPROACHED BY MS. GONZALEZ AND OTHERS. MS.
GONZALEZ AND OTHER UNKNOWN INDIVIDUALS BEGAN TAUNTING THE TWO DAVIS GIRLS
ABOUT BEING COMMUNIST AND FIDELISTAS. MS. GONZALEZ AND UNKNOWN INDIVIDUALS
BEGAN TO THREATEN BODILY INJURY TO THE TWO DAVIS GIRLS. THE UNKNOWN
INDIVIDUALS STATED THAT THEY WERE GOING TO BASH THEIR HEADS AGAINST THE
CONCRETE AT THE POOL SIDE. WHEN I SPOKE TO P. DAVIS SHE STATED SHE FEARED
FOR HER LIFE AND FELT THE THREATS COULD BE CARRIED OUT. MS. P. DAVIS CALLED
THE SONESTA HOTEL SECURITY. THE SONESTA HOTEL SECURITY DID NOT NOTIFY KEY
THE BISCAYNE POLICE DEPT. THE SONESTA HOTEL SECURITY DID NOT GATHER ANY
INFORMATION FROM THE SUBJECTS. NO FURTHER INFORMATION.

Key Biscayne police department report regarding threat of bodily injury and assault at the Sonesta Beach Hotel on July 11, 1994, upon my daughters, Maggie and Paula, fourteen and fifteen years old, as well as the failure of Sonesta Hotel security to take any action, including reporting it to police.

———

Not until I receive the police report do I learn that upon reaching home, Paula and Maggie walked to Key Biscayne police and filed a report. That during the attack, Paula had sought the protection of Sonesta Hotel Security. That as they waited poolside for hotel security to arrive, a woman— her name was Elsa Gonzalez—and several others threatened to beat them up and even bash their heads on the concrete by the pool. That according to the report, *Sonesta Hotel Security did not notify Key Biscayne Police Dept. The Sonesta Hotel Security did not gather any information from the subjects.*

It is a quiet weekday afternoon when I return to the beach with Ben. That jogs his memory, *That woman, a moron.* Or maybe not. Maybe it was already permanently inscribed.

A quarter century later, I will ask Ben what, if anything, he remembers. "People running up to our car, yelling at us." And the beach, he remembers the beach. Did he not think it strange, that his mom was the target of so much hate? "No, it was the world being a scary place, crazy. And people being mean." A view he holds to this day.

44

THE KID

———

The game room at the Sonesta. It's safe, it's underground, filled only with kids. Ben sits at the wheel of a pretend race car, a screen of fast-moving lane markers and sharp curves and detours before him. I sit on a stool bent over my work. Ben walks to me. "Mommy."

"Hold on, Ben."

"But Mommy." He tugs at my T-shirt.

"In a minute, Ben." Must finish this paragraph, thought, sentence.

"That kid, Mommy. He was being mean to me."

I hop off my stool, walk to one of the kids. One of three. And I light into him. Don't let up.

"I didn't do it," the kid says, in a most defensive way.

"Oh, you think you're the big shot, the bully." Then, "Asshole!"

The kid storms out, his friends in tow.

"Mommy," says Ben. "Mommy, that wasn't the kid."

I go back to my work. It takes me a good hour to realize the kid didn't do it. I bolt up the basement stairs, Ben straddled on my hip, run through the hotel lobby. Exit the beach. I look for the kid, look for clusters of three among the blues of sea and sky, umbrellas and blankets. "Have you seen a kid, so high?" I hold out my palm then realize I'm describing any kid.

I pant, I sweat, I *OhGodOhGodOhGod*. Ben is silent. A squiggly rope of seashore comes at us, away from us. I spot three preadolescent boys. "Excuse me, were you in the game room?" He could be one of these three and I wouldn't even recognize him.

They shake their heads no.

"I just wanted to apologize." If it is them, it got to him. My message. Apology. If it is them. But I don't know. Maybe they think I'm the crazy-bitch woman in the game room. And best they steer clear. I search the pool area. Not there either.

I don't find the kid.

"Oh God, Benny. Oh God."

———

In the morning, I find a note from Sadie, perched upright on my bathroom sink. It's addressed to Katy; *Tata*, what Cuban children call big sisters.

Note from my daughter, Sadie, age four, to her older sister, Katy, that Sadie left on my bathroom sink, summer 1994.

Dear Tata,
even thogh your not a
lawier even thogh I'm not
either.
would you rather
be yelled at
and not be able to stand
up for your self?
or would you rather just
be able to yell at your own
mother.
This story is about
mom and Abuella.
P.S. Please write
back

———

The kid. Sadie. The end of the work day and still. Still I'm remembering. The kid. Sadie. Yelling at my mother, I am yelling at my mother. *Which time?*
  Sadie. I am not *able* to stand up for myself. The times I've told myself: *Do you want your children to grow up and think you did nothing or that you fought?* And I am not able to stand up for myself.

45

MONSTER

———

I read to Ben and Sadie, their eyes wide with wonder, mine paper-thin with exhaustion. Paula lies on the other bed, listening in, a dreamy, infantile look about her. "Read me one more book," Ben moans. "No," I say. "Okay, then one more chapter . . . one page . . . a paragraph . . . a line . . . a word?"

I laugh at our usual drill, bury my face in his neck. But here comes Mami. "Beba," her voice projected, her hair wiry and wild about her, her false teeth already removed for the night. She turns up the volume of the radio Ira gave her last Chanukah.

"*Ay, Mami*," I say. "I don't want to hear *esa mierda*."

"Mom!" Paula says, "I don't believe you!" She storms out of the room.

"*Es que están hablando de ti*," Mami says. Talking about you. She puts a thick index finger on a radio-cassette button, holds it a few long seconds. "*Lo estoy grabando.*" Taping it.

"The life of Magda Montiel Davis is in danger," says one Ricardo Nuñez-Portuondo. "The same way Castro agents just murdered that woman psychic, they will kill Magda Montiel too." Ricardo Nuñez-Portuondo speaks in all-points-bulletin alarm. Five nights ago, a twenty-five-year-old psychic was gunned down in the parking lot of WCMQ exile radio station as her husband waited for her in the car. Her crime? Predicting on the air that Fidel would stay in power another year.

"There are *damas*" the broadcast continues, "and then there are *damas*"—ladies—"and Magda Montiel Da—" and Mami's radio dies. Just like that, it dies.

I look at the radio, press this button, this knob, hit it, shake it. Nothing. "At least we have the tape," I say. I check the cassette recorder. Mami pressed *Play*, not *Record*.

"*Perdoname, Chichi.* It's just that when I heard them talking about you—"

"Mom," Ben sniffles. "Read to me." Sadie edges closer.

Nerviosa, Mami says. "*Me puse nerviosa.*" She smells of stale cigarette smoke. "And they were saying, '*Y la Montiel no tiene madre.*'" That Montiel woman has no mother. "Why do they say those things?"

I feel so deeply sorry for Mami and for Ben and Sadie too, and the lump in my throat is hard and it hurts. I get up, fetch Ben and Sadie's Playskool radio-cassette player, find the WCMQ *Rumbo Sur* broadcast, and in spite of myself, in my most elementary, condescending tone, give Mami instructions. "You see this?" I press *Record*. "Do not touch it. If this button flips up, come and get me. When the broadcast is over, come and get me. You don't have to do anything except watch it, make sure none of the buttons I pressed pop up."

Then I tell her to leave, just like that, leave, so I can read to Ben and Sadie, all the while relieved that Paula didn't see it. And as she exits, shoulders bent, head to floor, "Just make sure you're still recording. Okay?"

And I know I should say sorry, and I want to say sorry, but I say nothing.

"If you gaze long into the abyss," said Nietzsche, "the abyss gazes also into you."

That's it, that's all, just sorry. Mami will take that. She'll take that. But nothing, I say nothing. "Whoever fights monsters," said Nietzsche, "should see to it that in the process he himself does not become a monster."

PART THREE

AL CARAJO

46

THE RETURN

DAY 84 OF 3 (MAYBE 5)

———

Yes, I am going to Cuba. Fuck it. And fuck them. *Al carajo.*

When I told Ira as much, he gave me a look, and I said, "And fuck you too."

"I'd like to," he said. "When?"

———

Sitting in the laugh-filled office of Foreign Minister Roberto Robaina—Robertico—amid tropical foliage and the singing and chirping of his caged birds, my right leg crossed over the left, swinging away, I talk to Cuba's UN ambassador, Fernando Remírez de Estenoz, Robaina, and a few others, when from the doorway, an assistant motions to Fernando. He shoots up, is gone a bit, comes back, sits, looks at me, smiles, leans elbows on long legs. "How important is that dinner engagement of yours tonight?"

"Not very." A mistake.

"Well then," says Fernando, "I have a surprise for you."

A flurry of *ahhs!* and animated murmurs and I know: that was Fidel, on the telephone. A one-on-one with Fidel may be a gift to others, but not to me, and not now.

———

I sit in the back seat of the tiny Lada, Fernando scrunched next to me. It is black inside the car. It is black outside, but even blacker inside. We stop at Hotel Sevilla so I can get Ive's number from my room. I know her number by heart—the same number since we were kids—but tonight I don't remember her number. When I hear her usual "*Oigo*," I speak quickly before I hear about the black beans she made me with a bit of sugar, just the way I like them. I don't have to tell Ive why I can't make it or where I will be. When I say I'll try to make it afterward, she says, "*Olvidate*, you'll be there all night."

———

In the lobby sits Roberto Carballo, who last I saw four months ago greeting Fidel at the videotaped reception. Roberto, ex-Bay of Pigs invader and CCD member. Me, ex-CCD treasurer, ex-CCD founder. Though once a founder, always a founder. Though I'm sure my name is no longer listed as cofounder or coanything, no longer mentioned at the CCD. One of those dark chapters nobody brings up.

When Roberto sees me, he rises. "*Hola, mi vida.*" A tight hug for me, loud slaps on the back for Fernando. I want to motion to Roberto, *Save me, take me away. Even if the CCD did kick me in the* culo, *even if you and the other cowards stayed silent, pull through for me this time, just once.* But I only smile, say hello.

———

The night is starless and hot. I make small talk with Fernando in the back seat of the dark Lada, putting up a cool front. We talk of the sixties and the Beatles and what fun those days were. The driver stick-shifts his way through the narrow streets and winding alleyways of Old Havana, and I will lose Ira, this time, for sure, I will lose Ira. And we talk of the Beatles.

The illuminated white marble statue of José Martí comes into view. And there it is, the Palace of the Revolution.

The Lada glides into an underground crescent-shaped driveway. Fernando opens the car door and pulls me gently from the back seat. Inside, I hand my Paloma Picasso backpack across the counter to one of three security officers. He fumbles to unclasp it. I take it from him, point to the hidden zipper in the back. "Easier to open this way."

Paloma Picasso splayed open on Fidel's Cold War security counter.

———

I sit with Fernando in a vast room teeming with tropical plants of translucent green, big rocks, and pebbled pathways. River rocks from the Sierra Maestra. Boulders chiseled into sitting benches.

I feel stillness, yet life. The life of the trees, the energy, still, of Celia Sánchez. Vast space between the lustrous marble floors and the flat ceiling. Such an impression of height would normally require a domed or cathedral ceiling, but here a flat ceiling conveys a sense of space nonetheless. Simplicity abounds: nothing ornate, nothing ostentatious, yet elegant like the essence of Cuba, the life force of her countryside. I sit amid the walls and floors and trees and rock gardens created by Celia Sánchez, the now deceased hero of the revolution, once Fidel's most trusted companion, Celia with her liquid black hair and unassuming face.

And I am dying a slow, quiet death, sitting here. My marriage will not survive this. Not this time. But still I am about to cross the line. Again, nevertheless. And I only sit here. And talk of the Beatles.

A woman aproned in white, the first woman I've seen all night, pushes a serving cart toward us. "*¿Café? ¿Jugo?*" I go for the coffee. It's going to be a long night.

"The first time I met Fidel," Fernando says, "I was a leader of the Communist Youth. I'd been warned that Fidel was very inquisitive and would ask the most minuscule question. So I spent days, nights, studying all there was to know about our organization: when it was established, all sorts of statistics, everything." He wipes his wet glass of mango juice with a paper napkin. "And when I met Fidel, the first thing he asked was, 'What percentage of your organization is comprised of women?'" Fernando laughs, "He threw me a curve ball. I had no idea."

And now, here they come for me, and my veins are going to break.

Someone, Fernando I think, stands over me, extends an arm, and I rise in numbed silence. Escorted to a tunnel-like passageway, I duck my head under a metal detector and think, How silly, the reflex to lower your head even when you know you have enough room.

A door opens, and there he is. Towering figure in olive-green uniform, black leather boots, pointy grey beard, fallen lids giving his eyes a sad look. Flashes of hot white light blind me through blotches and streaks of black, orange, purple, the kind that float inside your eyelids when you've been startled by a sudden crash, a bad fall. The *schlick!* of a camera shutter and then a *schlick!* and another *schlick!* Fidel hugging me, holding me away in a *let me take a look at you* raise of the eyebrows, Fidel kissing me on the cheek. *Schlick-schlick.* Fidel, the sparse grey locks brushed off the wide forehead, the watery dark eyes, the epaulet: a halved red-and-black diamond with a white star (signifying his military rank: *comandante*, major) over a yellow-gold olive branch. Instantly, a gripping sensation of fear: Oh God, do not let it happen again, *do not*, the pictures of me and Fidel, front page, in the *Miami Herald*, TV, newspaper, radio, the attacks, the hate, the danger on the streets, everywhere. What I have learned: Do not assume anything; at a perfect loss as to what's what, who's who, like the olive branch still swimming inside my eyelids from the hot white of the flash. And the dichotomy, the ambiguity the olive branch brings; move in one direction, soft, velvety; move in the opposite, a roughness, resistance to moving in your direction. And all I think of is Ira. Ira and the flashes of hot white light and this gripping sensation of fear. And that is the thing about fear, this feeling of aloneness, of ambiguity, of contradiction and confusion.

———————

With his arm on my shoulder, Fidel walks me to a seating area in his office. Motioning graciously for me to sit, he waits for me to choose, though the big tufted chair is obviously his. I opt for the sofa, upholstered in brown-haired animal skin, from one of his hunting expeditions with Hemingway perhaps or with Khrushchev, Fidel wrapped in thick fur, deep in Soviet snow, dangling a dead, furry catch upside down. Or maybe with financier Ted Turner.

"Would you like one?" He points to a plate of *croquetas* in the shape of a sundial.

"*No, gracias. Soy vegetariana.*"

"Well, then," he quips, "you can eat these. There's hardly any meat in them."

José Cabañas, from the foreign ministry, says, "*Comandante*, the talk in Miami today is a graphic description of what they will do to us when they take back the island."

"Well," says Fidel, still standing, "then they're going to have take us all dead." His arm makes a sweeping half circle that includes me in his range of motion.

Oy vey. *En este velorio, no quiero vela.*

He sits in his tufted chair at ninety-degree angle to me. Modern teak Scandinavian-style shelves are filled with books. An autographed baseball rests on a Lucite stand. A sculpture of a fierce, powerful bull stands on a corner of his desk. Did Fidel's *brujero* give it to him, *se lo preparó*, as Mami would say, prepared with flower and song and ritual and blood? Like the three-foot ceramic tiger Mami gave me when I began practicing law, an incisor-wielding tiger she told me always to keep in my office, and I do, even though it clashes with the décor.

Across his desk, on a matching teak stand, is a portable TV set. I envision Fidel watching me at the conference on that TV as I leaned into the standing microphone and asked, "How are we supposed to counter the *ultraderechistas*"—the extreme right—"when they assail us with recriminations about *los fusilados*?"

"*Los americanos* think I hate them," Fidel says. "I don't hate them. *Los americanos* put me on the map. If it weren't for *los americanos*, nobody would know who I am."

Sitting with us is Eusebio Leal, Fidel's contemporary and the city historian, who's restored colonial fortresses, centuries-old cathedrals, and hundreds of other landmark buildings in Old Havana, designated by UNESCO as a World Heritage site. With the collapse now of the Soviet Union and Cuba's loss of billions, the office of the historian was given the power to use revenue derived from tourism in Old Havana for the construction of schools, homes, and more hotels.

With us also are a couple more from the old guard who I know but never remember their names, and my contemporaries: Carlos Lage, Cuba's economic expert, who I last saw at the conference; José Cabañas from the foreign ministry; and Fernando. A young fellow introduced as Felipe Roque, who soon will replace Robaina as foreign minister, sits opposite Fidel, taking notes on a yellow legal pad resting on a crossed leg.

Everyone addresses Fidel in the formal *Usted*. Even the older guys, who fought and shit and pissed in the mountains with him, *Usted*. Everyone, except me. I say *Fidel*, I say *tu*. Instantly, a hushed silence that for a second makes me wonder, Did I cross the line? Do I switch to *Usted*? Hell, no. No switching. *Fidel* and *tu* it is. The man sitting before me, who put my life— is still putting my life—and the lives of my children in such grave danger, is *tu*. To Fidel, I am *Magda*, I am *tu*. Why should he be anything but *tu* and *Fidel* to me? He doesn't take offense at my *tu*; he seems comfortable, relieved even, having me address him as do the people on the streets— often, he orders his driver to stop, gets out, and mingles with the people or visits workplaces and classrooms unannounced.

Head down, scratching the back of his head, "How many kilometers comprise the Florida seacoast?" Fidel asks. Some strategic military planning? I shrug. "I don't know." Fernando gives me an *I told you so* twist of the lips.

"How many inhabitants in Miami?"

"Don't know, either." No, no strategic military planning. And he's not testing me, either. Fidel is just curious. He leads such an uncommon, protected life—can't go here, there; not freely anyway, nor alone; and if he goes, it must be unannounced—like a blind man, he wants to visualize it.

"Where do you and your husband go on vacation?"

"Depends. Every year we go to the immigration lawyers' conference." Watch him ask me how many members, the ethnic and gender breakdown . . . "We're too busy to plan anything in advance, so usually we just stay a few extra days, visit the surrounding area, you know, whatever comes up, whatever we feel like doing." And I shrug again. "We're just not the types to live with all that . . . predictability."

"I used to go away to the beach, but I don't anymore because of the current *situación* of the country." *Current* as in it'll go away. And it will.

I think of the perception my travels gave the staff—*ex*-staff: *Magda off again to the Ashram or Canyon Ranch for her day-long hikes and crystal-domed yoga; Magda flying to Europe, Latin America, or Cuba with Ira and her five kids, and here we are, working away; here we are, going nowhere.* Or so was the perception.

We talk about working out. I don't say anything about Streetdance, my ouster. But he knows. Not by way of intelligence reports on the *Miami mafia*, as he calls them. No need for that. My ouster from Streetdance was all over the *Herald*.

"How much does it cost to open a dance studio in Miami?" When I don't answer—how can I? I'm so taken aback—he turns to the men in the room.

"No, no." I shake my head, my hands, laugh a little bit. I can just see it: The Magda Montiel Dance Studio, underwritten by *el regimen comunista de Fidel.* Never mind egregious violations of the US embargo, of the Trading with the Enemy Act.

"And what do you do for exercise when you're away on vacation?" he asks.

"I run, like I do here—along el Malecón. *Divino.*"

"*Sí,*" he says. "*Sí es divino por el Malecón.*"

"But I don't like to run in Miami. And when I run here, my husband will say, 'Ah, you won't run with me in Miami but you'll run in Havana.'"

"You should run with your husband."

"Why? I—"

"*Está bien.*" He holds up both palms in surrender motion. I note he does not say okay, not the Cuban *o-kah*, not the Anglo "okay." His *español* is impeccable, though I can't imagine, like any self-respecting Cuban, his not using a good *coño, carajo*, and *cojones*. "You know what works well when you're away?" he says. "Going up and down stairs. That's what I do." From this day on, every time I climb stairs, that's what I'll remember, Fidel and this, our first meeting of many, and his going up and down stairs. I will see his long legs (in olive uniform still) determinedly going up one stair, then another and another.

He asks about the children, about Ira, everything, Fidel wants to know everything. He knows that Ira is Jewish, or maybe figured it out, from the name and the Brooklyn. Did I convert?

"Yes. But not to marry him," I forewarn.

"So," hands on crossed knees, "were I to invite you and your husband to dinner, what could you eat? You don't eat meat, you—"

"No." I chuckle. "We don't keep kosher."

He nods. "And how are your cases going?"

He means my exit visa cases. I recount the latest. "The *novia*, from Milwaukee, met *el cubano* when she flew here, just . . . on impulse, while vacationing with a girlfriend in Jamaica. He's a . . . fisherman; she . . . her dad has a lot of money, she has a few college degrees." An audible exhale. "The US Interests Section is giving us trouble because she's forty and he's eighteen."

"Mm." Fidel puts a long finger to his forehead. "Those kind of relationships don't work."

"What kind?"

"Younger men with older women."

"Why not? You men have been with younger women for years."

"It's just that as the woman ages, the man—"

"The man, what? Older men with younger women don't age?"

Again, he holds up his palms in surrender motion. "All right, all right." A light chuckle. "So why can't *el cubano* join his *americana* in Milwaukee?"

Why does Fidel say *americana*? Because he's old school . . . old guard? Or because he thinks *americana* is the only lingo to which I, the converted *americana*, relate? In keeping with the writings of José Martí, or at least their subtext, the US is not America; US-ers are not the *only* Americans, say present-day Cubans. The Americas belong to us all: North, South, Central,

Caribbean Americans. "*El cubano*," I tell Fidel, "needs a visa from the US Interests Section. And he needs an exit visa. From . . ." I start to say *you*, "from Cuba. He's eighteen, of military age."

Fidel looks over at his comrades. "*Pero ¿porque es así?* Why don't we let anyone who wants to leave, leave? The fisherman should be with his *americana*. I think our military is strong enough that it can withstand the loss of one fisherman."

Cabañas bows his head. "We will see to it, Comandante, that the fisherman gets his visa."

¡Metele, coco! My insides are jumping, but I keep a cool front. "Now it's just the US I have to worry about."

"Well, I can't help you there." Then he adds, amusedly, "US presidents don't talk to me till they're out of office."

———

Two, three hours later, the warm-up over, my potent dose of *café cubano* wearing off, Fidel transitions to the attacks. I begin with the first jolt, that first call home, the frantic scribbling in my journal, my bewilderment: who's who, what's what. My coming home, the ensuing days, everything. I talk hard, I talk fast.

He says nothing, only listens. Only once does he speak, and that is when I tell him about my first Friday home, the day before the Magda Parade, when two thousand demonstrators marched from one end of Key Biscayne to St. Agnes, "To celebrate mass for all the Cuban martyrs who died on our ocean floors seeking freedom." I tell him about the magnum-equipped soldiers, the SWAT team Ira hired.

"What did you do?"

"I left with my mother and the kids. My husband made me."

"Good. And what did your husband do?"

"He stayed. He said, 'Nobody's going to run me out of my house.'" I don't tell him that Ira ordered the SWAT team, "Anyone tries to enter our property, you shoot to kill."

"I want to meet that man." He points at me. "Next time you come, bring him."

What would Ira say if I told him Fidel told me to bring him? *Okay*, that's what he would say, *maybe when I have a chance*.

I press on, recount all. It feels good, that he should hear. That they should all hear. He needs to live this out with me, even if from afar, even if just a bit. Almost a catharsis, not yet a healing. Then the updates. "I went to a prison facility the other day to interview a client. As I was leaving, someone waiting to see an inmate said something about 'Magda Montiel,' and when I said something back to him, he said, "Hitler should have done away with all you people.' I thought he was going to chase me through the parking lot."

"Why did you say something back?"

"Because. I had to. Sometimes I do, sometimes I don't. Depending."

"Me too."

"People yell at you on the streets?"

"No. Miami reporters. Sometimes when I travel, Miami reporters are there. Sometimes I say something back, depending too. But you know the media, they invent stories, characters. Like one of Gabo's novels." García Márquez, Fidel's good friend.

He then asks about protection: quantity, quality, at all levels.

I press each finger as if counting. "FBI, city, county, police, bomb squad . . ."

"And *have* they protected you?"

"Yes." No. Only Key Biscayne.

Fidel's gaze is brimming with thought, and I can't tell: Is he disappointed at my *yes*? Gratified? He seems one—various—steps ahead: *Why are they protecting her?* I call up Ira's "Yeah, but is the FBI protecting you for you? Or for them?" To see what they can gather on the Miami Rosenberg couple.

"Aside from them, are there any more *que te cuidan*?" Watch over you. But in Spanish, it sounds better: not just watch over you, *take care* of you.

When I say *yes*, Fidel seems relieved. So he *doesn't* trust the FBI et al. to protect me. Why should he? After the thirty-plus attempts on his life and who knows what else.

"Otto," I say.

"Ah. *El fuerte.*" He lifts his arms akimbo emulating Otto's bulky physique. "What about your children, your mother? They have protection too? Your mother lives with you, right?"

Forget Ira—what would Mami say if she knew Fidel asked about her? Would she laugh? One of those *heh-heh-hehs* of hers? Or be quick to anger? "*Eh, y a Fidel ¿que coño le importa mi vida?*" Be fearful? "Come to Cuba with me, Mami," I often say to her. "*No puedo, mi'ja,*" she says, albeit in longing tone. Then she recounts the same story: she quit her teaching job without giving proper notice and was branded a *contrarevoluciónaria*. By this time, I've turned my back, am making a face—any sort of physical release. *"Ay, Mami, ¡por favor!* That was thirty-three"—or twenty-three, twenty-eight, whatever—"years ago."

Fidel waits for me to continue. "One of my daughter's teachers threw her exam paper on the floor. Months ago. I just found out." My lips quiver. "Nobody told me."

"What is her name?"

"Paula." Can't fathom the need for names, *pero bueno*, it seems to be Fidel's way: the total picture. "My mom won't leave the house, not even to go to the grocery store. And that was the only social life she had, really, going to the grocery store, talking to all the *cubanas* who work there. My aunt told me Mami's embarrassed to go." What Tíita told me is that Mami is more afraid that someone will say something *sucio* about me than of being insulted herself. Already my voice is shaky. I don't want tears to come. "And Sadie—"

"That's the four-year-old."

I nod. "Almost five. She had a dream her little brother's legs were blown off." I stop, bite the inside of my cheeks, force my mind to go elsewhere. "She said, 'And I woke up and looked under the sheets to make sure his legs were still there, and all the way to school I kept looking in the back seat to make sure he still had legs.'"

Fidel squeezes his eyes shut, leans his head to the side, rubs his forehead with three middle fingers. Eyes stay closed. Then he looks at me.

A silence overtakes the room.

"I am sorry," he says. "When they came and asked me, 'Comandante, do you have any objection to the release of the video?' I said no." He shrugs. Shoulders stay uplifted, arms held close to his sides. "I didn't think about the consequences for all those of you living in Miami. I am sorry," he says again.

Fidel, unthinking of the consequences? Leader of the revolution, mastermind of the 1953 attack on Batista's Moncada barracks that set the rebellion in motion? I was five months into this life. Fidel, as fallible as the rest of us? He winced at the description of the attacks against me, against the children, the effect on all of us, but hasn't he seen much worse? The eyes of a Moncada comrade, Abel Santamaría, set on a plate by Batista's men, then brought to his sister Haydée, also captured. Haydée's suicide years later. The dreams that, a quarter century after Ché's execution, Fidel still has of him. He sees him, Fidel says. They talk as if Ché existed in this life.

Ché's execution took place the morning of October 9, 1967. It was my mother's birthday, her forty-first, my age now. Already she'd been grossly deformed because of the pituitary tumor that after she left Cuba transformed her once-beautiful hands, hair, features to grotesque.

Ché's execution, Mami's disfigurement. Three weeks later, I met my first boyfriend. I was fourteen. It was a Sunday, the sixteenth of September, at the North Miami Armory Sunday-night dance. He asked me to dance. A boy, wanting me to dance. "Good Lovin'," raved the Young Rascals. "Good Lovin'." ("Too-roo-lo?" Mami said as she drove my friend Carol Cooperstein and me home in the family's Corvair. "Too-roo-lo? What is that hombre singing?") The boy was eighteen, so I took on my sister's persona. I was a cheerleader, I told him, at Miami Central High. My name was her name. "Groovin'," then "How Can I Be Sure?," then "A Girl Like You." And me, busy with my eighteen-year-old boy. Then "People Got to Be Free," but I was busy with my eighteen-year-old boy. By now, my father said I had to confess to the eighteen-year-old who I really was. Too soon, Ché was one-year dead. By now, my boy was nineteen and Ira at nineteen was on the other side of the world crossing a line against the bobby's order, uncivilly disobeying that and every mandate young people in the sixties disobeyed. But I was with my nineteen-year-old boy because I needed *someone*. My father was *sure* to leave us, *soon* to leave us, I sensed it, feared it, the abandonment. Another abandonment. First Cuba, my island homeland and its sun and steep hills and crystalline waters, its Malecón kilometers of curvy seawall, curvy girls kissing curvy boys on the curvy seawall. *Come On Up!* intoned the Young Rascals, and still I danced with my nineteen-year-old boy. *Come on u-u-u-u-up / And have a good time.* Fifteen, and tied to a boy of nineteen for twelve months. Then came Paul. Then came the Sunday night my father said he was leaving, yes, of course all those years I had imagined he was leaving, all along he had, in fact, already left us, long before. Then came nineteen, I was nineteen, and that September, I married Paul.

————

If Mami knew that Ché was killed on her birthday, she never mentioned it. We never discussed exile politics at home. Years before, my parents, certainly my sister and I (earlier, much earlier than our parents), had moved on. Put all that behind us.

I meet with Fidel on this ninth of August 1994. In ten years exactly, Mami dies. To most it may seem a banality, a mere coincidence. But Mami was always one for numbers. The lottery numbers that she played every week turned on all our birthdays and as a great-grandson came forth, Maggie's baby boy, his birthday as well. The great-grandchildren who followed she would not live to see.

Her numerical guide was La Charada, the Cuban lottery system dating back to the 1800s, when following Cuba's abolition of old slavery, new slavery arrived, Chinese laborers. Across the continents they brought with them La Charade China, drawings of a man whose body is covered in animals, their symbols, and corresponding numbers. Dream of a bicycle, play 52. See a *cucaracha* scurrying across the kitchen, play 5. *La policía*, 50. One day, I will wonder and smile winsomely: In the years following the *alboroto* of The Kiss, the *alboroto* of the *alboroto*, how many times did Mami play 50, *la policía*?

———————

I look at Fidel. Is his grimaced face—in reaction to my description of the attacks—genuine? Does it matter?

The question then is not about the release of the video, the whos or the whys. It is not and never has been about the video. It is said that Ché told the US-Bolivian commander, as the man entered the room, "*Sé que vienes a matarme.*" I know you are coming to kill me. "*Dispara, ¡cobarde! Sólo vas a matar un hombre.*" Shoot, coward! You are only going to kill one man. But it's not about who shoots whom, who's the coward, the hero. It's about what Ché said following that: Millions of others who walk this earth die unnecessarily every day.

It is, therefore, not about the video or Fidel or any man or woman. It's not about the firing squads during the early days of the revolution, nor is it about the torture inflicted by US authorities on Cuban soil at the US naval base at Guantanamo. Such actions are humankind at its worst. Rather, it is about my island nation's concern with the care and welfare of the Cuban people and of people throughout the world. The healing and ending or lessening of suffering provided by her doctors and other health-care workers. The sun-scorched *guajiro* who once had nothing but a machete to work the land and now his daughter is a *universitaria*. The housing, state pensions, and basic food staples every Cuban receives. The eradication of racial and other social injustices.

"How do you do it?" I ask Fidel, my voice almost a whisper. "Deal with those who have betrayed you?" I think of his close friends, confidantes who helped build the revolution, who fought by his side, who turned on him. I think of his sister, Juanita, living in Miami. Mellower lately, but quite the free-tongued media favorite during earlier days.

"Haven't there been some who have supported you?"

"Yes. Some."

Fidel snaps his fingers, points at me. "Then concentrate on those."

"So speak out on behalf of the revolution," he continues. "And don't be afraid. Had I been afraid, I would be dead by now." His hands are steepled across his chin. "Even if it means sacrificing your children."

I sink my fingernails into my palms. I say nothing. The conversation goes on. At times I respond, briefly, lightly. Or the men, briefly, lightly as well. And the longer I stay silent, the greater my sense of betrayal of the children.

He stands. I am relieved. I am exhausted. We walk to the elevator that opens into his office. Fidel's arm is draped loosely around my shoulder. The camera *schlick-schlicks* again, the lights flash hot, and I walk, heavy with the betrayal of my children, of not defending, not speaking up for them.

I mention something about the Sierra Maestra.

Fidel says, "Someday, *con mucho gusto*, I will tell you all about the Sierra Maestra."

But would Fidel sacrifice *his* children?

"So, anytime," Fidel says. "I'll be happy to talk to you about those *tiempos*." Those times. "*Nuestra lucha hacia la victoria*." Our collective struggle for victory. "Anytime."

We stand before the elevator doors. I step inside, Fernando, Cabañas, Carlos Lage, Eusebio Leal about me. And I know. It is now, has to be now. The elevator doors slide toward each other. And I know. This is it. Now. "Fidel." I find the ◄ | ► button, press long and hard. The doors open again. "You know how you said I must speak out, not be afraid?"

"*Sí.*" A nod.

I hear the silence from the men around me.

Fidel takes two, three steps toward me.

"When I speak out, I have to do that on my own terms, on my own time." I point my finger at him. "So, you know those photographs taken when I first came in? And the ones just now?"

And he nods again.

"I'd better not see them all over the front page of the *Miami Herald* tomorrow morning. Or ever. I'd better not see them anywhere." The grand finale. And now, a dead silence. Silence from Fernando and Lage and

Cabañas and Eusebio Leal. And from Fidel. A dead silence. And soon, a dead me?

After a few seconds, Fidel speaks. "How could you think I would do that to you? Were I to do that, I could never look you in the face again." A wistful smile, a wave—not a hearty one, just a tired lift of the hand—and the elevator doors bang shut.

EPÍLOGO

JANUARY 27, 2018
HAVANA

Tonight, on the eve of the one hundred sixty-fifth anniversary of José Martí's birth not far from here, I stand on the Escalinata, the long accordion of white marble steps gracing the entrance of the University of Havana. I stand awaiting the start of the Marcha de las Antorchas, when students carrying homemade torches walk from the university steps to the Malecón seawall, reciting Martí's poetry or passages from his essays or their own essays or protests.

This, the Escalinata, is where I waited with my *abuelo* for my mother to finish class, not quite comprehending what a grown-up, especially Mami, was doing still attending school. Finally Mami would exit, her *tacones* tap-tapping on the white-marble steps, her black hair French-twisted into an upsweep of sophistication, her mouth red-lipsticked and puckery, a trail of blue cigarette smoke behind her. When I call up that image, my mother wears the same dress, a creamy white A-line flaring from a tightly bound, wide-belted waist, bright orange polka dots moving as she moves; round, clip-on earrings the same size and orange as the polka dots on her dress.

The university, closed by Batista, had reopened soon after the rise of the revolution, and now Mami was back in school for her graduate degree. I wonder if she ever acknowledged it, Fidel's reopening the university. I wonder if she ever stood on these steps, marched the Marcha de las Antorchas, stood on the Malecón seawall.

On the streets, in death as in life, no park, hospital, or airport is named after Fidel. No statue, no school. But hanging from open windows and leafy scroll balconies are handmade signs: GRACIAS, COMANDANTE. In Old Havana is a small colonial park, where Michelle Obama planted a baby tree, now named after her and the only US president ever to have the backbone to have the Cuban flag raised over Washington, DC, and the US flag over Havana.

If I could see her again in this life, what would Mami say about all this? *¡Alaba'o sea Díos! Los americanos, ¿amigos con Fidel?* and let out that string of chuckles that always kept us wondering what she thought. But she would think I won. She would say to the pharmacist and the cashier at the grocery store, to everyone, *Mi hija, ¡gano!*

I wouldn't correct her.

I would walk along the Malecón seawall with her.

I would let her smoke.